QUICK
ESCAPES
from
Los Angeles

Quick Escapes Series
Second Edition

QUICK ESCAPES

from
Los Angeles

24 Weekend Trips from the Metro Area

by

Eleanor Harris

A Voyager Book

The Globe Pequot Press

Old Saybrook, Connecticut

Photo credits: P. 43: San Diego Convention and Visitors Bureau; p. 68: Knott's Berry Farm; p. 101: San Diego Wild Animal Park; p. 130: Royal Caribbean Cruise Lines; p. 141: Hearst Monument/Ken Ravelli; p. 143: J. Paul Getty Museum; pp. 243, 255: Las Vegas News Bureau. All others photos by the author.

Cover photo copyright © 1992 Susan Lapides

Library of Congress Cataloging-in-Publication Data

Harris, Eleanor
    Quick Escapes from Los Angeles: weekends from Los Angeles / by Eleanor Harris.--2nd ed.
        p. cm. (Quick escape series)
"A Voyager book."
Includes index.
ISBN 1-56440-982-1
1. California, Southern--Tours. 2. Los Angeles Region (Calif.)--Tours. 3. Automobile travel--California, Southern--Guidebooks.
I. Title.
F867.H27   1997   96-39384
917.94'90453--dc21   CIP

Manufactured in the United States of America
Second Edition/Special Printing

To Ben, the very best person in the world to escape with

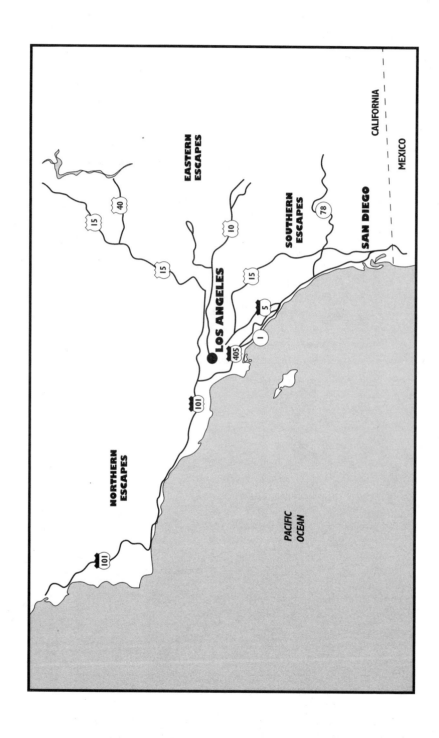

Contents

Acknowledgments

Many thanks to the kind people in various visitor bureaus and Chambers of Commerce, the patient staff at my local National Automobile Club, public relations personnel, and others who graciously shared local lore and helped me with the research and development of this book.

Introduction

This is a Southern California guide to select destinations of particular scenic beauty and year-round outdoor recreational attractions for overnight, weekend, or longer getaways. Each has something special to recommend it. Some places are deservedly well known, and others—small towns and villages—may be new discoveries you can claim for your own.

Each "escape" is presented as a detailed itinerary for the best of sightseeing, dining, and overnight accommodation in the featured area. Easy-to-follow, road-tested directions, including driving time and distance, get you there and back with the easiest, most direct route.

In all areas of its spectacular countryside, Southern California is an enchanting, carefree, warm, and sunny vacationland. The mild Mediterranean-like climate and weather are unfailingly wonderful. Usually there's no rain from mid-April to mid-October, so you can pretty much depend on blue skies for perfect vacations almost year-round.

Few places in the world are as beautiful and abundantly rich in natural scenic and geographic diversity. This book escorts you to the mile-high snowcapped mountains, sun-kissed deserts, romantic secluded beaches, sleepy rural villages, peaceful farmlands, and quiet harbors that are Southern California—all ideal change-of-pace getaways, where you can have fun, unwind and relax.

You'll visit parks, boat-filled marinas, zoos, a popular offshore island in the Pacific, avocado and orange groves, museums, a sunny all-Danish city, world-famous theme parks, art colonies, world-class championship golf and tennis resorts, a gold camp town, missions, a legendary private castle, a rural mile-high apple-growing community, and gaming casinos. A bonus is the region's proximity to Mexico, a foreign country just a few hours' drive from Los Angeles. One escape takes you to the world's most popular and exciting border city (a duty-free zone), and another continues farther south into the "real" Mexico to a lively bayside resort town along the seductive Mexican Riviera. U.S. and Canadian citizens do not need a passport or tourist card for a stay of less than seventy-two hours. Another, new escape is a luxurious four-day Pacific Ocean cruise from Los Angeles to Ensenada, Mexico, and Catalina Island, aboard a state-of-the-art cruiseship.

Hotels and resorts range from upscale, world-class, and glamorous with unlimited amenities to cozy quiet hideaways, all first-rate and nontouristy. Sports and fitness enthusiasts will find plenty of golf, tennis, bicycling, horseback riding, watersports, skiing, and hiking. The gourmet and the wine maven will be delighted, as will the sun-worshiper, the nature lover, and the culture-vulture. Shoppers will find

Nirvana, and children will find warm welcomes and much to keep them busy.

Since Southern California is the heart of the world's entertainment industry, film stars, celebrities, movies, and TV have long been an important part of its glamour and lifestyle. Many picturesque locales showcased throughout the years in films are highlighted in passing. Besides serendipitous spotting of celebrities at any time, anywhere, you're also apt to come upon film crews at work on location throughout the area, shooting a TV episode, commercials, or a movie.

Additionally, Southern California has a wealth of romance and history associated with its past and with its Spanish and Mexican heritage: the great rancheros, pioneer settlers, the Wild West, cowboys, missions, stagecoaches, gold strikes, and gold camp towns. History is kept alive and celebrated in many of the small cities with museum exhibits, living history events, and other special presentations.

The Los Angeles region has the finest freeway system in the world, enabling motorists to drive long distances in the shortest of times. Get to know the freeways and their routes as well as their traffic patterns. Odd-numbered freeways travel north and south, even numbered, east and west. Read maps and plot out your routes beforehand.

Take advantage of the seasons and what they offer. Contrary to what most people believe, Southern California has four distinct seasons. There's spring, when the air is soft and fragrant with lilacs and apple blossoms and the deserts are ablaze with wildflowers as far as one can see. In summer's long, lazy afternoons of daylight hours, you can travel farther distances or linger indefinitely at the beaches and lakesides to watch the sunsets. In fall the days become shorter, the air is brisk, and the landscape turns russet as golden leaves flutter to the ground and aromatic wisps of smoke curl from chimneys during apple harvests and merry Oktoberfests. Mild winter months bring a blustery nip to the breeze, crisp clear air, and endless vistas. The brief rainy season begins, and snowy mountain winter sports beckon, while the sunbaked desert, with warmer temperatures and less rain, is a brilliant colorwheel of lavender mountains, green golf courses, and blue swimming pools. Energetic vacationers can spend a morning skiing in a mountain resort and then bask in the warm desert sun or swim in the ocean a few hours later.

Throughout the year these getaways offer a happy grab-bag full of colorful regional, seasonal, historical, and holiday festivals, carnivals, fiestas, cook-offs, sports tournaments, ethnic and cultural celebrations, pageants, and other long-running events and activities of every kind to attend and enjoy.

There are actually forty-four escapes from Los Angeles in these twenty-four chapters, since many chapters include more than one destination. I have pointed out many places of interest and other cities along the way you may wish to visit as a side trip or mark for future exploration. Further, the destination cities follow in logical geographic and freeway sequence, so they're easy to revisit en route or returning from another getaway in the same general direction.

All the time-consuming and pesky details have been researched in each custom itinerary to offer the maximum freedom from stress on your escapes. Look for the special headings at the end of each chapter. *There's More* points out additional attractions to investigate this time or next visit. *Special Events* highlights local happenings and festivities that may be of interest. *Other Recommended Restaurants and Lodgings* offers fine alternative dining and accommodations not mentioned in the itinerary. Last, *For More Information* lists sources to contact for brochures, city maps, and further visitor attractions in each destination.

Fees and fares are mentioned but not quoted, as they are subject to change. Prices are reasonable unless otherwise indicated. While missions and museums usually charge admission, special "free" days are noted. Hotel reservations are definitely recommended (midweek anywhere is less crowded than weekends). Be sure to make your plans as early as possible for holidays and busy seasons.

A great deal of time and effort has gone into ensuring accuracy of information and honest appraisal of places mentioned in this guide. There may be, however, a change of ownership, a renumbered highway, or a place gone out of business altogether, and admission fees may be added where none existed at press time. It's always advisable to call establishments you plan to visit, before embarking on your escapes from Los Angeles.

Have a great time and drop me a post card in care of The Globe Pequot Press, P.O. Box 833, Old Saybrook, CT 06475!

Maps provided at the beginning of each section are for reference only and should be used in conjunction with a road map. Distances suggested are approximate.

All directions given in this book originate from downtown Los Angeles.

Southern Escapes

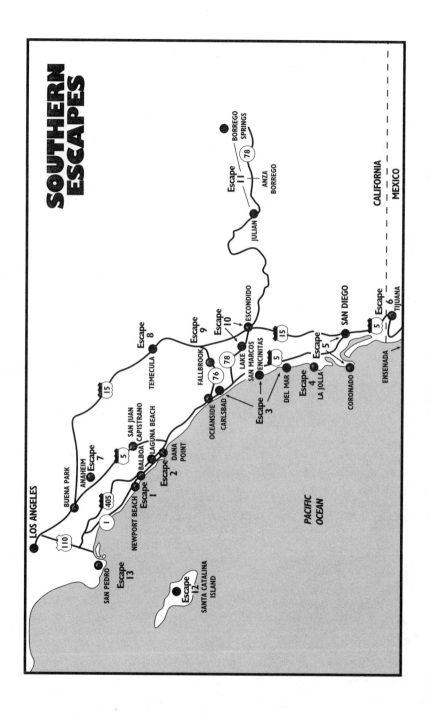

Newport Beach/Balboa

Car ferry crosses Newport Harbor in three minutes.

Living on the Water

—————————— 1 NIGHT ——————————

Beach • Piers• Boating• Harbor cruise
Decorative gardens• Shopping • Amusement park

This two-day getaway to a nearby exclusive resort city is short on mileage but long on diversion and year-round appeal. Catering to an elite lifestyle, about 9,000 sumptuous yachts preen in sparkling bays surrounded by miles of white sandy beaches. The friendly coastal city is a collection of several small villages offering watersports, world-class hotels, gourmet dining in some 300 restaurants, and fanciful shopping. Exploring individual islands and piers, you'll go on harbor cruises, lunch on a Mississippi-style paddlewheeler, relax at a waterfront amusement park, eat chocolate-dipped frozen bananas, and dine in bayside bistros.

Day 1

Morning

Take San Diego Freeway 405 south past the small beach cities—Manhattan Beach, Huntington Beach, and others—to Corona del Mar Freeway 55, which becomes Newport Boulevard. Continue on Newport Boulevard, cross the Pacific Coast Highway to Via Lido, and turn left to Lido Marina Village at the entrance to Balboa Peninsula, about 55 miles.

In **Lido Marina Village** stroll down Via Oporto, an attractive, curving red-brick-paved street of flowers, fountains, and flower baskets hanging from decorative streetlamps. In this delightful European-style waterfront area, dozens of shops and galleries back up to the boardwalk cafes, which face the water and offer pleasant outdoor dining on little tables overlooking the luxe yachts bobbing in their slips. Among the eateries are George's Cameo, for beer-batter fish-and-chips, and the Newport Marina Waterfront Deli, where they know how to make a hearty sandwich.

Lunch: **The Warehouse**, 4350 Via Oporto, Newport Beach. (714) 673–4700. Rustic wood siding and tin roof provide atmosphere. All tables enjoy a view of Newport Bay—or go for patio dining. Generous, inviting salad bar takes top billing, but sandwiches, hamburgers, and seafood cocktails are further good choices. Sunday Champagne buffet brunch. Monday through Friday Happy Hour features complimentary hors d'oeuvres. Free validated parking.

Afternoon

After lunch drive around the posh Lido Isle residential section. Then take Newport Boulevard to the Newport Pier area, passing the landmark 1952 Crab Cooker restaurant in its red building with a tall sidewalk clock out front, and continue past the Old Spaghetti Factory and popular Woody's Wharf, where some hungry guests arrive for lunch by boat. Newport Pier is where the historic Dory Fleet fishermen, the last on the West Coast, have arrived each morning since 1891 with their catch. Early risers can watch the dories roll in from the ocean and onto the beach, then watch the Dorymen prepare the fish for public sale in a small, enclosed open-air fish market on the sand behind their boats, where large gray pelicans patrol the rooftops waiting for handouts and gulls hover even closer. Lively McFadden Square has many snack places that are popular for fresh clam chowder and fish tacos, and Fishermen's Restaurant at the end of the pier is a congenial spot for cocktails, lunch, and dinner. In this area along Oceanfront, you'll also find Portofino Beach Hotel and Doryman's Inn.

As you drive along the 2.5-mile-long stretch of Balboa Peninsula from Newport Pier, Newport Boulevard changes to Balboa Boulevard. You'll notice that it becomes more crowded as you approach Balboa Village and the distinctive dome-shaped cupola silhouette of the famous **Balboa Pavilion,** where all the Big Bands played in the 1930s and 1940s. It was the hub of the peninsula, built in 1906 as a Victorian bathhouse and the Pacific Electric Red Car Terminal, where the big red cars delivered visitors from Los Angeles to spend the day. It now houses Tale of the Whale restaurant. The adjacent old-fashioned General Store, with its worn wooden flooring and large barrels of candy, is worth browsing for mementos.

Appealing **Balboa Village,** a compact area at the tip of the peninsula, with the pavilion on one side and the Balboa Inn on the other, has small-town flavor, with tall ficus trees, wooden benches, cafes, shops, and a bakery. Residents recommend Britta's Cafe for breakfast, but it seems busy all day. Across the street at Blue Sails, you'll find postcards, above-average souvenirs, windchimes, and books. Buy a postcard, sit down on a bench to write it, and drop it off at the post office a few doors away.

Next to Balboa Pavilion is where you board for your forty-five-minute narrated **harbor cruise** on the Mississippi-style riverboats, the *Pavilion Queen* and the *Pavilion Paddy,* which depart every half-hour from 10:00 A.M. to 7:00 P.M. (in winter from 11:00 A.M. to 3:00 P.M.; fare). You can take better photos and probably see a bit more up on the sundeck. During the cruise, which focuses on famous past or present movie stars' and celebrities' homes and luxury yachts berthed here, you see where John Wayne, Newport Beach's most famous resident, lived and anchored his boat, the *Wild Goose;* pass James Cagney's house and Joan Crawford's boat, the *Queen of Sheba;* and cruise past unpretentious million-dollar bayfront mansions with swimming pools, twenty-five-car garages, bowling alleys, and the like built beneath the homes due to shortage of land. At Edgar Bergen's house you see daughter Candice's (*Murphy Brown*) playhouse, a dollhouse-size sailboat.

You pass the Nautical Museum's Riverfront Cafe on the bay, see the sailboarder school with students in the water, and note where Jack Benny, George Burns, and Roy Rogers and Dale Evans lived. It's a lovely cruise, with the sun dancing on the water and kayaks and other boats of all sizes crisscrossing your path. The longer, ninety-minute cruise goes out of the harbor, where the seals cavort offshore and where *Gilligan's Island* and *Treasure Island* were filmed. This is one of the country's largest marinas and the launching site of the spectacular annual Newport-Ensenada race of more than 500 yachts of all sizes.

After your harbor cruise turn right and stroll down the oceanfront boardwalk to the **Balboa Fun Zone,** a miniature waterfront amuse-ment park built in 1956 as an old-fashioned California seaside attrac-tion. Watch the arcade games, ride the bumper cars, or take a turn on the Ferris wheel and small merry-go-round with its unmistakable cal-liope music. You'll find snackbars for ice cream and frozen yogurt as well as benches to sit on to watch the ocean or the Fun Zone action. Stop for a slice of pizza or the whole pie at Ginna's Pizza, or, if they're crowded, walk back a few steps to Pizza Pete's or Mrs. Field's Cook-ies. It's a happy scene, with boats in the water, people licking ice cream cones, pigeons fluttering about, skateboarders, rollerskaters, children, and strollers.

At Palm Avenue you can watch the historic Balboa ferry arrive at the pier and unload its three cars and its thirty passengers and bicy-clists and pick up more of the same to sail back across the harbor for the four-minute ride to **Balboa Island** for a modest fee. This is a nos-talgic way to get to the island. The privately owned car ferries date back to 1916, and probably the line of cars waiting to board began then too.

Following Main Street back toward Balboa Beach, **Kites, Etc.,** at 711 East Bay, is a marvel of kites of all sizes, shapes, and colors. Across the boulevard at Balboa Pier's end, Ruby's Diner has been a popular eatery since 1982. The broad beach is uncrowded, and the water is tempting. Time to stretch out on the sand around the pier and watch the waves, or go for a swim. This beautiful, clean beach can be yours for the afternoon.

Along Main Street at beachside, you'll find more restaurants and shops. Albatross general store is well stocked with clothing and beach supplies. The Balboa Inn, at 105 Main Street, built in 1929 on the beach, with Spanish-style architecture, was belle of the coast, a place where Errol Flynn, Howard Hughes, and other bons vivants overnighted. It's been remodeled and modernized many times and is still a popular hostelry.

Dinner: **Bistro 201,** 3333 West Pacific Coast Highway, Newport Beach. (714) 631–1551. Noted for zesty international home-style cooking, the restaurant is on the water's edge, with stunning harbor views. For starters go for the seared crab cakes with red bell pepper *coulis* and mixed green salad, followed by Bistro's meatloaf atop carmelized onion with mashed potatoes, or the salmon in potato crust on mushrooms, artichokes, and asparagus, with basil sauce. And top it off with the popular hot chocolate soufflé.

Lodging: **Newport Beach Marriott Hotel and Tennis Club,** 900 Newport Center Drive, Newport Beach, CA 92660. (800) 228–9290 (reservations only); (714) 640–4000. Excellent central location near Fashion Island, with 570 large, nicely furnished guestrooms and 15 suites with sitting areas, private patios, or balconies with views. TV with free in-room movies, clock, hair dryer, iron and ironing board, two heated swimming pools with spas, sauna, exercise room, eight tennis courts, restaurant, lounges, sushi bar, and business center.

Day 2

Morning

Breakfast: in **JW's** at Newport Beach Marriott Hotel or **Coco's** in Fashion Island, 151 Newport Center Drive, for more reasonably priced breakfast fare, with friendly but slow service—better bring a book or your knitting to keep you awake until your order arrives. Besides eggs and pancakes, there are many interesting breakfast specialties; lower-priced senior specials.

Fashion Island, in sleek Newport Center marked by Mediterranean-style architecture, fountains, courtyards, and tree-lined walkways, features major upscale department stores, hundreds of specialty shops, cinemas, boutiques, and many restaurants.

The soaring, dramatic Farmer's Market Atrium Court, rimmed with fast-fooderies, sweetshops, a deli, and a bakery, is a convenient and popular meeting place. Shop Fashion Island Monday through Friday from 10:00 A.M. to 9:00 P.M., Saturday from 10:00 A.M. to 6:00 P.M., and Sunday from noon to 5:00 P.M. (714) 721–2000 (concierge desk).

Take Newport Center Drive to the Coast Highway, turn right to Jamboree Road, and then turn left. Go over the short bridge to the small, lighthearted world of Balboa Island, which has seventy shops, galleries, cafes, and restaurants along its one main street, Marine Avenue—a funky, crowded, youth-oriented upbeat area where car traffic barely moves and parking spaces are hard to come by. Along Marine Avenue, with its tall, thick eucalyptus trees, munch on the island treat, frozen bananas dipped in chocolate, as you browse the small trendy shops and cafes. Amelia's, with fancy grillwork, is a longtime local dinner favorite, serving fine Italian cuisine. Starbucks is always available when you need a coffee break. Also here are Hershey's market on the corner of Park, a post office, Marcelle's Boutique, a bookstore, and jewelry, souvenir, and clothing shops. Strollers stand in line for the house specialty at Dad's Old Fashioned Ice Cream, watch the car ferries land, or stroll around the whole island, with its small beach cottages.

Lunch: **Riverboat Cafe,** in the Newport Harbor Nautical Museum, aboard the *Pride of Newport* (formerly the *Reuben E. Lee*), 151 East Coast Highway, Newport Beach. (714) 673–3425. Where else can you have lunch aboard a gleaming white paddlewheeler that offers unlimited views of the harbor, plus a tour of a charming museum? You'll find good variety in crisp salads, sandwiches, hamburgers, fish of the day, and clam chowder. A popular lunch choice is the California Chicken Sandwich of grilled chicken breast on toasted sourdough bread with *salsa fresca,* avocado, and melted Jack cheese, served with onion rings or french fries. After lunch, browse the small Nautical Museum for all manner of seafaring memorabilia. Lunch and dinner Tuesday through Friday, 11:00 A.M. to 9:00 P.M.; breakfast, lunch, and dinner Saturday and Sunday, 7:00 A.M. to 9:00 P.M. Ample free parking.

Afternoon

A special place to visit any time of year is **Roger's Gardens,** 2301 San Joaquin Hills Road, Corona del Mar (714–640–5800). Take Pacific Coast Highway south to MacArthur Boulevard and turn left to San Joaquin Hills Road; at the corner—turn right, into the entrance. Even nongardeners appreciate the spectacular beauty of the hundreds of colorful hanging flower baskets for which the nursery is famous. Its seasonal holiday decor in the large, well-stocked giftshop is inspiring. Pick up a brochure and garden map for self-guided tours of this seven-and-a-half-acre botanical showplace.

From here go back on MacArthur to Pacific Coast Highway and turn left (south) for a few blocks to the small, exclusive beach community of **Corona del Mar,** with its warm sands and parks that provide fine places to lounge, catch some sun, and watch Technicolor sunsets. East Coast Highway, the main street of this little city, is a long, browsable strip of boutiques, galleries, and restaurants, including noted silversmith Allan Adler's shop and the landmark dinner house, Five Crowns restaurant.

Next is **Sherman Library and Gardens,** 2547 East Pacific Coast Highway, Corona del Mar (714–673–2261), which covers an entire block in low-rise, California residential–style tan buildings. The library is a research center focusing on the development of the region. The gardens are stunning, in attractive settings of hanging baskets, fountains, a lathhouse, a serene tea garden, reflecting pools, and tall trees: a lovely escape from the city. The giftshop has cards, baskets, and books. Admission. Open daily, 10:30 A.M. to 4:00 P.M. (tea garden, 11:00 A.M. to 3:00 P.M.).

Retrace your way back to Los Angeles.

There's More

Golf. Two courses open to the public:

Newport Beach Golf Course, 3100 Irvine Avenue, Newport Beach. (714) 852–8681. Near the airport; 18-hole executive course lighted for night play, driving range, pro golf shop, restaurant, lounge.

Pelican Hill Golf Club, 22653 Pelican Hill Road South, Newport Beach. (714) 759–5190. Between Corona del Mar and Laguna Beach; two 18-hole championship golf courses with coastal hillsides and ocean bluff fairways; large clubhouse, practice range, and putting, pitching, and chipping greens.

Harbor cruises, whale-watching, Catalina Island cruise, sportfishing. Balboa Pavilion Ticket Office, Balboa. (714) 673–5245.

Newport Harbor Art Museum, 850 San Clemente Drive, Newport Beach. (714) 759–1122. Modern and contemporary art featured in changing exhibitions. Permanent collection focuses on post–World War II California art, including works by Richard Diebenkorn, Joe Goode, Billy Al Bengtsen. Bookstore offers art books, artisan showcase puppets. Museum open Tuesday through Sunday, 10:00 A.M. to 5:00 P.M.; free admission on Tuesday. Sculpture Garden Cafe open Monday through Friday, 11:30 A.M. to 2:30 P.M.

Newport Harbor Nautical Museum, 151 East Coast Highway, Newport Beach. (714) 673–3425. The museum has been relocated aboard the *Pride of Newport* paddlewheeler (formerly the *Reuben E. Lee*), docked in Newport Harbor, and holds nearly a century of Newport Beach history in photographs, artifacts, navigational and nautical instruments, boat models, ships in bottles, and other exhibits. Open Tuesday through Sunday, 10:00 A.M. to 5:00 P.M. Donations accepted. (The Riverboat Cafe, aboard the *Pride of Newport* offers dining with unsurpassed harbor views; see "Lunch.")

Parasailing. Davey's Locker, Balboa Pavilion. (714) 673–1434.

Tennis (all in Newport Beach); Palisades Tennis Club. (714) 644–1700.

Marriott Tennis Club. (714) 640–4000. Eight courts.

Newport Beach Tennis Club. (714) 644–0050.

Upper Newport Bay Ecological Reserve, Jamboree Road and Back Bay Drive. Surrounded by bluffs and cliffs that encircle Newport Back Bay, this 752-acre coastal wetland has been a designated wildlife preserve since 1975. Birdwatchers can spot nearly 200 bird species; additionally, from August to April up to 30,000 birds are present, including many endangered species. Popular for biking, hiking, fishing, boating, and horseback riding, with nature trails and free guided walking tours Saturday and Sunday. Information: Friends of Newport Bay, (714) 646–8009.

Special Events

Late February. Annual 5K/10K Spirit Run, Newport Center. (619) 434–2312.

March 21–31. Newport Beach International Film Festival. (714) 851–6555.

April/early May. Newport-to-Ensenada Race. More than 500 yachts participate in this spectacular race; watch them start from the cliffs or beach. (714) 435–9553.

May 1–7. Second annual Collectors and Classic Car Auction, Hyatt Newporter. (714) 729–1234.

May 5. Balboa Peninsula Car Show, Balboa Pier Park, 10:00 A.M. to 4:00 P.M. (714) 760–0929.

May 11–12. Newport Beach Jazz Festival, Hyatt Newporter. Advance tickets available. (714) 729–1234.

May 24. Twenty-third Annual California State Championship Chili Cookoff, Hyatt Newporter. Here's where you get to sample some of the best and spiciest chili. (714) 729–1234.

June 9. Heritage Regatta and Classic Boat Show, Newport Harbor Nautical Museum. (714) 673–3425.

July 4. Old Glory Boat Parade. Decorated boats tour Newport Harbor. (714) 673–5070.

July 12–28. Orange County Fair. A salute to the farming industry; carnival rides, rodeo, entertainment, food, arts and crafts, livestock. (714) 4708–FAIR (3247).

September 8–9, 28–29. Balboa Park Arts & Crafts Festival. (714) 644–3151.

Mid-September. Seafest. Exciting events include annual Newport Seafest Sand Sculpture Contest, Taste of Newport, boat races, kite festival, and more. (714) 729–4400.

October 6. Concourse D'Elegance. Judging of antique and classic cars, along with a muscle car exhibit. (714) 756–0993.

Mid-October to December 31. Christmas Fantasy at Roger's Gardens. (714) 640–5800.

December 17–23. Newport Harbor Christmas Boat Parade. More than 200 colorfully decorated and lighted boats tour the harbor. (714) 729–4400.

Other Recommended Restaurants and Lodgings

Newport Beach

The Cannery Restaurant, 3010 Lafayette Avenue. (714) 675–5777. The old cannery was razed and reopened as an architectural-award-winning restaurant using recycled machinery, catwalks, and other equipment as authentic decor. Dine at water level on the bay as boats drift dreamily past your Oriental chicken salad or shrimp Louis. Sunday Champagne brunch; Champagne brunch harbor cruises.

The Arches, 3334 West Coast Highway. (714) 645–7077. Handsome, comfortable restaurant—a local tradition since 1922 for good food, though a bit pricey. New York steak sandwich, Caesar salad prepared tableside.

Chili's Grill and Bar, 3300 West Coast Highway. (714) 631–7515. Easy atmosphere for southwestern specialties like grilled chicken, BBQ, baby back ribs, salads, burgers, and sandwiches.

Yankee Tavern, around the corner from Riverboat Cafe, 333 Bayside Drive. (714) 675–5333. Dinners highlight fresh seafood, salads, traditional Yankee pot roast with crisp potato pancakes, and steaks. Sunday brunch.

Hyatt Newporter Resort, 1107 Jamboree Road. (800) 233–1234; (714) 729–1234. Lush tropical landscaping and relaxed feeling in rambling low-rise buildings built in 1961 on twenty-six acres overlooking Newport's Back Bay. Offers 410 nicely furnished rooms, 20 suites with minibar and refrigerator, TV, free in-room movies, three swimming pools, three whirlpools, sauna, 9-hole executive golf course, sixteen lighted tennis courts, fitness room, jogging paths, three restaurants, lounge. Golf and getaway packages. Airport shuttle.

The Balboa Bay Club, 1221 West Coast Highway. (714) 645–5000. Exclusive bayfront beach resort with private beach, 121 rooms, 15 suites, heated swimming pool, sauna, exercise room, tennis courts, private golf course, restaurant, lounge. Outstanding Sunday Champagne buffet brunch.

Newport Dunes Resort, 1131 Back Bay Drive. (800) 288–0770; (714) 729–3863. Upscale RV park on one hundred acres, with full hookups, individual picnic area, cafe, swimming pool and spa, clubhouse, showers, laundry facilities, restrooms. Launch area; bring your own boat or rent one here.

For More Information

Newport Beach Conference and Visitors Bureau, 3300 West Coast Highway, Newport Beach, CA 92663. (800) 94–COAST; (714) 722–1611.

Laguna Beach/Dana Point/San Juan Capistrano

Replica of 1835 brig *Pilgrim* in Dana Point Harbor.

Swallows and Sunshine

1 NIGHT

Beaches • Art galleries • Museum • Watersports
Historic port • Marinas • Mission

This two-day seaside jaunt takes you to Southern California's most popular artists' enclave. In this small, friendly oceanside village, you'll visit galleries and a museum, enjoy superb watersports and wide beaches, go shopping, and relax in a coffee pub. You'll also wander through a romantic, historic port and continue on to the famous mission where the swallows return every year.

Day 1

Morning

Drive south on I-5, Santa Ana Freeway, passing the **Citadel Outlet Stores,** where you can pick up some designer bargains. You pass Anaheim and Disneyland. After Tustin, exit Highway 133 south, which becomes Laguna Canyon Road and winds down to Pacific Coast Highway and Laguna Beach.

Laguna Beach has been called the quintessential casual Southern California beach town, a small, unfettered, happy, and sunny place where houses roost atop steep ocean cliffs and where curving, narrow streets are graced with tall eucalyptus trees planted by pioneer homesteaders.

Busy Pacific Coast Highway, the main thoroughfare cutting through the city alongside the ocean, is flanked by a multitude of shops, restaurants, hotels, and businesses. Laguna Beach is as well known for its beautiful beaches and nonpareil surfing and other watersports as it is for its art galleries.

With its mild climate and windblown landscape of ocean and bluffs, Laguna Beach has been a successful artists' enclave since the early 1900s, when thirty or so artists began straggling in by horse-and-buggy or stagecoach. They came to paint the spectacularly scenic hills and untamed surf, and they tried to capture the clear and changing light in the manner of the French impressionists. But one doesn't have to be a Gauguin to appreciate the considerable natural beauty of Laguna Beach's 7-mile rocky canyon and craggy cliffs, which plunge dramatically some 40 feet down to the restless ocean. Though lively throughout the year, the little city fairly overflows with throngs of visitors during its annual eight-week summer art festivals, which attract about three million people (see "Special Events" at the end of this chapter).

Lunch: **The Terrace,** Hotel Laguna, 425 South Coast Highway, Laguna Beach. (714) 494–1151. In the middle of the village, the sun-filled Terrace, mere yards from the bounding surf, is unbeatable for a midday break. Menu selections range from hamburgers, pizza, and salads to seafood and sautéed chicken.

Afternoon

One of Laguna Beach's most pleasant small-town aspects is its intimate size. You can walk to everywhere (a good thing, since parking spaces are hard to find), from restaurants and beaches to shops along Pacific Coast Highway in the village. Stroll **Forest Avenue,** Laguna Beach's tree-shaded main street and gallery row, which expresses the city's friendly atmosphere in its bustle of people, flowers, sidewalk cafes, architecturally attractive multistory plazas, art galleries, restaurants, and boutiques. The window of Macalla's Pharmacy is jammed with straw hats; Thee Foxes Trot, at 264, features handcrafted home and personal accessories. Scandia Bakery and Deli, which sells bulk coffees and lunch, buzzes with hungry patrons.

Hollywood discovered Laguna Beach's photogenic attributes during the silent-film era, when moviemakers D. W. Griffith, Mack Sennett, and other legendary innovators substituted its craggy coastline for such foreign locales as the French Riviera, Hawaii, and Italian and Greek coastal villages. Errol Flynn's *Captain Blood* was shot near Three Arch Bay; *Robinson Crusoe* was filmed here in 1922; and many scenes in Harold Lloyd's movies took place on Forest Avenue. Between 1913 and 1930 more than fifty silent movies were filmed in Laguna Beach.

Through the years many Hollywood stars, authors, and other creative people have found the city to be a perfect escape. Among former residents are Mary Pickford, Bette Davis, Judy Garland, Rudolph Valentino, Charlie Chaplin, and Mickey Rooney. John Steinbeck wrote *Tortilla Flat* while hunkered down at 540 Park Avenue; Tennessee Williams was a pinsetter at the bowling alley. Many prominent celebrities still call Laguna home.

In the heart of downtown, at Broadway and Coast Highway, **Main Beach Park** resembles a sunlit, nostalgic Norman Rockwell painting of young, happy, sun-bronzed people enjoying themselves on the beach. This is the most "fun" beach for all ages, a place where everyone meets and mingles and plays basketball and volleyball, the bikini bunch swims and sunbathes, and towheaded kids soar on the swings.

Drive a few blocks north on Pacific Coast Highway, turning left on Cliff Drive to number 307, the **Laguna Art Museum** (714–494–6531), on a hilltop corner overlooking the ocean and beach. Site of the first gallery built in Laguna Beach, in 1929 for the Laguna Beach Art Association, the museum was extensively expanded and renovated in 1986. Its permanent collection focuses on the 1890-1920 period of California impressionist painters; changing exhibits are offered as well. The Museum Store sells art books, stationery, and jewelry. (Open Tuesday through Sunday, 11:00 A.M. to 5:00 P.M.; admission; kids free.)

Drive around to the right past the museum to **Heisler Park,** overlooking the ocean. Its long, narrow, grassy terrace edges the oceanside cliff above two of the city's most popular diving beaches—Bird Rock and Diver's Cove—and luminous turquoise bays. There's no finer spot for picnics, barbecues, sunset-watching, or sitting on a bench looking out at little boats on the horizon. The small, rustic gazebo, frequently used for weddings, offers closer viewing of the ocean and surfers below.

Dinner: **Dizz's as Is,** 2794 South Coast Highway, Laguna Beach. (714) 494–5250. Tucked in a small wooden cottage, typical Laguna style, this cozy, informal dinner hangout serves first-rate cuisine amid an eclectic 1930s and 1940s decor, photos of Marilyn Monroe, antique radios, and the like. International menu spotlights filet mignon with béarnaise sauce, rack of lamb, fresh seafood.

Lodging: **Surf and Sand Hotel,** 1555 South Coast Highway, Laguna Beach, CA 92651. (800) 524–8621 (nationwide), (714) 497–4477. At the southerly edge of town away from the hubbub, this hotel, which recently underwent a $20-million-plus renovation, offers 157 luxurious rooms, apartments, and penthouses on the ocean and sandy beach. Elegant rooms face ocean views from private balconies; minibar, refrigerator, in-room safe, marble bath, whirlpool tub, and hair dryer. Heated swimming pool, two restaurants, complimentary daily newspaper. Seasonal rates. Overnight parking fee.

Day 2

Morning

Breakfast: **Splashes Restaurant,** in Surf and Sands Hotel, a sophisticated room with glass-topped tables, cedar-beamed ceiling, and doors opening to the languid surf. Start your day with a power breakfast—order Swedish pancakes, oat bran waffles, *huevos rancheros,* or grilled salmon with poached eggs and spinach.

Drive south about 5 miles along Pacific Coast Highway to historic **Dana Point,** with its boats dancing in the harbor, awesome cliffs, and dreamy beaches. Turn right at Golden Lantern to **Mariner's Village,** where dozens of smart specialty shops and restaurants are connected by dining terraces and dockside walkways.

With 2,500 yachts and a sportfishing and charter fleet residing in the sunny marina, a slender white forest of masts swaying in the soft briny breeze invites you to linger awhile in this delightful romantic setting. Listen to the ships' bells and the water slapping against the docks as trim pleasureboats glide in and out of the harbor.

Lunch: **Delaney's Inc.,** 25001 Dana Drive, Dana Point. (714) 496–6195. Lunch is refreshing beneath a patio umbrella at the water's edge, with choice of sandwiches, seafood, salads, and a winner of a tostada shell filled with Caesar salad and topped with strips of blackened salmon.

Afternoon

The area is named for author Richard Harding Dana, a young Harvard law student who went to sea to improve his delicate health and wrote a successful book, *Two Years before the Mast,* exposing the severe hardships of life at sea during the 1800s and also describing the ports he visited. When his two-masted brigantine Pilgrim sailed into San Juan Port in 1835, Dana called the sheltered cove and promontory surrounded by tall protective bluffs "the only romantic spot in California." The book was made into a movie starring Alan Ladd.

The community was renamed after the writer. In 1971 the old anchorage was transformed into a popular recreation-oriented marina with a New England seacoast theme in honor of Dana's birthplace. At **Dana Wharf** watch the sportfishing boats set out mornings and afternoons for adventures at sea, or join a narrated harbor cruise. Or just relax on a bench along cobbled walkways, where anglers throw a line over the railing and fish, while you settle back to daydream about tall-ships drifting into the peaceful harbor.

Follow along Dana Point Harbor Drive past the small park and go over the bridge to **Dana Island** to see the large bronze statue of the author-seaman on a tall pedestal facing the cliffs. Then continue on Dana Point Harbor Drive around the bend of the water, where the 121-foot gleaming replica of Dana's brig *Pilgrim* stands tall in the calm water beneath the 100-foot, wind-eroded tawny cliffs mentioned in his book.

Alongside, the **Marine Institute,** at 24200 Dana Point Harbor Drive (714–496–2274), offers tours of the ship and is an oceanographic educational facility with many exhibits (open daily, 10:00 A.M. to 3:30 P.M.). **Doheny State Beach,** adjacent to the harbor, is California's most popular reserved camping park, with a long wide beach.

For the 3-mile run to **San Juan Capistrano,** head out Dana Point Drive, which turns into Del Obispo Street, which takes you into San Juan Capistrano; turn left on Camino Capistrano and proceed to the mission.

This quiet, small, sun-filled city was founded when the mission was built, in 1776, and their history runs together. San Juan Capistrano was a drowsy little farming pueblo growing oranges and walnuts. But during the 1930s townspeople began noticing the yearly March 19 return of flocks of tiny swallows that nested in the eaves of the old mission, stayed until October, then flew away.

It didn't take long before crowds of visitors began arriving every spring to witness this yearly phenomenon. The popular song "When the Swallows Come back to Capistrano" aroused national interest in the small town.

Mission San Juan Capistrano, on Ortega Highway at Camino Capistrano (714–493–1111), is called the "Mission of the Swallows." It was founded by Father Junípero Serra and is the seventh in the chain of California missions. Ask for a map as you enter, and try to allow sufficient time to explore the spacious, ten-acre grounds. The mission survived the 1812 earthquake, though its Great Stone Church was destroyed.

During California's Mexican rule, when all missions and their lands were confiscated, San Juan Capistrano became part of a large rancho. The mission was auctioned off to a family, who lived there for twenty years, until the U.S. government returned it to the Catholic church. Though the town grew, the mission was completely abandoned until 1895, when restoration was begun.

Beyond the entry plaza gravel paths lead to the broad courtyards and statue of Father Serra and a young Indian boy. Look for swallows' nests up under the eaves. Two nests are visible at the north corridor at the western end of the building. But you'll see many other historic sights and treasures in the old mission: the ancient graceful arches with the smooth worn stones beneath your feet; the rose garden and fountain; the strutting white pigeons; the gnarled, one-hundred-year-old pepper tree beside the padre's quarters; the huge millstone, used for grinding wheat and corn into flour and crushing olives for cooking oil and fuel for lanterns; and the sacred garden with its historic bells.

Three museum rooms and a bookstore contain archaeological finds and ancient artifacts. In Serra Chapel, built in 1777 and restored in the early 1920s, you can feel a strong tug of the past. It is the oldest building still in use in California and the only remaining chapel of the missions where Father Serra said Mass. In the long narrow chapel, with its 22-foot-high ceiling, paintings depict the Stations of the Cross. The shining reed organ dates from 1892, and the gilded cherrywood altar from Spain is more than 300 years old. The mission is open daily from 8:30 A.M. to 6:00 P.M. and later in the summer (admission).

When the swallows return every March 19 to build their nests, the sacred garden bells are rung and a week-long fiesta begins. Weekends are crowded year-round, but far more visitors arrive during spring. The birds remain to care for their young until October 23, when they begin their 6,000-mile journey back to Argentina.

Have a snack or dessert at **The Depot**, 26701 Verdugo Street (714–496–8181), either on the large patio or inside the old Capistrano Depot, built by the Santa Fe Railroad in 1894 and now a busy

Amtrak station. Attractive dining rooms, converted from the former baggage room, waiting room, and ticket office, feature sandwiches, salads, and Mexican food. If the Depot is closed between lunch and dinner hours and you're hungry or thirsty, go past the entrance about halfway along the building and up a short wooden stairway. Turn left and you're in the Main Bar of the old Freight House. You're also in the railroad station, with tracks on one side of the platform and unused passenger cars on the other. The Main Bar's menu offers good sandwiches and cheeseburgers with great fries.

You've still time to browse and shop along **Camino Capistrano,** the city's small main street. Ortega's Capistrano Trading Post, at number 31741, is a large, barn-red corner store selling Indian jewelry, souvenirs, and gifts. Moonrose, at 26715 Verdugo Street, has interesting windchimes, candles, antiques, jewelry, books, and music.

Every Sunday at 1:00 P.M., the Historical Society provides guided walking tours of the Los Rios Historic District adobes, built in the late 1700s and early 1800s. Tours begin at El Peon Plaza, across from the mission (fee).

Return to Los Angeles via I–5 North.

There's More

Shopping. The Pottery Shack, 1212 South Coast Highway, Laguna Beach. (714) 494–1141. With huge, lifelike deer on its roof, the place has been a local landmark since 1936. Catch the pottery and glass-blowing demonstrations.

Village Faire Shoppes, 1100 South Coast Highway, Laguna Beach. Ethnic restaurants, antiques, galleries, trendy fashions, and more in this large open-air shopping-dining complex.

Surfing. Bird Rock, below Heisler Park, Cliff Drive in Laguna Beach. Has the biggest waves.

Bodysurfing. Victoria Beach, West Street Beach, and Crescent Bay, all in Laguna Beach.

Diving. Glen E. Vedder Preserve, at Bird Rock, below Heisler Park in Laguna Beach. Good for reef diving.

Wood's Cove, 1 mile south of Main Beach, in Laguna Beach. Tree-kelp dives; made for scuba divers.

For other locations and diving and surfing conditions, call (714) 494–4573.

Golf. Aliso Creek Golf Course, 31105 South Coast Highway, Laguna Beach. (714) 499–1919. Nine-hole public course, clubhouse, Ben Brown's restaurant.

Monarch Beach Golf Course, 33080 Niguel Road, Dana Point. (714) 240–0247. Eighteen-hole public course overlooking the ocean.

Tennis. Laguna Beach High School, 625 Park Avenue, Laguna Beach. Eight lighted courts.

Irvine Bowl, next to Festival of Arts, Laguna Canyon, Laguna Beach. Two lighted courts.

Bicycle rentals. Dana Point Bicycle, 34155 Pacific Coast Highway, Dana Point. (714) 661–8356.

Boat cruises. Adventure Sailing Association, Dana Point Harbor. (714) 493–9493.

Harbor tours. Dana Island Yachts, Dana Point Harbor. (714) 248–7400.

Boat rentals. Dana Harbor Yachts, Dana Point. (714) 493–2011.

Sportfishing, whale-watching, parasailing. Dana Wharf Sportfishing, Dana Point Harbor. (714) 496–5794.

O'Neill Museum, 31831 Los Rios Street, San Juan Capistrano. (714) 493–8444. This wooden Victorian-era residence, built in the 1880s, has been restored and refurnished as San Juan Capistrano's Historical Society office. On view are old photographs and Indian artifacts. Closed Monday.

Special Events

Mid-February, early March, Late April, mid-May, and mid-June. Laguna Craft Guild Street Festival, Laguna Beach.

February and March. Festival of Whales, Dana Point.

First week in March. Heritage Festival, San Juan Capistrano.

Early March. Arts and Crafts Fair, Patriot's Day Parade, and Irish Festival of Art—all at Laguna Beach.

March 19. Return of the Swallows and Heritage Fair Fiesta, San Juan Capistrano. The first Saturday after March 19 is the Swallows Day Parade and Fiesta de los Dolondrinos. (714) 493–1976.

Late March. Laguna Club for Kids annual Wine Taste (714–494–5579).

May 5. Cinco de Mayo, San Juan Capistrano.

Mid-May. Laguna Charm House Tour, Laguna Beach.

July–September. Eight-week art celebration, from Fourth of July weekend through Labor Day, at Laguna Beach; admission varies. Events include the Festival of Arts, a juried art show featuring the area's finest artists and craftspeople; the Pageant of the Masters, a nightly event wherein live models re-create great works of art in paintings, sculpture, tapestries, and porcelain; the Sawdust Festival, an unjuried show of local artists and craftspeople (714–494–3030); and Art-a-Fair, a juried show open to artists from everywhere, free workshops, demonstrations, and entertainment (714–494–4514).

Mid-July, mid-August, and mid-September. San Juan Capistrano Symphony Orchestra concert, Dana Point Resort, Dana Point.

Early October. Oktoberfest, Laguna Beach.

October 23. Farewell to the Swallows, San Juan Capistrano.

Late October. Harvest Festival, San Juan Capistrano.

Thanksgiving Day. Turkey Trot, Dana Point.

Early December. Santa's Arrival and Hospitality Night, Laguna Beach. For specific dates call the Laguna Beach Chamber of Commerce at (714) 494–1018.

Other Recommended
Restaurants and Lodgings

Laguna Beach

Las Brisas, 361 Cliff Drive. (714) 497–4955. The blue-umbrella'd dining terrace above Main Beach is the popular luncheon and late-afternoon rendezvous, bubbly with that chic French Riviera look. Mexican cuisine emphasizes fresh seafood but also grilled New York steak with borracho beans. Stay for the sunsets. More formal dining inside. Sunday brunch.

Cedar Creek Inn, 384 Forest Avenue. (714) 497–8696. Old English–style, great-looking place, with fireplace and busy bar. From lunch salads, sandwiches, and pastas to dinner steak, prime rib, chicken, and pasta entrees. Two hours of free parking.

Hotel Laguna, 425 Coast Highway. (800) 524–2927 (in California); (714) 494–1151. Ideally located in the center of town on its private beach, adjacent to Main Beach Park; sixty-five rooms, most of which have been upgraded in this turn-of-the-century hotel. Two restaurants; continental breakfast is included in the room rate and served in a hospitality room on your floor. Seasonal rates.

Inn at Laguna Beach, 211 North Pacific Coast Highway. (800) 544–4479 (reservations); (714) 497–9722. Opened in 1990 on the hillside just below the museum, overlooking Main Beach. Seventy deluxe rooms, private balconies, TV, VCR, honor bar, minirefrigerator, hair dryer, bathrobes; most rooms include microwave ovens. Heated swimming pool and spa. Complimentary continental breakfast served in your room with daily *Los Angeles Times*. Seasonal rates.

Dana Point

Cannon's, 34344 Green Lantern. (714) 496–6146. That romantic view over the harbor just doesn't quit. The lunch bunch goes for chicken Cajun sandwiches, excellent Cobb salad; the dinner bunch, for the grilled salmon with lobster tails. Sunday brunch.

Dana Point Resort, 25135 Park Lantern. (800) 533–9748 (United States and Canada); (714) 661–5000. Rambling, Cape Cod–style resort on forty-two acres of lawn and flowers; 350 rooms; 17 suites with TV, hospitality bar/minirefrigerator; two heated swimming pools, spas, health club; three lighted tennis courts; restaurant. Two- and three-night packages offer various complimentary amenities.

The Ritz Carlton, Laguna Niguel, 33533 Ritz Carlton Drive. (800) 241–3333 (reservations); (714) 240–2000. Luxurious pricey resort atop a 152-foot ocean bluff; 362 rooms, 31 suites with private balconies, two bathrooms, hair dryer, bathrobes, TV, honor bar, minirefrigerator; two heated swimming pools, two Jacuzis, seven lighted tennis courts, fitness center, salon; three restaurants, lounge, library; golf nearby; overnight parking fee. Special midweek rates and perks.

San Juan Capistrano

Sarducci's Cafe, 31751 Camino Capistrano. (714) 493–9593. Besides sandwiches and pastas in the attractive cafe, special selections include veal *piccata,* blackened halibut with Cajun spices. Large dining patio.

El Adobe de Capistrano, 31891 Camino Capistrano. (714) 493–1163. Noted for good Mexican food; formerly a stagecoach stop.

BJ's Chicago Pizzeria, 31781 Camino Capistrano. The place for thick-crust pizza.

Amsterdam Coffeehouse, 31781 Camino Capistrano. (714) 489–0221. A European-style coffeehouse with specialty coffee drinks, pastries, sandwiches, and snacks.

Best Western Capistrano Inn, 27174 Ortega Highway. (800) 441–9438; (714) 493–5661. Features 108 units, in-room coffee, some kitchenettes; heated swimming pool, spa: Monday through Friday, complimentary full breakfast in poolside Cafe Capistrano, plus two complimentary drinks during 5:30 to 7:30 P.M. Happy Hour. Daily and seasonal rates.

Mission Inn (motel), 26891 Ortega Highway. (714) 493–1151. Across from the mission; twenty-one rooms, all with microwave oven, refrigerator, in-room coffeemaker, VCR; heated swimming pool, Jacuzzi. On four acres with sixty-five orange trees; picking encouraged.

For More Information

Laguna Beach Chamber of Commerce, 357 Glenneyre, Laguna Beach, CA 92651. (714) 494–1018.

Dana Point Chamber of Commerce, P.O. Box 12, Dana Point, CA 92629. (714) 496–1555.

Dana Point Harbor Association, P.O. Box 548, Dana Point, CA 92629. (714) 496–6040.

San Juan Capistrano Chamber of Commerce, 31931 Camino Capistrano (corner of Del Obispo), San Juan Capistrano, CA 92675. (714) 493–4700.

Mission Visitor Center, 31882 Camino Capistrano, San Juan Capistrano, CA 92675. (714) 248–2049.

Carlsbad/Encinitas/Del Mar

Del Mar is noted for gentle surf and warm sandy beaches.

Flower-Filled Seaside

_____ 1 NIGHT _____

Uncrowded beaches • Surfing • Fine dining • Antiques
Flowers • Fairs • Horse racing/horse shows • Hot air ballooning

One of Southern California's greatest assets is its beautiful and inviting coastline, bordered by wide, secluded beaches with gentle surf and small, slower-paced villages with fine restaurants and world-class accommodations. This two-day itinerary covers just over 100 miles as it takes you south to a small and charming European-style seaside village; through the "Flower Capital of the World," where in spring and fall hillsides are ablaze with millions of poinsettias, ranunculas, and gladioli; and to a quiet but posh coastal community noted for its celebrity racetrack and county fair.

Day 1

Morning

Drive south on I–5, past Anaheim and Santa Ana, and then follow the coastline, continuing through San Clemente, which was Richard Nixon's Western White House, and passing the San Onofre Nuclear Generating Station on the beach. It is then a 20-mile drive alongside **Camp Pendleton,** the largest U.S. amphibious Marine Corps training base in the world. For a self-guided tour of the camp, exit at the main gate on I–5 and ask for the "Windshield Tour," or phone (760) 725–4111. As you continue your coastal drive, you'll see drowsy lagoons and farms reaching to the sea. Following Oceanside, take the Carlsbad Village Drive/Elm Drive exit, turn right toward the ocean, and turn left on Pacific Coast Highway. Continue about 0.5 mile and you're at the ocean. The heart of Carlsbad Village is just up the road.

Carlsbad, known as the "Village by the Sea," has an Old European style—a friendly small town with the ocean at its front door, clear soft air, and blue skies, a place where visitors come for a day and stay for weeks or months.

You'll want to stroll Carlsbad's uncrowded beaches, swim and surf in its calm water, unwind watching fiery sunsets over the horizon, and discover restaurants and fine lodgings. The small, attractive downtown village area, with sidewalk cafes, fountains, benches, and flowers, was named for a health spa in Karlsbad, Bohemia. In 1883 a farmer's well tapped both artesian and mineral water, which the farmer then sold to parched railroad passengers, who found it palliative. A hotel was built near the well, and guests indulged in mineral baths. Later, when the water was analyzed and found to contain properties similar to those of the European spa, the spelling was Americanized and the city became Carlsbad.

Among other delights, Carlsbad's twice-yearly Village Faires, held on the first Sunday in May and November, are California's largest street fairs. Although the railroad doesn't stop here any longer, the old-fashioned, 1887 depot is now home of the Carlsbad Convention & Visitors Bureau. The city is also the home of the plush, internationally known celebrity favorite La Costa Resort and Spa, about 3 miles inland.

A historic reminder of the town's beginning is the site of Frazier's Well, in front of the **Alte Karlsbad Hanse House,** 2802 Carlsbad Boulevard. The three-story, half-timbered, medieval-style building, which resembles part of a foreign-movie set, contains a museum and giftshop. Its basement leads to the old well location.

Lunch: **Neiman's Restaurant,** 2978 Carlsbad Boulevard, Carlsbad. (760) 729–4131. The town's centerpiece is this 1802, refurbished three-story gray-and-white landmark mansion, complete with turrets, cupolas, and flags waving from towers. It was formerly the home of a city cofounder and a popular overnight inn during the 1920s. Lunch in the bright American Bar Cafe and Brasserie lends itself to sandwiches, pastas, and chicken. The Neimanburger is a charbroiled top sirloin served on sourdough. Sunday brunch is outstanding.

Afternoon

Browse through Victorian-style **Village Faire** shops behind the restaurant.

Carlsbad's **State Street** is noted for its antiques and is a magnet for treasure hunters and decorators. The 3 blocks between Oak Avenue and Laguna Drive have about twenty-five antiques shops along both sides of the street, with some outdoor galleries as well. Among those starting north from Oak Avenue are the Wooden Indian, at number 3019, with Native American jewelry and art; Lion & Lamb Cottage Shops, (3060); State Street Antiques, (2946); International Imports, (2084); and Carlsbad House of Antiques and Dolls, in Antique Art Plaza, (2752).

Take time to stroll around this sparkling, compact village area packed with a variety of restaurants, shops, and streets named for presidents. Then drive or walk back to the ocean just across Carlsbad Boulevard. Its paved seawall or sidewalk above the low ocean bluffs is where you can join joggers, walkers, runners, and those pushing baby strollers. Or find a bench, sit, and watch people on the beach, surfers riding the waves, pelicans doing their daredevil dives, and the magical sunsets. The beautiful beaches are uncrowded, clean, and irresistible. Follow the broad staircase leading down to the warm sand and relax as you watch the slow, easy surf rolling in.

Dinner: **Coyote Bar & Grill,** 300 Carlsbad Village Drive, Carlsbad. (760) 729–4695. In the Village Faire shops. With its striking decor, it's a steady favorite for tasty southwestern cuisine. Rotisserie chicken is served with tortilla, beans, rice, *salsa fresca,* and cheddar cheese.

Enjoy dinner or lunch in the good-looking dining room with cozy fireplaces or on the patio around inviting fire pits. Nightly entertainment except Monday.

Lodging: **Tamarack Beach Resort,** 3200 Carlsbad Boulevard, Carlsbad, CA 92008. (800) 334–2199 (United States and Canada); (760) 729–3500. Opened in 1986; just across from the ocean. Sprawling, Spanish-style architecture; the seventy-seven rooms include twenty-three large hotel rooms and fifty-four one- and two-bedroom condominium suites rentable nightly or weekly. Spacious guestrooms, most with ocean views, have private balconies, honor bar/minirefrigerator, TV, and VCR; complimentary VCR library in Recreation Room. Gym, heated pool, two spas; barbecues, restaurant. Seasonal rates. Hotel/guest activities include daytrips to nearby attractions—Tijuana, Catalina, and so on—plus complimentary wine-and-cheese parties and reduced dining rates to select village restaurants.

Day 2

Morning

Breakfast: **Mariah's Westwind Restaurant and Bakery,** 377 Carlsbad Village Drive, Carlsbad. (760) 729–6040. Breakfast is served all day at this busy neighborhood place. Pancake specialties, breakfast combinations, and 150 omelet suggestions. Patio dining if you prefer.

With its mild climate, Carlsbad has been a major flower-growing center since the 1920s, when its flower and bulb industry of gladioli, ranunculas, and irises began and was commercially successful. From mid-March through April, about a hundred acres on the hillsides behind Pea Soup Andersen's restaurant are an explosion of multicolored ranunculas. The city became a prime avocado-growing center after a nurseryman planted the first avocado groves in 1916 and developed different varieties Other avocado growers followed and prospered through 1948. But when water shortages arose, growers began selling their land to developers for better profit than farming offered. The first bird of paradise flowers were grown here after seeds planted in greenhouses were transferred to an old avocado grove; the exotic bird of paradise is now Carlsbad's official city flower, appearing in colorful sidewalk and building murals.

The drive south on Carlsbad Boulevard to Encinitas and Del Mar is more pleasant along the ocean than on the freeway, despite the San Diego Gas and Electric Power station that intrudes on the lovely coastal vistas. At times it seems that everyone is on holiday. The bikepath has plenty of pedalers, men fish at the water's edge, and other people swim and wade in the calm frothy surf or relax on the uncrowded beach and watch large brown pelicans dive-bomb like arrows into the water. **South Carlsbad State Beach,** where colorful umbrellas dot the beach, is popular with campers.

Seasonally, this coastal highway (State Highway 21) explodes with dazzling yellow, orange, and purple ranunculas and other multicolored flowers grown in the area. A roadside grove of tall, noble eucalyptus trees ushers you into **Leucadia, Encinitas, Cardiff by-the-Sea,** and **Olivenhain.** These four small cities were consolidated in 1986 as the city of Encinitas, though each retains its individual attractions and lifestyle.

In the 1870s Leucadia's early settlers were English spiritualists seeking freedom of worship, and they named their community after a Greek island whose name means "paradise." Many streets have names of Greek gods. The 1881 founder of Encinitas gave his town a Spanish name meaning "little live oaks." When Cardiff was homesteaded in 1875, its developer named it after a large city in Wales. Olivenhain was settled in 1884 by a small group of Germans; their old meeting hall is one of its attractions.

With Encinitas's millions of commercially grown gladioli, ranunculas, and poinsettias, the area has been dubbed "Flower Capital of the World." In spring and fall the Chamber of Commerce conducts tours of those greenhouses or nurseries open to the public. Call (760) 753–6041 in February or September for information.

Along this lively road are cafes, lodgings, many antiques stores (D Street), and the Self-Realization Fellowship Retreat and Hermitage. 1st Street has a strip of Italian restaurants and the good-looking Lumberyard Center's restaurants and shops.

The fine beaches along here are known for great surfing and provide scenic views from the bluffs. The train whistles right through Encinitas, where Moonlight Beach is a favorite family picnic area. These are all wonderful little beach towns you will want to revisit and explore.

Continue south on I–5 past acres of greenhouses, and in ten minutes you'll have arrived in **Del Mar.** Take the Via de la Valle exit to Jimmy Durante Drive (the "Schnozz" was a former resident and mayor). Turn left past the Del Mar Race Track and Fairgrounds, then drive along the town's broad main street, Camino del Mar, to 15th Street and the heart of this small, low-key, genteel town, with its Old World atmosphere and architecture.

Lunch: **Bully's,** 1404 Camino Del Mar in Del Mar. (760) 755–1660. Small, dimly lighted, with roomy red leather booths and a congenial bar, Bully's is an old-fashioned steakhouse and the local watering hole, a place known since 1967 for consistently good food. The succulent Barbecue Beef Bones with fiery barbecue sauce and the excellent french fries are worth the trip. Other options include steaks, prime rib, chicken, seafood, burgers, and sandwiches. There's patio dining in the rear.

Afternoon

Del Mar began in 1885 as a beach resort town and evolved as a vacation getaway for Los Angeles's elite. It's still easy to relax in this amiable, well-heeled residential beach city, which follows a scenic 2.5 miles of curving coastline studded with top-notch restaurants, specialty shops, and noteworthy accommodations. Del Marians also invite you to enjoy their broad beaches for great swimming, fine scuba diving, and matchless surfing atop those long tubular waves that keep rolling in from Hawaii. From sea to sky is a thrilling transition for hot air balloon enthusiasts, who can enjoy panoramic views as they drift quietly over the glittering coastline in sunrise and sunset flights.

To see more of the city, begin your stroll along Camino del Mar at 15th Street, where you'll find **Stratford Square,** a mock-Tudor building encompassing shops and restaurants. Carlos and Annie's corner sidewalk cafe is a busy hangout for southwestern dishes and burgers beneath its umbrellas. Earth Song Bookstore favors best-sellers with celebrity book-signing parties, in addition to stocking a selection of architecture, art, and children's books. Through an archway, Ocean Song Gallery, a wonderful, offbeat boutique specializing in world music, has tables piled with fine import pieces, rugs, ethnic records, and cards.

Across the boulevard is the popular **Del Mar Plaza,** an open-air, multilevel, upscale dining and shopping center. Among its dozens of shops are Peaches en Regalia luxe apparel, Esmeralda's Bookstore/Cafe, and Daniel's gourmet market. Its fashionable Italian-style indoor/outdoor restaurants boast smashing ocean-view terraces and chic epicurean variety. There's underground parking; an elevator is in the rear.

The city is famous as home of the **Del Mar Race Track** ("where the turf meets the surf") and Fairgrounds. Launched in 1937 by actors Bing Crosby and Pat O'Brien, who lived in the area and began its Hollywood glamour and celebrity status, Del Mar was established as a new playground of the stars, notably Lucille Ball and Desi Arnaz, Harry James, Betty Grable, Jimmy Durante, and Bob Hope. Del Mar buzzes in summer with the annual big Fair and Thoroughbred Racing and year-round satellite wagering.

Walk or drive downhill on 15th Street the few short blocks to the ocean, where **Seagrove Park,** with stately palm trees, overlooks the beach just a few steps down the bluff. Side by side at the beach on Coast Boulevard, two of Del Mar's waterfront dining institutions, Jake's and the Poseidon, offer beachfront terrace dining and are generally packed with seafood aficionados.

Amtrak's small (1882) beachside station, popular since bygone days when Hollywood movie stars such as Mary Pickford, Charlie Chaplin, Rudolph Valentino, Douglas Fairbanks and other film stars and vacationers arrived from Los Angeles by train, has recently been moved north to Solana Beach. Passengers can taxi back to Del Mar or arrange for hotel pickup.

The wide beach with gentle waves spilling onto the sand is too hard to resist. To better savor beautiful Del Mar, you need to spend some time strolling barefoot in the sand . . . sit and relax for a while and watch the bathers, listen for the train whistle, and let the sun work its magic.

Return to Los Angeles by heading back inland on Via de la Valle to connect with I–5 north.

There's More

Smith-Shipley-Magee House, 258 Beech Avenue, Carlsbad. The 1887 home of Samuel Church Smith is now headquarters for the Carlsbad Historical Society.

Shipley-Magee Barn, Magee Park, Carlsbad. Collection of old farming implements and a cistern.

St. Michael's Episcopal Church, 2775 Carlsbad Boulevard, Carlsbad. Small redwood chapel, built in 1896.

Carlsbad Raceway, at the city's eastern edge, is the site of weekend world-class motocross racing; elaborate skateboard area. Year-round. For information call (760) 727–1171 (recording).

Watersports. Snug Harbor Marina, in Agua Hedionda Lagoon, 4215 Harrison Street, Carlsbad. (760) 434–3089. Water-ski, jet-ski, waverunner rentals.

Golf. Rancho Carlsbad Golf Course, 5200 El Camino Real, Carlsbad. (760) 438–1772. Executive, 18-hole public course.

Tennis and Golf. Carlsbad High School, 3557 Monroe Street, Carlsbad. Nine courts; open after school and evenings.

Del Mar Recreation Center, 15555 Turf Road, Del Mar. (760) 481–0363. Eight lighted courts and lighted golf driving range.

Stage Coach Park, 3420 Camino de los Coches, Carlsbad. (760) 434–2895. Four courts; open evenings.

Hadley Fruit Orchards, 6115 Paseo del Norte/I–5 Palomar Airport Road, Carlsbad. (800) 854–5655; (760) 438–1260. Free catalog. Large selection of California dried fruits and nuts, giftpacks, wine cellar/tasting room.

Hot-air ballooning. Skysurfer Balloon Company, 1221 Camino del Mar, Del Mar. (760) 481–6800. Sunrise and sunset flights over the scenic canyons and coastline, followed by Champagne party. Reservations required.

Farmer's markets. Public parking lot on Roosevelt Avenue between Carlsbad Village Drive and Grand Avenue, Carlsbad Village. Every Wednesday from 2:00 to 5:00 P.M. Farm-fresh and organically grown fruits and vegetables, herbs, spices, flowers.

City Hall parking lot, 1050 Camino del Mar, Del Mar. Every Saturday, 1:00 to 4:00 P.M. Fresh produce, beautiful fresh flowers, plants, honey, avocados, and eggs.

Barnstorming Adventures, Ltd., 6743 Montia Court, Carlsbad, CA 92009. (800) 759–5667; (760) 438–7680. Don helmet and goggles and thrill to open-cockpit biplane rides with certified pilots in daily flights over the beautiful coastline.

Coast Express Rail Line. The new Coaster runs daily from Oceanside to San Diego with stops in Carlsbad. (800) 262–7837.

Special Events

Early January. Five-day Mercedes championship golf, La Costa Resort and Spa, Carlsbad.

Late January. San Diego Marathon, Carlsbad.

Late March. Carlsbad 5000 (5K race). Attracts the world's fastest distance runners.

Late April. North San Diego Rockhoppers Volksmarch (10K walk), Carlsbad.

April 25 to May 12. Del Mar National Horse Show, Del Mar Fairgrounds, Del Mar. (760) 296–1441.

Early May. Strawberry Festival, St. Michael's by the Sea, Carlsbad.

First Sunday in May. Carlsbad Village Faire. Largest one-day street fair in California.

Late June through August. Evening jazz concerts in the park, Carlsbad.

Mid-June to early July. Del Mar Fair, Del Mar Fairgrounds.

Mid-July. Summer Village Art Festival, Carlsbad.

Second Sunday in July. Carlsbad Triathlon, Carlsbad.

End of July through September. Thoroughbred racing, Del Mar. Closed Tuesday.

Late August. Toshiba Tennis Classic, La Costa Resort and Spa, Carlsbad.

Early October. Oktoberfest, Carlsbad.

Mid-October. Two-day Southern California Grand Prix, Del Mar.

First Sunday in November. Carlsbad Village Faire. Largest one-day street fair in California.

Early December. Christmas tree lighting, Carlsbad.

Other Recommended Restaurants and Lodgings

Carlsbad

Armenian Cafe, 3126 Carlsbad Boulevard. (760) 720–2233. Small cottage features Belgian and other waffles for breakfast, plus Armenian specialties—pita bread, lamb, and so on. Closed Monday and Tuesday.

Daily News Cafe, 3001 Carlsbad Boulevard. (760) 729–1023. At the Carlsbad Inn. Place your order at the counter and food is brought to your table inside or on the busy patio. Cute menu. Omelets, buttermilk pancakes, salads, sandwiches, freshly made croissants, cinnamon rolls, Belly Bombers (burgers). Breakfast and lunch only.

Jay's Gourmet Restaurant, 2975 Carlsbad Boulevard. (760) 720–9668. Opposite Neiman's. Prepare to stand in line at this small, checkered-tablecloth beehive for its seafood, pizza, calzone, pastas, and veal dishes, with homemade sauces.

Kafana Coffee, 3076 Carlsbad Boulevard, Carlsbad. (760) 720–0074. Convenient for coffee breaks and snacks around the clock or quick breakfast. Extensive selection of fine coffees ground to order. They roast their own beans on the premises. Fresh pastries, bagels; snack inside or on front patio. Nightly entertainment.

The Alley, 401 Grand Avenue, Carlsbad. (760) 434–1173. By the railroad tracks. Congenial after-hours cocktails and dancing nightly; piano bar.

Carlsbad Inn, 3075 Carlsbad Boulevard. (800) 235–3939 (United States and Canada); (760) 434–7020. Across from the beach in the center of town; 50 hotel rooms, half with kitchenettes, and 132 condominiums. In-room coffeemakers, TV, video players, satellite TV;

heated swimming pool, Jacuzzi, health club gym-sauna. Picnic cabana on the beach.

La Costa Resort and Spa, Costa del Mar Road. (800) 854–5000 (national); (760) 438–9111. Internationally known luxury celebrity resort of 478 rooms, suites, and private residences on 400 acres. Five restaurants, Tournament of Champions lounge; two championship golf courses, twenty-one tennis courts, beauty/health spa; shopping gallery, salon, movie theater. Golf, tennis, and spa packages.

Encinitas

Raddison Hotel, 85 Encinitas Boulevard. (800) 333-3333 (worldwide); (760) 942–7455. Dramatically situated atop a bluff overlooking the ocean. Ninety-one rooms and suites, some with kitchenettes, all with balconies, cable TV. Heated swimming pool, whirlpool; coffeeshop and restaurant. Complimentary continental breakfast in coffeeshop or lobby, plus daily newspaper.

Del Mar

En Fuego, 1342 Camino del Mar. (760) 792–6551. Patio diners prefer the great chicken *fajita* salad and Mexican specialties.

Del Mar Inn, 720 Camino del Mar (at 9th Street). (800) 453–4411 (in California); (800) 451–4515 (elsewhere); (760) 755–9765. Warm, English-style architecture and country decor; eighty good-size rooms, half with kitchenettes, overlook ocean or garden. Satellite TV and free movie channel; heated swimming pool, spa; complimentary continental breakfast served in your room; complimentary afternoon English Tea and Cakes in the cozy library.

L'Auberge Del Mar, 1540 Camino del Mar. (800) 553–1336; (760) 259–1515. Opened in 1989, on the site of the landmark old Hotel Del Mar. Luxurious amenities in French country decor in 123 rooms and suites, many with coastal views, large balconies, minibar and refrigerator, marble baths. Two heated swimming pools, fitness center, beauty spa; two tennis courts; restaurant. Sunday brunch. Special getaway packages.

For More Information

Carlsbad Convention and Visitors Bureau, P.O. Box 1246, Carlsbad, CA 92008. (800) 227–5722; (760) 434–6093.

Encinitas, North Coast Chamber of Commerce, 138 Encinitas Boulevard., Encinitas, CA 92024. (760) 753–6041.

Self-Realization Fellowship Retreat and Hermitage, 215 K Street, Encinitas, CA 92024. (760) 753–1181.

Greater Del Mar Chamber of Commerce, 1104 Camino del Mar, Del Mar, CA 92014. (760) 755–4844.

La Jolla

The sheltered La Jolla Cove

Coves and Caves

_____ 1 NIGHT _____

Beaches • Watersports • Dining • Shopping
Museums • Parks • Galleries • Hang gliding • Aquarium

Here's a two-day itinerary south to an energetic little seaside resort perched atop the edge of the Pacific Ocean. In addition to all manner of watersports, golf, tennis, and hang gliding, you'll have a tantalizing choice of good dining, visit an ocean-view museum and a delightful aquarium, picnic in the park, prowl upscale galleries, poke around chic boutiques, relax, sun and swim in a protected cove, and pedal a bike on a scenic path along the ever-present ocean.

Day 1

Morning

Drive south on I–5 about 115 miles to **La Jolla.** Exit at La Jolla Shores Drive, continue to Torrey Pines Road, turn left, and stay on it to Girard Avenue, in the heart of downtown.

Though La Jolla (pronounced "La Hoya") is probably best known for its variety of summer activities, any season is perfect for a visit. In an exuberance of natural beauty, its 7 miles of sandy beaches are wrapped around a spectacular coastline of towering cliffs, scraggy coves, and hilly terrain. Often referred to as a quaint little village, La Jolla is about as quaint as Clint Eastwood.

Creative people have long been attracted to the scenic locale. The first group of artists and actors seduced by the windswept coast and long lonely stretches of beach settled here in the 1930s. They created the legendary **Green Dragon Colony** on Prospect Street, with homes and studios overlooking the peaceful cove. Art is still a major part of village life, with dozens of galleries tucked throughout the city.

Additionally, La Jolla is a renowned think-tank hub, framed by the prestigious Salk Institute for Biological Studies, with its Nobel laureates; the University of California at San Diego campus; and Scripps Institution of Oceanography, whose enchanting aquarium attracts some 300,000 visitors yearly.

With its rolling hills, lush tropical planting, palms and tall aromatic eucalyptus trees, winding streets, posh hotels, dazzling ocean vistas, world-class shopping, and cheery sidewalk cafes, the effervescent city just 15 miles north of San Diego has a decidedly Mediterranean flavor and is frequently compared with the French Riviera.

Lunch: **Putnam's,** 910 Prospect Street, La Jolla. (619) 454–2181. In the Colonial Inn. A classy, popular pub with marble floors and a warm setting. You'll find friendly service and good hearty food, continental-American style, in pastas, sandwiches, and fresh seafood. Moderately priced; free valet parking.

Afternoon

The best thing about La Jolla is that its small downtown area is so compact you can explore the city by foot, thus avoiding the busy traffic and hard-to-find parking spaces. Even the beaches are an easy stroll from downtown.

Begin with stately **Girard Avenue,** the city's main thoroughfare. This lovely broad street, lined with tall palms and eucalyptus trees, is vaguely reminiscent of Santa Barbara, with its landscaped areas and wrought-iron benches. Shoppers' favorites along this stretch include Polo Ralph Lauren; Gallery Alexander, with ever-creative exhibits and collections; a preponderance of fine jewelry shops; and Banana Republic.

Girard leads into lively, attractive **Prospect Street,** a sweeping terrace atop the cliffs that overlooks the ocean and offers a complete change of ambience. You won't find many streets quite like this one, where shops and restaurants facing the water present spectacular views of the cove and the famous La Jolla Caves. It's a bustling, pedestrian-oriented street for shopping, dining, and browsing, filled with sleek boutiques, galleries, sidewalk cafes and posh restaurants, people, and traffic.

On the ocean side the pink-domed landmark La Valencia Hotel is flanked by cafes and shops. The Chart House Restaurant, 1270 Prospect Street, leads into **Coast Walk,** where boutiques and galleries housed in small cottages set far back from the sidewalk on wide expanses of lawn and brick-paved courtyards, pretty gazebos, and wide shade trees are the legacies of the famed Green Dragon Art Colony. The Collector, a fine jewelry shop, is a prime source for pink tourmalines mined in San Diego, tanzanite from Africa, and other gemstones as well as decorative mineral specimens. (A sister store is in Fallbrook). The Gallery of Two Sisters shows a pleasing selection of oil paintings, watercolors, stoneware, and ironwood sculpture by California artists, at good prices.

Shoppers and adventurers won't want to miss La Jolla Cave & Shell Shop, 1325 Coast Walk (619–454–6080), one of the city's oldest shops. Ensconced atop the cliffs since 1903, the shop features decorative and specimen shells, jewelry, and the like from all over the world. From the shop you can descend the 133 steps built into a man-made, lighted tunnel to **Sunny Jim Cave,** the largest of La Jolla's original seven sea-level smugglers' caves and the only one that can be entered (fee charged for the adventure).

At the end of Coast Walk, follow bikers, joggers, and strollers along the curving and scenic Cliff Walk atop the bluffs overlooking **La Jolla Cove,** the center of attraction for residents and visitors alike. The small protected beach, with its calm and crystalline water, is the favorite area for swimming, scuba diving, snorkeling, sunbathing, and socializing. Cliff Walk also overlooks La Jolla's notorious smugglers' caves in the shallow water below, and from here you can watch people clambering all over them. Especially Sunny Jim Cave.

Wander farther down to the **Ellen Browning Scripps Park** at the foot of Coast Walk bordering the cove. Here you're apt to find an old-fashioned tableau of people picnicking or lazily sprawled on the warm grass in the dappled shade of slender palms and the lofty Torrey pines, evoking a feeling of having stumbled into an impressionist painting. La Jolla's balmy climate nurtures the rare, prehistoric, sea-loving Torrey pines, which exist in only one other place on earth: Santa Rosa Island off Santa Barbara. Bring your own picnic lunch or snack, stake out a bench or patch of grass, and enjoy the superb ocean view or watch the surfers. Many picnickers arrive as late as 5:00 P.M. with food hampers and blankets to enjoy the blazing sunsets over the ocean.

Dinner: **Sammy's California Woodfired Pizza Kitchen,** 702 Pearl (corner of Draper), La Jolla. (619) 456–5222. One of the most popular places in town. They don't take reservations, so feel lucky to find a seat at the counter, where you can watch the chefs make designer pizzas and generous salads; both can be shared.

Lodging: **The Empress Hotel,** 7766 Fay Avenue, La Jolla, CA 92037. (800) 525–6552 (nationwide); (619) 454–3001. In the heart of the village, sixty-eight oversize ocean-view rooms and four suites offer complimentary continental breakfast in a hospitality room. In-room coffeemaker, refrigerator, cable TV with in-room movies, daily newspaper; restaurant; sauna, Jacuzzi, exercise room; sundeck. The suites feature glamorous marble Jacuzzi tubs in the bedrooms.

Day 2

Morning

Breakfast: Enjoy the complimentary continental breakfast in your hotel.

Walk or drive to the recently remodeled and expanded **San Diego Museum of Contemporary Art,** 700 Prospect Street, (619) 454–3541. The long, low structure with sculpture garden overlooking the ocean is the former home of heiress Ellen B. Scripps, the city's benefactress; built in 1916 and designed by noted architect Irving Gill, who designed many other buildings in La Jolla. The enlarged Book Shop features a fine selection of children's books about artists in addition to adult material. The museum's extensive remodeling includes a cafe and a large new entrance lobby. Open Tuesday through Saturday from 10:00 A.M. to 5:00 P.M., Sunday from noon to 5:00 P.M. Closed Monday. Admission.

Two doors away, John Cole's Book Shop, 7800 Prospect Street, tucked in a historic wisteria-covered cottage, is a bookworm's haven, offering a wide selection of titles, in addition to folk art, imported toys, ocean views, and a cozy fire.

Lunch: **The Spot,** 1005 Prospect Street, La Jolla. (619) 349–0800. A local favorite, friendly and casual for sandwiches, good Chicago-style pizza, salad, barbecued baby back ribs, and daily gourmet chef special.

Afternoon

Drive north on Torrey Pines Road to Expedition Way, off La Jolla Village Drive; turn left toward the ocean and south to the **Stephen Birch Aquarium Museum** (619–534–FISH), on the campus of the University of California at Diego in **Scripps Institution of Oceanography,** one of the oldest, largest, and most important centers for marine science research. This new, $14-million facility, which opened in September 1992, is larger and more impressive than the Scripps Aquarium it replaced.

The boulder-decked outdoor tide pool that overlooks the sparkling coastline captivates children looking for starfish, mussels, and other small local sea animals. Inside, the aquarium features thirty-three tanks displaying more than 3,000 colorful fish from tropical waters as well as from the chill waters of the Pacific Northwest.

Among the stunning, shimmering variety of rainbow-colored fish and plants are a giant octopus; elegant vertical seahorses; fast-moving sharks, which always draw considerable interest; spooky moray eels; and venomous yellow-and-brown lionfish. A dramatic, 16-foot-deep kelp forest in a 50,000-gallon tank is viewed through a 21-by-13-foot acrylic wall.

The museum features the largest oceanographic exhibit in the United States. The bookshop offers more than 1,500 gifts, as well as extensive science and oceanographic literature. Open daily except Christmas Day, from 9:00 A.M. to 5:00 P.M. Admission.

Salk Institute for Biological Studies, 10010 North Torrey Pines Road (619–453–4100), on a promontory adjacent to the University of California at San Diego, is renowned for medical research, and foremost biologists come here to study. The powerful building was designed by the late architect Louis Kahn specifically for Dr. Jonas Salk, its founding director. The sprawling complex is a dramatic masterwork of poured concrete, glass, and travertine and is visited by many architects. Public tours are available weekdays at 10:00 A.M., 11:00 A.M., and noon.

For those interested in **hang gliding,** Torrey Pines Gliderport, La Jolla Village Farms Road (619–457–9093)—a popular, expert-rated launching site for hang gliders—is just up the road from the Salk Institute. Drive up the coastal hilltop and park on the towering bluff 300 feet above the ocean (overlooking Black's Nude Beach). Walk up to the knoll and watch the hang gliders assemble their craft, which they bring rolled up like tall masts in long zippered cases. Then watch them take flight in their fragile, multicolored craft like giant butterflies, as the wind off the sea lifts them from cliff's edge and they ride the updrafts to altitudes up to 1,500 feet, soaring over the cliffs and sand out to sea. Weekends are the best time to watch. In spring, when winds are strong, many hang gliders are in the air at once. Whatever the season, the best hours are between noon and 5:00 P.M., when the updrafts are strongest. For rentals, sales, and instruction, contact the Hang Gliding Center, 4206 Sorrento Valley Center, Del Mar (619–450–9008).

From here retrace your way back to Los Angeles on I–5 north.

There's More

Golf. Try the 9-hole Pitch & Putt course at Spindrift Golf Course, 2000 Spindrift Drive (619–454–7126). Torrey Pines Municipal Course, 11480 Torrey Pines Road (619–453–0381), will remind you of Pebble Beach, where cliffside fairways on two 18-hole championship courses overlook the blue Pacific.

Bike riding. Follow the marked scenic route along the coast or through town.

Skin and scuba diving. The craggy coves of Bird Rock, La Jolla Underwater Park, and underwater Scripps Canyon are the best areas for skin and scuba diving.

Surfing. Windansea Beach, considered one of the best surfing beaches along the West Coast, is at the end of Nautilus Street, between the village and Bird Rock to the south. For gear contact San Diego Diver's Supply, 7522 La Jolla Boulevard (619–459–2691).

Snorkeling/swimming. Can't beat La Jolla Cove.

Tennis. La Jolla Recreation Center, 615 Prospect Street (619–454–2071); La Jolla YMCA, 8355 Cliffridge Drive (619–453–3483); La Jolla High School, 750 Nautilus Street (619–454–2071).

Special Events

First week in June. La Jolla Festival of the Arts & Food Faire.

June through September. Concerts by the Sea, in Scripps Park series.

Last Sunday in August. Off the Wall Street Party.
Second Sunday in September. Annual Rough Waterswim, at La Jolla Cove.
Late September. La Jolla Arts Festival.
First Sunday in December. Holiday Festival Arts & Crafts Fair.

Other Recommended Restaurants and Lodgings

La Jolla

Alphonso's of La Jolla, 1251 Prospect Street. (619) 454–2232. A lively, crowded hangout for Mexican specialties but hard to get in the door or find a seat at a patio table.

Avanti Ristorante, 875 Prospect Street. (619) 454–4288. Locals recommend the fine cuisine of this elegant, black-and-white art deco room with pink tablecloths and dim lighting. Tuxedoed waiters are familiar with its northern Italian menu.

George's at the Cove, 1250 Prospect Street. (619) 454–4244. A long-time convivial favorite for creative regional cuisine amid romantic candlelit tables overlooking the cove. Dressy and expensive. Sunday brunch. Free valet parking.

Harry's Coffee Shop, 7545 Girard Avenue. (619) 454–7381. Where late risers go for breakfast. Sometimes everyone in town shows up when you do. Admire the wall paintings while waiting for your eggs or hamburgers. Park in the rear; open Monday through Saturday, 6:00 A.M. to 3:00 P.M., and Sunday until 2:00 P.M.

John's Waffle Shop, 7906 Girard Avenue. (619) 454–7371. A busy breakfast landmark for waffles, pancakes, and omelets. If you sit at the counter in this small cafe, you can watch your order sizzling. Breakfast served, with luncheon specialties included; open Monday through Saturday, 7:00 A.M. to 3:00 P.M.

Top O' the Cove, 1216 Prospect Street. (619) 454–7779. Set high on the bluffs in an ocean-view bungalow with candlelit tables; expensive but a consistent winner for fine continental cuisine and sublime desserts.

El Crab Catcher, 1298 Prospect Street. (619) 454–9587. Overlooking the coastline, featuring a variety of fresh crab and seafood entrees. Pleasant service. Sunday brunch.

Manhattan of La Jolla, 7766 Fay Avenue. (619) 454–1182. In the Empress Hotel. Sleekly sophisticated northern Italian cuisine in a New

York setting. Sink into an upholstered booth and watch the tropical fish drift by. Pasta, seafood, steaks, and chicken in generous portions; attentive waiters.

La Valencia Hotel, 1132 Prospect Street. (800) 451–0772; (619) 454–0771. Eighty-nine rooms and eleven suites, heart-shaped swimming pool—the choice of distinguished visitors since Garbo and other stars used to hide out in the 1930s. TV, clock radio, hair dryer, coffeemaker, minibar, refrigerator, daily newspaper, nightly turndown service; twenty-four-hour room service; three restaurants, lounge. Overnight parking fee. The Mediterranean Room's tropical, palm-fringed patio is a lively rendezvous for breakfast, lunch, dinner, and Sunday brunch. (619) 454–1199.

Colonial Inn, 910 Prospect Street. (800) 826–1278 (California); (800) 832–5525 (nationwide); (619) 454–2181. Fully restored, historic 1913 landmark in Victorian-style hotel, 1 block from the beach. Sixty-seven elegantly appointed rooms and eight suites; TV, clock radio, refrigerator on request (no charge), daily newspaper, complimentary continental breakfast in Putnam's; turndown service. Heated swimming pool. Complimentary valet and self-parking.

Inn by the Sea (Best Western), 7830 Fay Avenue. (800) 526–4545; (619) 459–4461. In the heart of the village. Private balconies for 132 rooms and 2 suites; TV with movie channels, clock radio, minirefrigerator available on request (no charge), hair dryer, room service, complimentary continental breakfast in lobby. Heated swimming pool, spa, fitness room; restaurant; conference facilities; complimentary valet and self-parking.

For More Information

Official Visitor's Bureau, La Jolla Town Council, 1055 Wall Street (corner of Herschel Street), La Jolla, CA 92037. (619) 454–1444.

La Jolla Historical Society, 7846 Eads Avenue, La Jolla, CA 92037. (619) 459–5335 Open Tuesday and Thursday, 2:00 to 4:00 P.M., or write to Box 2085, La Jolla, CA 92038.

San Diego/Coronado

Balboa Park is the cultural hub of San Diego.

Lively Seafront Holiday

2 NIGHTS

Zoo • Parks • Old Town • Trolley Tours • History
Historic hotels • Museums • Harbor cruise • Marine park

In this two-night, three-day excursion, you'll barely get to sample all the highlights of this versatile seaport city where California was born in 1769. Cheer a performing killer whale; ride a ferry across the sparkling bay to a tony Victorian resort enclave. Historic San Diego has been host to Franciscan Father Junípero Serra, Wyatt Earp, Charles Lindbergh, the Prince of Wales, Clint Eastwood, and Marilyn Monroe.

Day 1

Morning

Drive south on I–5, the Santa Ana Freeway, for this 120-mile excursion, which should take about two and a half to three hours, depending on freeway traffic. The scenic drive passes through orange groves, farms, little beach cities, and rolling countryside of low, cinnamon-colored foothills and sweet, soft air.

At the northern edge of San Diego, adjacent to I–5, that gleaming, elaborate, white Gothic-style structure with 190-foot-tall twin spires is the landmark San Diego Mormon Temple. As you near San Diego, you can see the skyline high-rise beyond the water-skiers and sailboats. Your first stop is the world-famous **zoo** in Balboa Park.

Take the Civic Center/10th Avenue exit to A Street, turn left, and turn left again at 12th/Park. Follow signs to the zoo and parking area along President's Way. The zoo, spread over one hundred well-landscaped acres, is the city's most popular attraction, noted for its exotic and rare wildlife. Cuddly teddy-bear koalas and playful pygmy chimpanzees are among its collection of 3,200 animals of 800 species. Most are in barless, moated enclosures resembling their natural habitats.

You can wander about on your own or pay a bit more for admission that includes the forty-minute, narrated 3-mile double-deck bus tour (better view from the upper deck) that roams through 60 percent of the zoo.

Besides the galaxy of graceful flamingos poised for photos near the entrance, among animals you'll see on the bus tour are the 500-pound pygmy hippos, California sea lions working on their suntans, the elusive Chinese leopard, Alaskan brown bears, zebras, 17-foot-tall giraffes, and the slinky jaguar. Roosters and chickens strut and fly freely throughout.

Though the bus tour covers a lot, by taking it you'll miss the world's largest collection of monkeys and apes, the children's petting zoo, the birds, and the Skyfari Aerial Tram. The bus tour also makes it difficult to see many animals that aren't out front and center, or to see above or through groups of people along the paths. Though walking may become tiring, you can stop, watch animals of interest, and take photos. (Open daily from 9:00 A.M.; closing hours vary and are extended in summer. Admission; free parking. Public information,

619–234–3153.)

To see more of the park's attractions drive out Park Boulevard, turn right on President's Way, and turn right again at the first boulevard; park behind the Spreckels Organ Pavilion.

Lunch: **Sculpture Garden Cafe,** 1450 El Prado Way (619) 232–7931. At the San Diego Museum of Art. Have lunch with the sculptors—Henry Moore, Joan Miró, Barbara Hepworth, and Alexander Calder—in a charming garden courtyard, a popular midday gathering place for enjoying lovely salads, various sandwiches, and pasta dishes. Open Tuesday through Friday from 10:00 A.M. to 3:00 P.M. and Saturday from 9:00 A.M. to 4:30 P.M.; closed Monday.

Afternoon

Balboa Park is a lush, 1,400-acre visual and cultural treasure one can happily spend several days exploring, with its hub of museums, theaters, and cafes. The ornate Spreckels Organ Pavilion, with curving, colonnaded walks and large outdoor organ, offers free concerts Sundays at 2:00 P.M. and Monday evenings in summer.

The park's rich, sixteenth-century Spanish-Moorish baroque architecture is enhanced with ornamental gardens and fountains, arched walkways, and a 200-foot bell tower. Ride the free red tram shuttling from one plaza to another, with frequent stops.

The Prado, across the center of the park, is embroidered with a cluster of ten museums and two art galleries winding through plazas, rose gardens, and a lily pond. The **San Diego Museum of Art**'s extensive collection ranges from pre-Columbian to twentieth-century art; it also has a Sculpture Court and Garden and a charming cafe (closed Mondays). The Reuben H. Fleet Space Theater and Science Center envelops you in a giant domed screen showing 3-D Omnimax films.

Some museums charge admission; hours vary, but most are open daily from 10:00 A.M. to 4:30 P.M. You can buy a map and guide for 60 cents at the **Balboa Park Visitors Center,** 1549 El Prado (619–239–0512). The renowned **Old Globe Theater,** designed in round, sixteenth-century style, is part of a three-theater complex presenting Shakespeare and musicals. Purchase same-day tickets at the box office if they are available (information, 619–239–2255), or buy half-price, day-of-performance tickets at Time's Art Tix downtown at the Horton Plaza ticket booth (619–497–5000). With Balboa Park's evening theater performances, plus many cafes and snackbars, you can spend a pleasurable, stimulating day and evening here.

Dinner: **Fifth and Hawthorn,** 515 Hawthorn (corner of 5th Avenue), San Diego. (619) 544–0940. Convenient uptown location close to the park; smart-looking, with white napery on candlelit tables. The menu favors California cuisine of fresh seafood, innovative salads, and light summer or smaller-portion entrees (also lower-priced) like filet mignon and pasta.

After dinner head south to Coronado Island on I–5 to Highway 75, which comes up very soon; take 75 over the San Diego–Coronado Bridge. Stay to the right as you approach the toll gates at the exit, to avoid paying the toll. (There's no toll returning to San Diego.)

Lodging: **Le Meridien San Diego at Coronado,** 2000 2nd Street, Coronado, CA 92118. (800) 543–4300; (619) 435–3000. French elegance throughout this sixteen-acre world-class hotel. Features 300 deluxe spacious rooms with sitting area, 7 suites, and 28 villas in country French decor; terraces, TV, minibar/refrigerator, hair dryer, terry robes, marble bathroom with tub and stall shower, excellent lighting, concierge service. Three heated swimming pools, two whirlpools, six lighted tennis courts, beauty spa, health club. Two restaurants and a cocktail lounge. Overnight parking fee.

Day 2

Morning

Breakfast: At the hotel. Or, if it's Sunday, investigate the buffet brunch at the noted **Hotel Del Coronado,** 1500 Orange Avenue, Coronado (619–522–8000). Each Sunday buffet brunch features a different international theme menu, served in the famed, enormous (156-by-66-foot) Crown Room. Brunch is a lavish array of hot and cold dishes, including salad bar, omelet station, hand-carved prime rib, sizzling pasta station, and incomparable desserts. Purchase your brunch tickets in the lobby. (Brunch served Sunday from 9:00 A.M. to 2:00 P.M.; reservations suggested; free validated parking.)

Following brunch explore this rambling, 1888 Victorian hotel, whose famous guests have included Edward, the Prince of Wales (said to have met Wallis Simpson, the future Duchess of Windsor, here in 1920), Charles Lindbergh, fourteen presidents, and Thomas Edison, who reportedly supervised the incandescent light installation. This is also the locale of *Some Like It Hot* and other films. The "Del" is a grand old showpiece, with its red cone-shaped roof, gleaming white trim, cupolas, and turrets (see "Other Recommended Restaurants and Lodgings"). Take the birdcage elevator to the lower-lobby level and browse the Galleria shops. Wander through the hotel's public rooms, beautiful gardens, and wide beach.

To see more of Coronado's downtown area, from 8th Street to the "Del," stay on Orange Avenue, the main street of the village and Coronado's "restaurant row." Coronado Visitor Information is upstairs at 1111 Orange Avenue (800–622–8300; 619–437–8788). Use the convenient sidewalk gondola, crammed with brochures and information.

Coronado is San Diego's resort community, graced by lovely parks and tree-lined streets; it has a relaxed, small-town flavor and offers luxury hotels, golf, tennis, bikepaths, and boating. It also has a history of famous guests and residents, such as millionaire John D. Spreckels, whose former mansion is now the vintage Glorietta Bay Inn, and L. Frank Baum, who wrote the classic *Wizard of Oz*. In 1927 Charles Lindbergh, the "Lone Eagle," took off from Coronado's North Island for his famous solo New York to Paris flight and was feted at the Hotel Del Coronado on his triumphant return.

Continue along Orange Avenue until it ends and then turn right, continuing 2^1/$_2$ blocks to **Ferry Landing Marketplace**, 1201 1st Street at B Avenue, with its Victorian-style white buildings with red roofs. This lively shopping-dining complex and fishing/ferry pier has a grassy park and a small swimming beach fronting along San Diego Bay. Sailboats crisscross the water; there's a great view of the downtown San Diego skyline, as well as of the sweeping San Diego–Coronado Bridge.

But the best part is watching the passenger ferry arrive at the pier hourly from San Diego. Before the San Diego–Coronado Bridge was built in 1969, Coronado could be reached only by ferry. The service was discontinued for almost twenty years, but now the popular ferry again carries pedestrians and bikes across the bay.

Drive back to San Diego over the 2-mile-long San Diego–Coronado Bridge; go north on I–5 to **Seaport Village**, 849 West Harbor Drive at Kettner Boulevard (619–235–4014).

Lunch: **Harbor House**, 831 West Harbor Drive, Seaport Village, on the boardwalk. (619) 232–1141. Along with its stunning harbor view, the Harbor House is noted for mesquite-grilled seafood, fresh salads, prime ribs, and steaks. The Topside Gallery lounge offers cocktails and lighter fare.

Afternoon

Enjoy Seaport Village's old-style harbor setting, with a Victorian clock tower and a lighthouse. Landscaped cobbled walks lead around restaurants; shoppers are in heaven with about sixty-five stores to browse for gourmet cookware, Scandinavian imports, and souvenirs. Saddle up on the hundred-year-old merry-go-round, then stroll the wooden boardwalk along the water.

See the highlights of San Diego aboard **Old Town Trolley Tours,** which includes Seaport Village among its ten different stops, for a stimulating, informative ninety-minute city tour encompassing Balboa Park, the zoo, Old Town, and Coronado. You can get off at any place of interest, then reboard another trolley to complete your tour. Knowledgeable drivers sprinkle entertaining commentary with anecdotes, chitchat, and history. Clint Eastwood made his day in *Dirty Harry* at Seaport Village; Wyatt Earp lived in the Gaslamp Quarter in 1850 and owned the most popular bordello in the West. You note where Charles Lindbergh stayed while his plane *Spirit of St. Louis* was being built nearby (619–298–8687; daily tours; fee).

Take Harbor Drive to the Embarcadero at the Cruise Ship Terminal, where the **Maritime Museum**'s trio of historic ships are permanently anchored along the waterfront. The magnificent tallship windjammer *Star of India,* built in 1863, is the oldest iron-hulled merchant ship afloat. Alongside are the 1890 steam ferryboat *Berkeley* and the 1904 steam yacht *Medea.*

Downtown's dynamic **Horton Plaza** dominates a 7-block stretch between Broadway and G Street. This shopping-dining hub houses 3 department stores and some 150 shops, as well as restaurants, theaters, and a multilingual International Visitors Information Center. The **Paladion,** 777 Front Street, dubbed the Rodeo Drive of San Diego, is an enclave of such prestigious designer names as Cartier, Tiffany, Ferragamo, Gianni Versace, Bernini, and Alfred Dunhill.

You're within a few blocks of the historic and lively **Gaslamp Quarter,** bounded by Broadway to Harbor Drive, 4th Avenue to 6th. This historic district dates back to the end of the Civil War. After a neglected period it has been restored—its Victorian 1880 buildings now house trendy shops and ethnic restaurants, galleries, and bistros—and is one of the most popular areas in the city. Come for lunch or dinner and stay to hear the jazz the quarter is noted for. Along 5th Avenue the 700 and 800 blocks appear to have more attractive restaurants. Parking is a problem, though many have valet parking, and the one-way streets make it difficult for hungry visitors.

Dinner: **Panevino Ostario,** 732 5th Avenue, San Diego. (619) 598–7959. In the lively Gaslamp Quarter, small and inviting, with a warm decor of brick walls and small, granite-topped tables. Veal specialties, ravioli, rigatoni. Delicious bread is served with your salad, and you can watch the chef bake your pizza in the brick oven.

Lodging: Le Meridien San Diego at Coronado.

Day 3

Morning

Breakfast: **Bay Beach Cafe,** at Ferry Landing Marketplace, Coronado. (619) 435–4900. Just north of your hotel. Dine indoors or enjoy the balmy breeze on the cheery deck overlooking San Diego Bay as sailboats drift past your morning coffee or mimosa. Egg specialties are served with potatoes or refried beans.

Leave for **Old Town.** Cross the San Diego–Coronado Bridge, take I–5 north to the Old Town Avenue exit, turn right, follow the signs, and turn left on San Diego Avenue. As you cross the bridge, the air is so clear you can see far across to the mountains framing the city.

San Diego began in Old Town in 1769, when Father Junípero Serra established California's first mission, Mission San Diego de Alcala, and the Presidio, a military installation on a hilltop overlooking San Diego Bay. Soldiers' families and early settlers gradually moved down to the flatland, and the old pueblo is the 6-block area of Old Town. The **old central plaza** along San Diego Avenue, the main street, is lined with restaurants, shops, and history. Along here are several cafes including the Old Town Mexican Cafe, where you can watch the tortilla ladies in the window making fresh tortillas, patting them between their hands. Shopping variety includes Mexican Imports and Apache Indian Art. Free walking tours of Old Town are given daily at 2:00 P.M. from the Old Town State Park Information Center, 4002 Wallace Street (619) 220–5424.

Around the corner, **Heritage Park** is a delightful cluster of multi-story, restored Victorian-era mansions of bright colors, ivory white trim, cupolas, balconies, verandas, and old-fashioned gardens. They house antiques and dolls and offer romantic overnighting at Heritage Park Bed and Breakfast (619–299–6832). From here turn right on Twiggs and left on Juan Street in Old Town to reach Bazaar del Mundo.

Lunch: **Casa De Bandini,** 2660 Calhoun Street, Old Town San Diego. (619) 297–8211. Dine in the courtyard of Juan Bandini's restored 1823 adobe mansion, a State Historic Site. Relax beneath a shady umbrella as you sip a cool margarita in this pretty place near a splashing fountain. Gourmet Mexican and seafood specialties.

Afternoon

Bazaar del Mundo, next door at 2754 Calhoun Street, is a festive dining-shopping garden marketplace of sixteen international shops for handcrafted gifts, Guatemalan fashions, jewelry, pottery, and folk art. Restaurants here are Casa de Pico, Lino's Italian Cuisine, and Rancho El Nopal Restaurant & Cantina for Mexican/American specialties. Shops are open daily from 10:00 A.M. to 9:00 P.M. (619) 296–3161.

To get to **Sea World,** take I–5 north to the Sea World Drive exit and turn left. The 150-acre marine park is located on Mission Bay.

Plan to stay several hours to see the six major shows staged during the day, featuring performing killer whales, seals, otters, sea lions, dolphins, and penguins. Shamu, the three-ton terpsichorean killer whale, is the pride of Sea World. Read your guide map and review the show schedule so you'll know which way to go in this spread-out park. Between showtimes you can visit twenty marine animal exhibits and three aquariums.

Spend the rest of the day in Sea World. Browse the pleasant shops, snack in the cafes, and cool off with ice cream or frozen yogurt. Open daily, 9:00 A.M. to dusk and to 11:00 P.M. in summer; admission; free parking. (714) 939–6212; (619) 226–3901.

There's More

San Diego Harbor Excursions, 1050 North Harbor Drive at Broadway, San Diego. (800) 442–7847; (619) 234–4111. Take in a one- or two-hour narrated cruise of San Diego Bay; food and drink aboard. Fee.

Cabrillo National Monument and Visitor Center, on the tip of Point Loma, San Diego. (619) 557–5450. The statue of Juan Rodriguez Cabrillo commemorates his 1542 discovery of California. The old Point Loma lighthouse provides an unbeatable panoramic view out to sea and is a prime spot for whale-watching.

Mission San Diego de Alcala, 10818 San Diego Mission Road, San Diego. (619) 281–8449. The first of California's twenty-one Franciscan missions, established by Father Junípero Serra on Presidio Hill in 1769. The mission houses Father Serra's original records and an ecclesiastical art museum. Self-guided tour; services daily; admission.

San Diego Trolley, Santa Fe Depot. Broadway and Kettner Boulevard, San Diego. (619) 231–8549 or 233–3004. The red trolley takes you on a 16-mile trip from downtown to the Mexican border. Every quarter-hour daily, from 5:00 A.M. to 1:00 A.M.; $1.75 each way.

San Diego Factory Outlet Center at the International Border, 4498 Camino de la Plaza, San Ysidro. (619) 690–2999. Well-known manufacturers offer factory-outlet prices in designer clothing, housewares, toys, shoes, leathergoods, and more. Open daily. Exit I–5 at the sign LAST U.S. EXIT and turn right; proceed 1 block.

Spreckels Park, Orange Avenue between 6th and 7th streets, Coronado. Donated by John D. Spreckels, a charming park, with children's playground and nostalgic bandstand for Sunday-evening summer concerts.

Tidelands Park. Twenty-two acres of shoreline below the San Diego–Coronado Bridge in Coronado. A lively spot to swim, picnic, walk, and bicycle; children's playground.

Art-in-the-Park. Where local artists display work in Spreckels Park, Coronado, the first and third Sunday of the month, from 10:00 A.M. to 4:00 P.M.

Farmer's market, Ferry Landing Marketplace, 1st and B Street, Coronado. Every Tuesday 2:30 to 6:00 P.M.; fresh fruits and vegetables.

Special Events

Mid-January to mid-May. San Diego Opera Season.

Mid-March. Annual St Patrick's Day Parade, San Diego.

Early April. Annual San Diego Crew Classic.

Early April through early October. San Diego Padres baseball season home games, Jack Murphy Stadium. (619) 283–4494.

Mid-April. Annual Coronado Flower and Garden Show.

Early May. Annual Cinco de Mayo Festival, Old Town San Diego State Park.

Early June. Annual Greek Festival, Miss California Pageant, (619–497–0430), San Diego.

Late June. San Diego International Triathlon. (619) 233–8797.

July 4. Annual Coronado Independence Day Celebration.

Mid-July. Bastille Day Celebration, Balboa Park, San Diego.

Mid-August. Annual World Body Surfing Championships. Oceanside.

Early September. Annual National Bodyboard Championship Pro Am Invitational, Oceanside.

September through May. California Ballet Season, San Diego.

September through December. San Diego Chargers football home games. (619) 563–8281.

Mid-September. Annual Greek Festival, Annual All-Star Basketball Classic, San Diego.

Late September to early October. Metropolitan Tennis Championships, San Diego.

Early October. Oktoberfest, Zoo Founders Day, free day at the zoo, 9:00 A.M. to 4:00 P.M., San Diego.

Mid-October. Annual Columbus Day Parade, Festa Bella Italian Festival, San Diego.

Mid-November. Annual San Diego International Boat Show.

End of November. Annual San Diego Thanksgiving Dixieland Jazz Festival.

Early December. Coronado Christmas Open House and Parade, Annual Christmas on the Prado, Balboa Park, San Diego.

Mid-December. Annual San Diego Harbor Parade of Lights.
December 15 through February. Whale-watching, Point Loma, San Diego.

Other Recommended Restaurants and Lodgings

Gaslamp Quarter

La Strada, 701 5th Avenue. (619) 239–3400. Chic trattoria, large room, white tablecloths, open kitchen to pizza oven and grill, northern Italian cuisine.

Fio's, 801 5th Avenue, on corner. (619) 234–FIOS. Local favorite; sleek and sophisticated. Northern Italian cuisine, homemade pastas, wood-burning pizza oven, calzone, grilled chicken, meats. Valet parking.

Croce's Restaurant and Jazz Bar, 802 5th Avenue at F Street. (619) 233–4355. American southwestern and American-international cuisine.

The Horton Grand Hotel, 311 Island Avenue. (800) 542–1886; (619) 544–1886. Belle of the lively Gaslamp Quarter. Guests favor the cozy intimacy of this renovated, 1886 Victorian hotel. All 132 rooms, including 25 suites, have antique decor, cozy fireplaces, and TV (but rather small bathrooms). Suites feature microwave ovens, wetbar, two TVs. Restaurant, lounge, bar, afternoon tea, evening jazz. Overnight parking fee.

Downtown

California Cafe Bar and Grill, 502 Horton Plaza. (619) 238–5440. Great view over the harbor from the top of Horton Plaza. California cuisine, nightly piano entertainment, Sunday brunch.

Coronado

Peohe's at the Ferry Landing Marketplace, 1201 1st Street. (619) 437–4474. Dine on deck or inside beneath the skylight and amid indoor waterfalls and palm trees. Pricey menu features New York steak, grilled citrus scallops, rack of lamb. Sunday brunch.

Hotel Del Coronado, 1500 Orange Avenue. (619) 522–8000. Landmark 1888 Victorian charmer, with distinctive red, cone-shaped roof, as well as dormer windows, turrets, and cupolas. Sprawled along thirty-three beachfront acres; 692 rooms with TV, minibar, some with hair dryers and balconies. Beautiful gardens, two heated swimming pools, spas, six lighted tennis courts. Four restaurants and a deli. Overnight parking fee.

Loews Coronado Bay Resort, 4000 Coronado Bay Road. (800) 815–6399; (619) 424–4000. Four-diamond AAA and four-star *Mobil Travel Guide* awards for this luxury waterfront resort spread on a private fifteen-acre peninsula. Its 440 rooms, including thirty-seven suites with private balconies, are custom-furnished with minibar and refrigerator, two telephones, TV, spacious bathroom with oversize tub and separate shower; twenty-four-hour room service. Enjoy the good life around three heated swimming pools, spas, a fitness center, five bayside tennis courts, and an eighty-slip marina. Award-winning restaurant with a cafe and deli. Children's activities; getaway packages; overnight parking fee.

For More Information

San Diego Convention and Visitors Bureau, International Visitor Information Center, 11 Horton Plaza, San Diego, CA 92101. (619) 236–1212.

Old Town Chamber of Commerce, 3965 Artista, San Diego, CA 92110. (619) 291–4903.

Coronado Visitors Bureau, 1111 Orange Avenue, Suite A, Coronado, CA 92118. (800) 622–8300; (619) 437–8788.

Tijuana/Ensenada

Mariachis serenade diners in Ensenada.

South of the Border Serenade

_____ 3 NIGHTS _____

Duty-free shopping • Authentic Mexican cuisine
Beaches • Winery • Mariachis • Fishing • Discos

This three-night, four-day adventure south of the border from San Diego to sunny, friendly Mexico affords an interesting change in culture, language, currency, food, drink, and scenery. You don't have to take a plane to get to a foreign country, when Mexico is within a few hours' drive of Los Angeles. U.S. citizens do not need a passport for this short visit to Baja, California, a duty-free zone. In teeming Tijuana, the internationally famous U.S.-Mexican border town, and in Ensenada, a smaller resort town 70 miles farther south, you experience a different lifestyle as you are serenaded by mariachis; shop for bargains in perfume, cosmetics, and Mexican-made liquor, jewelry, pottery, and other imports; and tour a 104-year-old winery. (*Note:* Each U.S. citizen may bring back $400 worth of purchases, duty-free; adults may each bring back one liter of alcohol. And good news for bargain hunters is the recent devaluation of the Mexican peso, an event that has more than doubled our dollar's buying power. At this writing the dollar is worth seven pesos, and the value of the peso is still drifting downward.)

These aren't two sleepy, dusty little Mexican villages. Tijuana is a gaudy, vibrant jumble of noise, traffic, and people. Ensenada, though more laid-back, is a vital, upbeat, friendly port that never wants to sleep.

For a more enjoyable Mexican sojourn, bring along a gallon of drinking water to have on hand. The best way to avoid stomach upsets or traveler's diarrhea is to not drink the tap water. Stick to sealed bottles or cans of beer or soda. (Mexican beers are great.) Drink these beverages right out of the bottle. Never use ice in your drinks. Avoid salads, raw fish, raw meat, and raw vegetables; eat only fruits you can peel. Coffee and tea are safe when made with boiled water. Brush your teeth with mouthwash or bottled water. Tuck some Pepto-Bismol, Lomotil, and/or Imodium in your travel med-kit in the event of any stomach upsets.

Tank up before you cross the border into Mexico. Be certain to purchase Mexican auto insurance, as your U.S. insurance does not cover you for liability or property damage in Mexico.

Day 1

Morning

From Los Angeles drive south on I-5, the Santa Ana Freeway, to San Diego—about 120 miles—and then drive 15 to 20 miles farther to cross the Mexican border, skirting Tijuana now and visiting it on your return from Ensenada, when you can allow whatever amount of time you'd like to spend there. Ensenada can be reached via a free road and also a toll (*cuota*) road. This escape is via the well-maintained, less crowded toll road from Tijuana.

On I–5 south just past Carlsbad, take the Encinitas Boulevard exit to have lunch in this city, an easy freeway exit and return.

Lunch: **Hungry Hunter,** 305 Encinitas Boulevard, Encinitas. (619) 753–8870. Half-hidden by a Texaco station at the edge of a large, unobtrusive shopping center, this enjoyable restaurant is where they create a delicious salad bar at your table and then you go on to well-prepared sandwiches or steaks. Alternatively, **Allie's** next door offers an inexpensive buffet brunch feast with an extensive variety of delicious hot and cold dishes.

Afternoon

Return to I–5 and continue south through San Diego and to the Mexican border. They wave you right through, but on your return to the United States you must stop for customs inspection, though not every car is inspected. Be prepared for a long wait at that time. Congestion at the border can take more than two hours during the week and longer on weekends and holidays. Try to avoid crossing the border at those times. Although it is not mandatory, you should purchase Mexican auto insurance, since your U.S. insurance does not cover you for liability and property damage in Mexico. You can obtain it through your auto club in advance of your trip or on both sides of the border. It is easiest to buy it on the U.S. side. You'll see many signs along the way; most are near fast-food eateries and convenient to the freeway. Have your auto registration slip in hand, since if you have to trot back to the car for it you'll lose your place in line. This insurance typically costs about $10 a day for a three-day visit.

At the border leaving the United States, you want to be in the Rosarito/Ensenada lane; stay to the right. You also want the *cuota* (toll) road. If at any time you need to verify directions, do so at the toll booth as you pay your $1.50 for each toll (three times each way) Ask your question quickly, before you pay, as they hustle you right through.

Speed limits and distances are posted in kilometers and easy to convert into miles. Just multiply the kilometers by six and move the decimal point one space to the left. Watch all road signs carefully for directions or you may wind up in Mexicali or Tecate.

The scenic, well-kept transpeninsular highway curving along the blue-green ocean skims above lonesome sandy beaches. There is a turnoff to Rosarito Beach, about 17 miles south of Tijuana. If you want to drive through to see this popular beach city, the road intersects back to the Ensenada toll road. Magnificent vistas accompany you all the way down the coast on this uncrowded highway. You pay your last *cuota* at **Ensenada,** 7 miles from town, as you catch a glimpse of beautiful Bahia de Todos Santos (Bay of All Saints).

Check into your hotel to get your bearings, then go on out to explore downtown Ensenada. When driving, you'll soon note that not all streets have names, but some are identified at major intersections on the horizontal light bars in the center of the street. Remember that Avenida Lopez Mateos is 1st Street, and Ruiz Street and Castillo are the north and south downtown boundaries. Boulevard Costero, also known as Lazaro Cardenas, is the divided highway along the ocean.

Ensenada's vitality is contagious, marked by the town's liveliness, its friendly, hospitable people, and its endless shopping and dining attractions. Stores and restaurants all accept U.S. dollars. (*Note:* An easy way to figure the peso is to divide the peso by seven for an approximate amount and add a bit.) There is a good deal of traffic and not too many parking spaces, so you might prefer wandering about on foot along Avenida Lopez Mateos, the city's main drag.

Dinner: **La Casa del Abulon** Restaurant and Club, at the end of Boulevard Costero, Ensenada. Phone: 6–57–85. (Take Castillo Boulevard west toward the ocean to Costero Boulevard, the divided highway that follows the bay. Turn left on Costero and continue for about 1 mile to the restaurant at the curve of the road; a large sign out front also says IBIS DISCO.) La Casa del Abulon is one of the city's finest dining places—a comfortable room with ocean views, dim lighting, good food, and attentive service. Patrons dress casually, often in shorts and T-shirts. The moderately priced menu highlights baked abalone, fresh Pacific lobster, prime rib, chicken, filet mignon, and Mexican dishes. Treat yourself to a flaming dessert of delicious crepes suzette, prepared tableside.

Lodging: **Hotel Villa Marina,** Avenida Lopez Mateos and Blancarte Street, Ensenada, Baja California, Mexico 8–33–21. (U.S. mailing address: P.O. Box 727, Bonita, CA 91908). Attractive, five-year-old twelve-story hotel is a convenient downtown landmark; 146 rooms, well-furnished, nice bathrooms; some private balconies have bay views. Cable TV, air conditioning, room service, heated swimming pool, Jacuzzi. Shopping gallery; cafeteria coffeeshop and penthouse restaurant; security parking lot.

Day 2

Morning

Breakfast: Full breakfast at the hotel's coffeeshop. Includes hotcakes, eggs American or Mexican style.

Avenida Lopez Mateos is alive with little shops and restaurants; **Farmacias** (pharmacies), where you can buy prescription drugs over-the-counter without prescription at substantially lower prices than in the U.S. Cosmetics and perfumes are less-expensive, too. Mariachis stroll along with guitars and trumpets enroute to serenade diners in cantinas and restaurants. **Licores** (liquor) stores offer attractive prices, particularly in Mexican-made Kahlua; corner food carts feature local specialities for hungry patrons. Merchandise is not as inexpensive as it used to be, though prices are said to be lower than those in Tijuana. You'll find good values in ironwood sculpture, pottery, T-shirts, sterling silver jewelry stamped 925, Mexican handicrafts, and leather apparel. Sidewalk vendors offer windchimes, jewelry, and novelty items. At the corner of Avenida Lopez Mateos and Avenida Ruiz, in **Plaza Hussong**—an attractive multistory shopping center—you can explore some of the newer shops and then relax on shady wide wooden benches and watch the traffic stream by.

You'll probably hear the noise coming from **Hussong's Cantina,** a few doors away, at Ruiz 113, before you see it. Just as in the movie *Casablanca* in which "everybody goes to Rick's," everyone who visits Ensenada goes to the legendary swinging Hussong's. This plain-looking saloon with a long bar, sawdust on the floor, and mariachi entertainment caters to a boisterous young crowd; it has been the town's number-one watering hole and hangout since it opened in 1892, and still shatters records for crowds and noise.

Across Ruiz from Hussong's, **Papas and Beer** is where all that loud rhythmic music pours from. Visit its busy upstairs bar and disco, where you can join congenial locals munching on the cafe's tasty signature french fries *(papas),* washed down with cool Mexican beer. A few doors away, **Dorian's Department Store** has long been an upscale choice for cosmetics, jewelry, and clothing.

Lunch: **Las Brasas Restaurant (Pollos Rostizado),** Avenida Lopez Mateos 486, between Avenida Gastelum and Avenida Ruiz, Ensenada. 8–11–95. Here's where they roast 220 chickens a day, and from the sidewalk you can watch the golden birds spinning on the rotisserie (60 at a time), while tortilla ladies deftly pat and shape dough into perfectly round thin tortillas, using something similar to a hamburger press. Dine inside or on the sunny patio. One-half roast chicken is served with fries, tortillas, and beans. Other selections include seafood and Mexican specialties. (Closed Tuesdays.)

Afternoon

Ensenada has delicious bread, *bollilos* (rolls), and pastries to snack on or buy to take home and stash in the freezer. Look for the PANADE-RIA (bakery) sign. Among others are Panaderia La Mexican, on Castillo Street; Panaderia el Nuevo Cristal, just off Benito Juarez at Calle Sexta (6th Street), next to the cathedral; and one on Ruiz, near Hussong's.

Tour **Bodegas de Santo Tomas,** Avenida Miramar 666 (8–25–09), Baja California's oldest winery, established in 1888. Take Lopez Mateos to Miramar and turn right, proceeding about 6 blocks to the sprawling winery. Forty-five-minute guided, narrated tours wind up with complimentary wine-tastings and samplings of assorted breads and cheeses, all available for purchase. The Gift Shop and Wine Store are stocked with logo T-shirts, glasses, and other attractive souvenirs. (Open daily at 11:00 A.M., 1:00 P.M., and 3:00 P.M. but closed at all other times; $2.00 per person.)

In this festive, lighthearted city, the better shopping area on Lopez Mateos is from Blancarte around the Hotel Villa Marina to Castillo Street. **Sara's** elegant, cool shop features cosmetics, perfumes (including Ralph Lauren, Calvin Klein, and Chanel), charming Lladro figurines; boutique clothing is downstairs. In this stretch you'll also find Casa Crystal's sleek silver jewelry and art objects. The Hunter is stocked with leathergoods, and Mario's Silver Shop gleams with lovely gold and silver jewelry, handbags, and fine guitars. Explore Asin's large selection of Lladro figurines from Spain as well as Mexican wood carvings at good prices. Across the street, Old Pier Block is reliable for T-shirts, straw hats, and handbags. Shoppers should also look for open-air markets and vendor stands on some of the side streets. Many stores offer discounts or are open to negotiation.

Dinner: **Las Cazuelas restaurant/bar,** Boulevard Costero and Sangines (next to La Casa del Abulon), Ensenada. 6–54–60. Drive to Costero Boulevard, turn left, and continue about 1 mile. This is another locals' and visitors' favorite, with excellent cuisine and service that spoils you. Moderately priced menu features Mexican dishes—delicate burritos, shrimp ranchero, *chipotle,* and so on—and also prime rib, filet mignon, lobster, fresh seafood, and New York steak. Live rhythmic lounge music enhances your dinner as will a dessert of peach Melba prepared and flambéed tableside.

Lodging: Hotel Villa Marina.

Day 3

Morning

Breakfast: **Sorrento Restaurant,** on Avenida Lopez Mateos next to the Cortez Motor Hotel, Ensenada. Regular American breakfast fare of bacon and eggs can be recharged with *chiliquiles,* hot red sauce, chorizo, and Salsa Ketchup. But the pancakes are delicious—light and fluffy.

After breakfast browse around this exciting part of downtown. If you're driving, note that parking meters are not in effect on Saturday and Sunday; the green zones are free to park in while shopping in the nearby stores. The busy sidewalks and roads are clean, and along Avenida Lopez Mateos arcades protect shops and shoppers from the sun. For cold drinks and snacks, Blanco, a large supermarket, is on Gastelum off Lopez Mateos.

Follow Boulevard Lazaro Cardenas along the blue crescent-shaped bay to Estero Beach, 6 miles south of Ensenada, for lunch at tony **Estero Beach Resort.** You'll pass a military base, groves of olive trees, roadside stores, and vendors selling baskets and pottery. Turn right at the sign for Estero Beach and then left to the resort.

Built in 1937, the resort is a sprawling, cushy complex of villas, elegant shops, a restaurant, and a museum. Drive down the long, impressive entrance road lined with tall palm trees and tropical plantings, and park toward the rear near the restaurant.

Lunch: **Las Terrazas Restaurant,** Estero Beach Hotel and Resort, Ensenada. 6–62–30. Dine on the beachfront cafe's charming patio beneath crisp white parasols. Try the shrimp or lobster cocktail or sample other menu specialties of fried chicken, fish, hamburgers, and Mexican dishes.

Afternoon

Walk past the restaurant, villas, and cottages for a glimpse of the ocean and the stunning blue lagoon. Follow the broad terrace that edges the private bay to its curved viewpoint beneath a large thatched umbrella encircled by stone benches. Relax awhile in this idyllic tropical setting and watch the swimmers in the bay and the small boats in the ocean beyond.

Your next stop is the museum, or **Exhibition Center,** to see the outstanding Mexican Cultural Exhibit, an extensive collection of pre-Columbian sculpture and ancient art. Then take time to explore the hotel's two elegant shops, offering fine merchandise totally unexpected in this semiremote beach area.

Bazar Mexicano is a treasure-house of a large variety of selective merchandise from all over Mexico, including handicrafts, ironwood sculpture, art objects, hand-embroidered clothing, silver, and jewelry. Most notable is the beautiful hand-painted pottery from Tonala, Tlaquepaque, and elsewhere in Mexico—pitchers, vases, birds, and other designs in soft luminous colors and glazes. An adjoining room displays more pottery, enormous paper flowers, and other handicrafts beneath a huge skylight. Prices seem good throughout, but you may do better in the roadside shops en route back to Ensenada.

Near the resort entrance, the striking Mayan-style **Import Shop,** framed by huge stone pillars, showcases exquisite and expensive merchandise, including fine crystal, Rolex watches, silver and gold jewelry, designer clothing, and other imports from Brazil, Portugal, Israel, Italy, Sweden, and India, among other countries as well as Mexican glassware. Both shops are open daily from 9:00 A.M. to 6:00 P.M.

On the way back to Ensenada, look for roadside shops offering lower-priced baskets, pottery, and other native handicrafts. Here's the place to employ your bargaining skills. **Galeria Mexicana** has a large selection of well-priced vases and other pottery, and the owner welcomes your patronage. Across the road, **Bazaar de Mexico** offers clothing, jewelry, and pottery. Additionally, several small roadside markets also sell reasonably priced Mexican art, pottery, and clothing. Look for Ramon's sign for *HIELO* (ice—and cold drinks), where shelves are stacked with pottery at very good prices.

Dinner: **El Rey Sol,** Avenida Lopez Mateos No. 1000 (corner of Blancarte), Ensenada. 8–17–33. Blue awnings highlight this 1947 landmark French restaurant, long considered Ensenada's finest. Rather expensive gourmet entrees include chicken mole, filet mignon, and New York steak. Service can be indifferent, but—ole!—mariachis serenade diners and the steaks are tender.

On your last evening in Ensenada, stroll along effervescent Avenida Lopez Mateos, which has considerably more car traffic at night than during the daytime. The air is balmy, and lilting music filters from the cantinas and from the radios in the uninterrupted lines of cars. The sidewalk is crowded with people out for an evening promenade. It's a very upbeat scene that will leave you with a warm memory of Ensenada.

Lodging: Hotel Villa Marina.

Day 4

Morning

Breakfast: At the hotel.

Leave Ensenada early, taking the toll road north to **Tijuana.** Allow sufficient time to spend in Tijuana, plus a good couple of hours crossing the border back into the United States. It's a magnificent drive on the divided highway that rolls gently between the tawny cliffs and the peaceful ocean.

As you drive into Tijuana, look for **Avenida Revolución,** the well-known main tourist street. You'll know when you've reached it, because of the crush of cars and people; the restaurants, bars, liquor stores, shopping plazas, and sidewalk vendors; and the non-stop movement.

Dynamic Tijuana claims that more Americans visit it than any other foreign city, and, like you, they're all looking for somewhere to park. This vibrant town with twenty-two million border crossings annually is a shopper's best friend, offering lower, duty-free prices in French perfume, cosmetics, liquor, designer clothing, and other imports. It's further noted for sizzling nightlife and lively spectator sports, such as jai alai, horse and dog racing, and bullfights.

Exciting, tawdry, and raucous Tijuana gained notoriety and glamour during the 1920s Prohibition era, when excitement-loving, thirsty Hollywood stars flocked to its bars and gambling casinos. The city was expensively renovated in the 1970s—streets were widened, potholes filled, and street vendors deposited in indoor malls and arcades. Tune up your bargaining skills—this is the major league.

Sara's tony store on Avenida Revolución, at 4th, is known for discounted cosmetics, perfume, crystal, and Lladro figurines. Take the elevator upstairs for designer fashions and ongoing sales. A parking structure is just up 4th Street.

Trendy **Le Drug Store,** with a sidewalk cafe at Revolución and 4th, is a good source for souvenirs and postcards. Near the corner you can have your photo taken astride a festively clad donkey, for a fee. Ever-popular Caesar's Restaurant, at 4th Street, the originator of the Caesar salad, serves continental cuisine.

Bargain hunters will find outlet stores located in the large new plazas away from the crowded city center. But there are familiar, prestigious names to shop along Avenida Revolución. Note that in all outlet stores, you should examine your selections carefully before purchase to be sure they're in new condition. Further, be aware that some designer names may be bogus or rip-offs.

Guess? has two attractive outlet stores, one at 540 Avenida Revolución between 1st and 2nd streets diagonally across from the Hard Rock Cafe and another at 1105 Avenida Revolución between 7th and 8th streets across from the Jai Alai Palace. Although these stores are fun to browse, they don't seem to offer any substantial bargains, as prices are fairly close to those in Los Angeles.

You'll fare better at **Benetton Factory Outlet**'s very large store, which sprawls between 6th and 7th streets on Avenida Revolución. Good values can usually be found in its two floors filled with heavily discounted merchandise.

Ralph Lauren Outlet Store, in a miniplaza on 7th Street between Avenida Revolución, Madero, and Negrete, offers low discounts on its popular polo shirts, cologne, neckties, shirts, and men's suits. Look for women's sweaters, cotton knit dresses, and other items at the rear of the shop.

Ellesse Outlet Shop is in the same miniplaza as Lauren, on 7th Street between Avenida Revolución, Madero, and Negrete. It features some Calvin Klein merchandise along with other designer labels, though not all may be the real thing.

Lunch: **Hard Rock Cafe,** Avenida Revolución at 2nd Street. 85–02–06. This addition to the popular chain, with its distinctive signature red car halfway through its roof as in other locations, opened in May 1992. You'll find the typically long lines of patrons waiting for a table, hamburgers, and fries, as well as familiar Hard Rock decor and noise.

Afternoon

Go down Revolución to 2nd Street, turn right, and continue 2 blocks to **Mexitlan,** 8901D, Ocampo, and 2nd Street. This fun, fascinating theme park opened in August 1991 and features some 200 miniature replicas of Mexico's famous archaeological sites, plus restaurants, shops, and entertainment. (Open Wednesday through Monday from 10:00 A.M. to 6:00 P.M. admission; free parking; information, 38–41–44).

To visit the striking **Tijuana Cultural Center,** at Paseo de los Héroes and Avenida Mina in the Tijuana Rio Zone, turn right on 2nd Street to Paseo de los Héroes, go around the circle, go back 1 block, and then turn right on Mina. Easily recognized by its monumental dome and powerful architecture, the center houses Omnimax theater films, exhibit halls, a performing arts theater, a restaurant, and shops. (Open daily except Monday from 10:00 A.M. to 8:00 P.M.)

Across the street, modern **Plaza Rio's shopping mall** has a diversity of restaurants, department and specialty stores, a supermarket, and the popular Suzett Bakery. The unusual **Plaza del Zapata** across the way features only shoes, of all types, from many outlets.

To get to the San Ysidro border, make a right on Paseo de los Héroes and go straight until you see the sign for San Diego, which leads to the crowded border, where you'll find about six lanes of cars, crossing to the U.S. side. Watch for signs above the individual gateways indicating the lanes for cars with two passengers or carpools of four people, and get in the correct lane. Otherwise, as you near the gate you'll have to edge your way in line ahead of other drivers, who may not be too gracious about letting you get in front of them.

When you've crossed the border, you are on I–5 north. Stay on it until you reach Los Angeles, or cut over to 405.

There's More

Riviera Del Pacifico, Boulevard Costero, Ensenada. The sprawling building with graceful arches was a famous 1930s plush gambling casino patronized by Hollywood film stars and is now a social and cultural center. Enjoy a drink to yesteryear on Patio Bugambilia and stroll the lushly landscaped grounds.

La Bufadora, Ensenada's most famous attraction, is 20 miles south, to the tip of Punta Banda Peninsula. At this dramatic and natural "blowhole" carved into the cliffs, when the tides are high the ocean crashing into the rocks spouts a geyser of foam and water almost 100 feet high.

Flea markets and swap meets, Ensenada. Los Globos is the largest, outdoors on Calle 9, 3 blocks east of Reforma. Open daily; weekends are better.

Additional outdoor weekend swap meet at Riveroll and Calle 6.

Chapultepec Hills, Ensenada. Drive north on Calle 2 to the residential area for a stunning panoramic view of Ensenada and its beautiful bay.

Bullfights are a rich part of Mexico's heritage. Tijuana has two major bullrings, downtown at Plaza de Toros, 100 Caliente Boulevard, and at the Bullring-by-the-Sea. Season runs May through November; open Sunday at 4:30 P.M.; closed in June. For specific dates call 80–18–08; for tickets and transportation call (619) 232–5049.

Jai Alai Palace, Avenida Revolución and 7th Street, Tijuana. 800–PIK–BAJA. Watch the fastest sport in the world, year-round, Thursday through Tuesday, 7:30 P.M. Admission.

Racetrack. Just south of Paseo de Los Héroes, Tijuana. Agua Caliente racetrack offers year-round thoroughbred horse racing and greyhound racing. Horse races are held Saturday and Sunday at noon; greyhound racing, nightly at 7:45 P.M. Admission. The U.S. information and hotline number is (619) 231–1910.

Golf. Tijuana Golf and Country Club on Agua Caliente Boulevard dates back to the 1920s, when young Arnold Palmer teed off here.

Plaza Civica, downtown, on Boulevard Costero, Ensenada. In attractively landscaped Three Heads Park, a broad terrace displays giant (12-foot) sculptured busts of Mexico's greatest heroes; Benito Juárez, Miguel Hidalgo, and Venustiano Carranza.

Special Events

End of January. Annual Caesar Salad Festival, Tijuana.

January, February, and early March. Whale-watching trips, Ensenada.

Mid-February. Hussong's Centenary Fishing Tournament, two days, Ensenada.

Late February to early March. National Surfing Championship, Caribbean Mardi Gras, Ensenada.

Mid-March. Benito Juárez Birthday, Ensenada.

March 25–26. Tijuana-Rosarito-Ensenada Bicycle Race, Tijuana.

Early April and late September. Rosarito-Ensenada Fun Bicycle Ride, Gastronomic Fair, Ensenada.

Early May. Annual Regatta Newport–Ensenada, Mountain Bike Ride. Batalla de Puebla, Ensenada.

Mid-May. Annual Tecate to Ensenada "Viva Baja" Bike Ride, two days, Ensenada.

Early June. Baja 500 Off-Road Race, three days, Ensenada.

Mid-June. Annual International Karate Championship; Wine Harvest Festival; triathlon, Ensenada.

Late June to early July. Expo Ensenada, eighteen days, Ensenada.

Mid-July. First Half Marathon by Cross Country, Ensenada. 100K Race—Tijuana-Rosarito-Ensenada.

Early August. Regatta Todos Santos, two days, Ensenada. Ensenada 200K Off-Road Race, wine festival.

Middle to end of August. Fair of the Californias, Tijuana.

Late August. Gran Carrera de Ensenada, two days, Ensenada.

Early September. Congress of Investigation Sea of Cortez, four days; annual seafood festival; annual three-day Fiesta Viva Expo, Ensenada.

September 18. Mexican Food Fair, Ensenada.

Mid-September. Independence Day, Ensenada Discovery, annual Chili Cook-Off, Ensenada.

Early October. Southwestern Yacht Regatta, three days. Mountain Bike Ride, Sordomudo Ranch, Ensenada.

Mid-October. Chili Cook-Off, Octoberfest, Cantina Hussong's Centenary, three days, Ensenada Gran Prix, Ensenada.

Late October. Expo Fiesta Viva, Second Cross Country Biathlon and Mountain Bike Ride, Ensenada.

Mid-November. Annual Score Ford/Tecate Baja 1000, Ensenada, Revolution Day, Ensenada.

Mid-December. Club Amigos de Ensenada Christmas Parade, Ensenada

December 16–18. Christmas Posadas, Tijuana.

Other Recommended
Restaurants and Lodgings

Ensenada

La Cueva de Los Tigres (Tigers' Cave). Acapulco and Las Palmas streets in Playa Hermosa District. Romantic seaside hideaway 1 mile south of the city. A steady local and tourist favorite for tender abalone, steaks, and shrimp.

Baja Inn Hotel, Boulevard Costero 1536. 7–22–55. Sunday Mexican-American Buffet Brunch includes fresh fruit platter, egg specialties, *chilaquiles,* refried beans, French toast, 7:00 A.M. to 1:00 P.M. Opened in July 1992; fifty-one nicely furnished rooms, three suites, satellite TV, heated swimming pool, restaurant, bar, underground garage, twenty-four-hour security guard.

Macho's, Boulevard Costero and Macheros. 4–02–68. Moderately priced and popular for grilled steak (*carne asada*), and seafood.

Corona Hotel, Boulevard Costero 1442 (U.S. mailing address: 482 West San Ysidro Boulevard, Suite 303, San Ysidro, CA 92173). 6–09–01. Sweeping four-story modern hotel; heated swimming pool, lobby bar, room service.

Cortez Motor Hotel (Best Western), Avenida Lopez Mateos 1089. 8–23–07; (800) 528–1284 (reservations). Excellent location, spacious guestrooms and bathrooms, cable TV, heated swimming pool, restaurant, cocktail lounge, underground security parking.

Estero Beach Hotel Resort, P.O. Box 86. (800) 762–2494. Luxury beachfront resort; 107 rooms, cottages, villas, and suites, with private terraces overlooking Estero Bay. Museum, shops, tennis courts, lagoon, restaurant, exclusive RV park.

Tijuana

Como Bueno; 75 Sanchez Taboada Boulevard, in the Tijuana Rio Zone. Good menu; variety of excellent Mexican dishes and fresh seafood.

La Lena, 4560 Caliente Boulevard. 86–29–20. Near the golf club. It's busy because everybody goes for the tender, tasty New York and T-bone steaks.

Grand Hotel Tijuana, 4500 Caliente Boulevard. 01152–6681–7000. Sophisticated, modern, twenty-five-story five-star hotel; 422 deluxe rooms and suites. Heated swimming pool, Jacuzzi, tennis courts; three restaurants, bars; conference center.

For More Information

Note: To phone Mexico from the United States, dial 011–52 plus the city prefix number, unless otherwise noted.

Ensenada State Secretary of Tourism, corner of Calle las Rocas and Costero Boulevard, Ensenada. 53–667–6–22–22.

Tijuana Tourism and Convention Bureau, Paseo de Los Héroes, 9365–201 (U.S. mailing address: P.O. Box 434523, San Diego, CA 92143–4523). 01152–606–8405–37, or (800) 522–1516.

Tijuana Information Booth at the San Ysidro border is open daily from 8:00 A.M. to 7:00 P.M. The information booth for pedestrians is 1 block past the border, on the right-hand side.

Tijuana Information Center Downtown, Avenida Revolución and 1st. 52–66–85–84–72. Open daily from 9:00 A.M. to 7:00 P.M.

USA Office of Information for Baja California (International Marketing/Promotions Associates, Inc.) 7860 Mission Center Court (#202), San Diego, CA 92108. (619) 298–4105; (800) 522–1516 (in California) (800) 225–2786 (in the rest of the United States).

Fonda Mixto de Ensenada (located in San Ysidro, California). (800) 319–5687.

Disneyland/Anaheim/Knott's Berry Farm/Buena Park

Bigfoot Rapids offers excitement at Knott's Berry Farm.

Amusement Park Heaven

1 NIGHT

Amusement parks • Theme parks • Shopping • Parades

Though Southern California has many superattractions, this light-hearted escape to two world-famous amusement parks is the ultimate in fun, fantasy, and entertainment. Let the years roll back as you soar on a rocket jet, ride roller coasters upside down, watch parades, and amble through a lively Old West mining town. One visit is never enough, especially for children. You and your family will want to return again and again.

Day 1

Morning

From Los Angeles take I–5, the Santa Ana Freeway, south for the short (27-mile) drive to Buena Park for Knott's Berry Farm and down the road to Anaheim for Disneyland. This area is generally slightly warmer than Los Angeles, so you might dress accordingly. Allow about an hour and a half in travel time, depending on traffic.

To reach Knott's Berry Farm, take the Beach Boulevard exit, turn right, and stay on Beach Boulevard, passing the Movieland Wax Museum, the Medieval Times Dinner and Tournament, and the Ripley's Believe It or Not Museum. You'll soon see some of Knott's high-flying amusement rides. Stay to the right, drive beneath the large Knott's Berry Farm banner, and pull into the parking lot on the left. (Free three-hour parking for customers of Mrs. Knott's Chicken Dinner Restaurant and California Marketplace; fee for theme-park parking.)

Knott's Berry Farm, at 8039 Beach Boulevard in Buena Park (714–220–5200), grew from a mom-and-pop roadside berry stand and small farm in the 1920s to a mega-million-dollar roller-coaster-thriller attraction. Knott's Berry Farm is a story with a happy ending that began when Walter Knott started gathering a few abandoned derelict buildings from deserted western towns and moved them to the farm around 1940, as a diversion for diners waiting in line for his wife Cordelia's fried chicken dinners and delectable boysenberry pie. Ghost Town, a California mining town, gradually took shape as more rustic buildings were added and the theme further embroidered. Other entertainment areas followed. Visitors still stand in line for the fried chicken, and the berry farm is one of Southern California's leading attractions.

Lunch: **Mrs. Knott's Chicken Dinner Restaurant,** Knott's Berry Farm, Buena Park. (714) 220–5080. You may have to wait for a table (reservations are for parties of fifteen or more), but since there are six dining rooms it shouldn't be long. They serve one and a half million chicken dinners a year, so go with the favorite: Mrs. Knott's Traditional Chicken Dinner, served from 11:00 A.M. A basket of hot buttermilk biscuits is followed by chunky chicken noodle soup or cherry rhubarb appetizer, next is a mixed green salad, and then the large, thick-crusted, golden pieces of fried chicken with mashed potatoes, country gravy, and vegetable. For dessert it's boysenberry, apple, or peach pie; ice cream; or boysenberry sherbet.

Afternoon

The country's oldest themed park is actively geared to family enjoyment, offering six distinctive entertainment areas: Camp Snoopy, Fiesta Village, Roaring 20's, Ghost Town, Wild Water Wilderness, and the Indian Trails. Each features its own restaurants, specialty shops, exciting rides, shows, and other attractions.

Pick up a map at the entrance to help guide you through the 150-acre park and to check the daily showtime schedule. Go to the right for **Camp Snoopy,** a special wonderland and petting farm for small children. Then work your way around the park. In **Fiesta Village,** with its bright Marketplace and mariachis, zoom on Montezooma's Revenge, a thrilling upside-down-and-backward ride. **Jaguar!**—the 2,700-foot-long big cat of roller coasters—soars 60 feet into the air, then dives, twists, circles, and swoops high above the ground. The **Boardwalk,** a thrilling new attraction, transforms the Roaring 20s area into a beach-themed roller coaster featuring **HammerHead,** a rousing high-intensity water-oriented ride that spins riders from a shark grotto to a height of 80 feet, at times riding upside down and sideways. In this area the high-speed Boomerang roller coaster turns you upside down six times in a minute. If you crave more excitement, strap yourself into the Parachute Sky Jump. Before you can say "Geronimo," you're in a daring, twenty-story parachute fall.

Move on to **Ghost Town,** where lively country music fills the air and where rural Main Street, with its covered wagons, Old West saloon, and blacksmith at the forge, evokes a sense of history. Browse for knickknacks at the General Store. Tall, leafy eucalyptus trees provide generous shade, and masses of bright flowers soften the hundred-year-old weathered wooden buildings, with their wide verandas and sagging doorways, moved here from forgotten towns. Though there may be hundreds of people about, somehow you don't feel crowded in this low-key, comfortable ambience

Just beyond Ghost Town, **Indian Trails** explores the heritage of American Indians from four geographic areas. Artisans from each region demonstrate handicrafts, including canoe carving, mask and totem-pole making, beadwork, weaving, and pottery. While storytellers spin legends, kids can have their faces painted. The Native American food is good here, particularly the Indian fry bread and the Navajo tacos.

It's wise to visit **Wild Water Wilderness** last, as you do get wet in this turn-of-the-century California river wilderness park. The highspot is Bigfoot Rapids, a wet and wild ride where passengers are bounced and splashed as they ride down a long, turbulent man-made river, spinning in fast-moving currents and shooting under waterfalls. The

Mystery Lodge attraction, alongside the rushing waters of Thunder Falls, takes you on a mystical, magical journey deep into the Northwest Pacific Coast, exploring Native American scenes and exhibits. (Hours: Memorial Day weekend to Labor Day weekend, open Sunday through Thursday, 9:00 A.M. to midnight daily. Labor Day weekend to Memorial Day weekend, open weekdays from 10:00 A.M. to 6:00 P.M., Saturday to 10:00 P.M., and Sunday to 7:00 P.M. Closed Christmas Day; admission, free parking.)

Leave Knott's Berry Farm and drive to Disneyland Park and the Disneyland Hotel, about 10 miles away. The easiest route to the Disneyland Hotel is to get back on I–5 south and take the Ball Road exit. Turn right to West Street, then turn left; the Disneyland Hotel is on the right, at the corner of Cerritos and West (check-in is after 3:00 P.M.). Stop in the main lobby to purchase your tickets/passports to Disneyland and then board the tram, which drops you at the Main Gate, or ride the monorail, which deposits you in Tomorrowland. Both go round-trip all day until the park closes.

Disneyland is the most popular attraction in the world—a must-see, ever since it opened in 1955, for statesmen, royalty, celebrities, and just about everyone else who visits or resides in Southern California. It offers more than sixty adventures in eight different themed lands. Wandering through its eighty acres is not just another stroll in the park; in *this* park you take your imagination along to visit Tomorrowland, Fantasyland, Adventureland, Critter Country, Frontierland, New Orleans Square, Mickey's Toontown, and Main Street U.S.A., a nostalgic prototype of a circa 1900 small town, where the streetlamps are 150 years old.

The folks at Disneyland recommend that no matter the season, the best times to see the most popular attractions are before noon and after dinner. Restaurants are busiest at lunch and dinner hours—same as at home—so try to eat early or late. You'll also find weekdays less crowded than Saturday and Sunday.

Enter the park and receive your free *Disneyland Today* schedule of daily entertainment and a handy map showing attractions plus dining and shopping in each area. Board a double-decker minibus or a horse-drawn trolley or else stroll up Main Street to romantic Sleeping Beauty Castle, the entrance to **Fantasyland.** As you cross the drawbridge over the moat where swans glide elegantly, keep looking for Mickey and Minnie Mouse, Goofy, Pluto, and Chip 'n' Dale, Disneyland's official greeters, who love to have their picture taken with visitors.

Along Main Street stop at the inviting plaza, with benches, flowers, and trees, to relax, people-watch, and listen to the ragtime pianist expertly playing old tunes in toe-tapping rhythm. You'll find musicians throughout the park, playing various instruments to entertain visitors.

There's certainly no place like Disneyland—big, sunny, clean, and busy, where people of all ages amble in different directions to browse, eat, shop, snack, board another ride, and greet a new adventure. There are happy music, flowers, and lots of smiling children. If you feel lines are too long at your favorite ride, you can soon find another and return later. Listen and watch for the parade of elaborate floats down Main Street, with Mickey and other Disney figures singing and swaying to rollicking music.

Dinner: At Disneyland Park, Anaheim. There are satisfying, healthful eating places throughout the park. Consult your guidebook if you don't spot someplace you'd like to try. At Cafe Orleans in New Orleans Square, the dinner menu features beef Bourguignon, Seafood Parisienne served over rice, or spicy chicken with pasta.

Lodging: **Disneyland Hotel,** 1150 West Cerritos Avenue, Anaheim, CA 92802. (714) 788–6600 or (714) 956–6400 (reservations). Newly refurbished, this sixty-acre, tropical garden resort features 1,131 rooms, 62 suites, and 2 concierge floors. Color TV has closed-circuit channel and free Disney Channel. Snack/beverage bar in room. Three heated swimming pools, Jacuzzi, marina playground, sandy beach, ten lighted tennis courts. Eleven restaurants and lounges. Shops, nightly entertainment, family video-game center. Complimentary monorail and tram service to Disneyland Park; overnight parking fee. Seasonal one- and two-night packages include Disneyland passports and hotel parking.

Day 2

Morning

Breakfast: In hotel, at **Goofy's Kitchen.** Children enjoy meeting Minnie Mouse, Goofy, and other Disney favorites who visit at tables. All-You-Can-Eat Buffet features waffles, egg specialties, cereals, and fruits. Kids receive a special memento.

Take the tram or the futuristic monorail back to Disneyland Park to enjoy a full day of fun and adventure. Just past the entrance, walk up the wide staircase to ride the **Disneyland Railroad,** pulled by a genuine steam locomotive. The train visits all the different lands in a restful, fifteen-minute narrated ride during which you can see the cars ahead as you round a curve and hear the nostalgic train whistle. You can get off at any stop or stay aboard until you're back at your station.

Lunch: **Plaza Inn on Main Street,** Disneyland Park, Anaheim. This busy buffeteria has a Victorian decor of pink umbrellas and white furniture. Attractive, wholesome-looking foods include baked chicken, spaghetti, salads, and meat-and-cheese sandwiches with pasta salad; children's menu. It's pleasantly cool inside, but you can also tote your tray out to the terrace.

Afternoon

Spend the rest of the day and evening or as long as you like visiting other themed areas. Ride the **Matterhorn** bobsled that zips in and around the tall mountain in a fast roller-coaster ride. Tuck into **It's a Small World,** a delightful child-oriented ride, and sail around a glitzy ornamental world while festively costumed figures sing a happy tune. Embark on **Star Tours,** a thrilling flight-simulated spaceship journey into space. Then follow the Indiana Jones adventure in an intriguing new expedition through the **Fabled Temple of the Forbidden Eye.**

During summer evenings and weekends, the Light Magic Parade of music and special lighting effects is a treat. It's followed by sensational fireworks. After dark go to Frontierland, to experience **Fantasmic,** Mickey Mouse's imaginative new musical spectacular of fire-breathing dragons, laser storms, heroes, and villains.

From mid-June to mid-September, the park is open daily from 8:00 A.M. to 1:00 A.M. From mid-September to mid-June, hours are Monday through Friday, 10:00 A.M. to 6:00 P.M., and Saturday and Sunday, 9:00 A.M. to midnight. Special holiday hours are offered; to verify them, call (714) 999–4565. Passport/ticket admission includes unlimited use of the attractions (except Arcades); one-, two-, and three-day passports are available, as are seniors', annual, seasonal, and summer passports. There is a parking fee.

Return to Los Angeles via I–5 north.

There's More

Medieval Times Dinner and Tournament, 7662 Beach Boulevard, Buena Park. (714) 521–4740; (800) 899–6600 (nationwide). Enjoy a hearty four-course feast in a huge (1,134-seat) indoor ceremonial arena of an eleventh-century-style castle. Dine while watching a lively two-hour pageant of knights in colorful raiment, astride costumed horses, competing in daring equestrian tournaments, sword fights, and jousting. Dinner, served by friendly "serfs" and "wenches," begins with a fruit wine cocktail and appetizers. No silverware was used in A.D. 1539, so drink your tasty vegetable soup from its small metal bowl and tear your hot and tasty whole roast chicken, spare ribs, and potato apart with your fingers, just like Henry VIII. Dinner includes two rounds of beer, a wine cocktail, or soft drinks as well as a pastry dessert and coffee. There are lots of encouraging shouts and cheers for favorite knights as they gallop heroically through the arena. Performances seven nights; seasonal matinees Sunday. Phone for showtimes; reservations are required. Free parking; ask your hotel about bus service.

Movieland Wax Museum, 7711 Beach Boulevard, Buena Park. (714) 522–1154. One block north of Knott's Berry Farm. Everyone wants to see movie stars, and after a visit here you can brag about seeing plenty of Hollywood favorites, along with more than 270 other celebrity wax figures wearing movie costumes in authentic soundstage sets. Take a two-hour self-guided tour through the dimly lighted, mirrored corridors, where you'll hear recorded music and voices of some of the stars: Mae West singing in a sequinned gown, W. C. Fields telling stories. Clint Eastwood emerges from a saloon, gun in hand. Judy Garland, in *Wizard of Oz* costume, is flanked by the Tin Man and Scarecrow.

Nearly every famous movie star is here, portrayed life-size with realistic facial likeness. Open daily, including holidays (in summer from 9:00 A.M. to 9:30 P.M. and in winter from 10:00 A.M.; box office closes one and a half hours earlier). Admission. Combination tickets available for Ripley's Believe It or Not Museum across the street.

Ripley's Believe It or Not Museum, 7850 Beach Boulevard, Buena Park. (714) 522–7045. One block north of Knott's Berry Farm, across from the Movieland Wax Museum, you'll see an amazing, entertaining collection of curiosities that are true, strange, and bizarre, from Ubangi women whose lips are pierced to have saucers inserted to a Chinese shrunken head about the size of a lemon. These and many other oddities displayed in glass showcases were accumulated by Robert Ripley, TV and radio pioneer and syndicated newspaper columnist, during his world travels.

Anaheim Stadium, 2000 State College Boulevard, Anaheim. (714) 937–6750. This 70,000-seat stadium hosts events year-round. Two miles east of Disneyland, the stadium is home to two professional sports teams.

Baseball. The California Angels season runs from April through September. Tickets are usually available before each game. (714) 634–2000.

Golf. H. G. "Dad" Miller, 430 North Gilbert Street, Anaheim. (714) 774–8055. Eighteen-hole public course with natural lake. Night-lighted driving range, restaurant, cocktail lounge. Reservations recommended.

Miniature golf. Golf'n Stuff, 1656 South Harbor Boulevard, Anaheim. (714) 778–4100. Across from Disneyland, two 18-hole miniature golf courses with an arcade center. Open daily. Birthday groups and family rates.

Wild Bill's Western Dinner Extravaganza, 7600 Beach Boulevard, Buena Park. (800) 883–1546 (reservations); (714) 522–6611. Lively two-hour western variety review and hearty all-American four-course dinner; family-style entertainment and fun. Performances nightly Monday through Friday at 7:00 P.M.; Saturday at 2:00, 5:00, and 8:00 P.M.; and Sunday at 1:00, 4:00, and 7:00 P.M.

Ice skating. Glacial Garden Ice Arena, 1000 East Anaheim Avenue, Anaheim. (714) 502–9023. Two spacious rinks open nightly; daily skating lessons, birthday parties, hockey. Hours vary.

Disney Ice, 300 West Lincoln Avenue, Anaheim. (714) 535–7465. The newest rink in Orange County, offering public-skating, hockey, and figure-skating lessons.

Anaheim Indoor Marketplace, 1440 South Anaheim Boulevard, Anaheim. (714) 999–0888. Largest swap meet in the area, with some 200 variety shops that sell below retail and warehouse prices. International food court, miniconcerts, family fun. Open daily except Tuesday.

Doll City USA, 2080 South Harbor Boulevard (at corner of Orangewood, 0.5 mile south of Disneyland), Anaheim. (714) 750–3585. Some 4,000 dolls, including Barbie and collectibles.

Hobby City, 1238 South Beach Boulevard (2 miles south of Knott's Berry Farm), Anaheim. (714) 527–2323. One of the world's largest hobby centers, with doll and toy museum, hobby and craft shops, restaurant, and miniature train ride.

Mott Miniature Museum and Doll House Shop, 7700 #8 Orangethorpe Avenue, Buena Park. (714) 994–5979. Here's where to find miniature items to build, decorate, and furnish any dollhouse.

Special Events

March 30–April 14. Annual Easter EggMazeMent, Knott's Berry Farm, Buena Park.

Early April. Freeway Baseball Series, Anaheim Stadium, Anaheim. (714) 634–2000. California Angels Baseball Opening Day, Anaheim Stadium.

May through September. Arena football, Anaheim Piranhas, Anaheim Pond of Anaheim. (714) 254–3000.

June to September 8. Disneyland opens summer season with Light Magic Parade and Fantasy in the Sky, Anaheim.

July 4. Independence Day Festival. Knott's Berry Farm, Buena Park.

Mid-August. Annual Southern California Home and Garden Show, Anaheim Convention Center, Anaheim. (714) 978–8888.

October. Mickey's Halloween Treat, Disneyland. (714) 999–4565. Camp Snoopy (selected dates), Knott's Berry Farm, Buena Park. (714) 220–5200.

October through April. Hockey, Mighty Ducks of Anaheim, Anaheim Pond of Anaheim. (714) 704–2500.

Middle through late October (selected dates). Halloween Haunt, Knott's Berry Farm, Buena Park. (Not recommended for children under twelve.) (714) 220–5200.

November 26. Thanksgiving Day, New Year's Week, Very Merry Christmas Parade, Disneyland, Anaheim. (714) 999–4565.

Late November. Anaheim Harvest Festival, Anaheim Convention Center, Anaheim. (800) 321–1213.

Late November to December 24. Knott's Berry Farm Christmas Crafts Festival, Buena Park. (714) 827–1776.

Other Recommended
Restaurants and Lodgings

Anaheim

The Anaheim Hilton and Towers, 777 Convention Way. (800) HILTONS; (800) 233–6094 (in California); (714) 750–4321. Has 1,600 deluxe guestrooms and 100 suites, cable TV, three rooftop recreation gardens, sundecks, heated swimming pool, four spas, pool bar, 25,000-foot sports and fitness center with pool and basketball court, golf center, pitching range, putting green. Concierge service. Post office. Eleven restaurants and lounges. Free shuttle to Disneyland Park all day until closing. Various packages. Overnight parking fee.

Anaheim Marriott, 700 West Convention Way, Anaheim. (800) 228–9290 (reservations); (714) 750–8000. Has 1,039 guestrooms, including 72 suites, 2 concierge levels. AM/FM radio, cable TV, in-room pay movies. Heated indoor and outdoor swimming pools, two hydrotherapy pools, fitness facility and sunning decks, video-game room. Giftshop, two restaurants, two lounges. Complimentary trolley to and from Disneyland Park. Family vacation and other packages. Overnight parking fee.

For More Information

Anaheim/Orange County Visitor and Convention Bureau, 800 West Katella Avenue, Anaheim, CA 92802. (714) 999–8999.

Visitor Information Line. (714) 999–8999, ext. 9888.

Anaheim Convention Center, 800 West Katella Avenue, P.O. Box 4270, Anaheim, CA 92803. (714) 999–8963.

Temecula and Wineries

Vineyards flourish in fertile Temecula Valley.

The Old West and the Wine Road

2 NIGHTS

Antiques • Dining • Museum • Golf
Resort • Wineries • History • Tennis

In this two-night itinerary, you wander through a restored 1890 cowboy town with a colorful past of Indians and the Butterfield Overland Stage, walk through historic buildings and visit a museum filled with mementos of the city's beginnings and Old West lifestyle, hunt for antiques and collectibles, have lunch in a bank vault, taste-tour a dozen wineries and learn the romance of the grape, play golf and tennis, and spend the night in a casual/luxe resort.

Day 1

Morning

From Los Angeles take I–5 south to Riverside Freeway 91 (before Fullerton). Head east on 91 (past Corona) and pick up I–15 south to **Temecula,** about 90 miles. Take the Rancho California Road exit to Old Town Temecula/Front Street and turn right.

Park your car and then amble down **Front Street,** the main thoroughfare of rambling wooden buildings with thick wood-plank verandas out front. The new buildings are skillfully designed to blend in well with the old 1890s structures. Temecula is curb-to-curb antiques shops and a collector's mecca, with all manner of memorabilia. In addition to many individually run stores, groups of dealers are housed together in various antiques malls. Even if you're not an antiques maven, you will enjoy the stores. Each has something different and appealing to offer, and the furniture, in particular, gleams in richly polished woods and is nicely displayed.

Old Town Temecula is a pleasant, relaxing, happy place to browse; walk around and poke into its shops. The small, 6-block-long area along Front Street and some sidestreets retains its flavor of the Old West between the 1800s and the 1900s. The city is often called Southern California's "New Frontier"; its first inhabitants, the Shoshonean Indian tribe, christened it "Land Where the Sun Shines through the Mist," or Temecula.

Temecula's history began in 1797, when its Indian village was discovered by Father Juan Santiago from San Juan Capistrano, who was looking for a new mission site. Santiago wrote to King Charles IV describing the Indian village. The king named the area Rancho Temecula, and it became one of several Spanish land grants.

In 1845, during the Mexican-American War when the missions were secularized, Rancho Temecula was given to Felix Valdez and the great ranches were divided into smaller parcels with private ownership. This was the beginning of the romantic era of the rancheros and vaqueros of early California.

After the first Butterfield Overland Stage arrived in September 1858 and became a regular stop on the route between St. Louis and San Francisco, new homesteaders began settling in. Mail service began, and in April 1859 the first inland Southern California post office was established in Temecula. The Civil War brought an end to the Butterfield Overland Stage service, and transportation was limited until January 1882, when a rail line was completed from National City to Temecula. As large numbers of people began migrating west, the city's business and population increased, but a series of floods in the late 1880s destroyed the railroad tracks and the old Temecula depot was abandoned.

Temecula dozed until 1904, when Walter Vail came to town and purchased most of the land in the valley (87,500 acres) for Vail Ranch, his cattle empire headquarters. The great cattle drives began, and the city became a focal point for shipping cattle and grain. For the next sixty years, Temecula was a lusty, prosperous cow town with a population of about 200 and a western lifestyle of ranchers and cowboys hanging out at the Swing Inn, Long Branch Saloon, and other watering holes. In 1964, when the Los Angeles–San Diego Freeway, I–5, was completed, the Vail Ranch was sold to developers. It was subdivided as a master-planned community and became incorporated as a city in 1989.

With its fertile soil and mild climate, the vast grazing land has been planted in vineyards and in citrus and avocado groves. It's still a noted horse-raising area.

Lunch: **The Bank of Mexican Food,** corner of Front and Main streets, Old Town, Temecula. (909) 676–6160. Built in 1914, it housed the First National Bank of Temecula for thirty years, until it closed in 1941 and became an antiques shop. In 1978 it was refurbished as an authentic home-style Mexican restaurant. Despite the building's rather hideous green exterior color, it's pleasantly cool inside the tall wood-beamed dining room with comfy booths, and the food is good. Menu selections include tostadas, crab enchiladas, burritos, and luncheon specials.

Afternoon

After lunch you can check into your hotel and play a round of golf or stay and browse **Old Town Temecula's shops and antiques stores.** Strolling down Front Street, you'll come to Temecula Market and Bakery and Barbeku, 28693 Front Street, with its wide wooden verandas. Here you can purchase local farmers' fresh produce, buy some baked goods or made-to-order sandwiches, and snack outside on the veranda facing Front Street while you watch the dudes go by.

Farther along are several antiques stores and giftshops; Rocky Mountain House features crystal, American Indian art, and jewelry.

The Welty Building, between Third and Main streets, was a former store and saloon built by the Welty family in 1902. It later became the Ramona Inn, then a prizefighters' gym where Sharkey, Dempsey, and other heavyweights worked out. Now it's an antiques store and deli. More antiques are around each corner and in the malls. ABC Trading Company features bottles and other collectibles; Far East Collection shows Oriental imports; and A to Z Antiques and Country Seller highlights country curtains, antiques, and furniture. The large, impressive Welty Temecula Hotel, on Main Street, was built in 1882 by the Welty family. It is now a private residence.

Across the street, Temecula Mercantile, at 42049 Main Street, is a marvelous place to browse. Built in 1891, it was a general store patronized by local ranchers for sixty years. Now it's a fascinating antiques store to explore for dishes, crystal, furniture, pottery, bric-a-brac merchandise, and jewelry. Most regular customers are collectors; the upstairs room is for special-interest collectibles.

Between Main and 4th streets, Calico Coffee Company is the place for fine gourmet coffees, teas, kitchen gifts, candy, aprons, and well-priced wines from local wineries. Old Town Antique Faire houses thirty antiques dealers, whose wares include collectibles and vintage oak furniture. Chapparal Antique Mall, at 28645 Front Street, distinguished by a large wooden wagon out front, is a complex of more than seventy dealers, offering pottery, china, folk art, toys, quilts, and many more old-time collectibles.

Stroll both sides of Front Street. The Machados store is another historic site, built by the owner in 1892 as a general store. It later became the local post office, with the owner as postmaster; had a good life as the Long Branch Saloon for many years; and now is a mall of about eighteen antiques dealers.

Stop by the **Temecula Valley Museum,** recently relocated and now at Front Street and Moreno Road, at the north end of town in Sam Hicks Park. Like a visit to great-grandmother's attic, this is a gem to visit, with artifacts dating back to the days of the Indians and old-fashioned household and farm items of the 1800s and early 1900s, collected locally. Wall shelves display fascinating turn-of-the-century items, including an old telephone, grand old typewriters and cameras, irons, a treadle sewing machine, buckets, pottery, branding irons, and old saddles. Tables display large scrapbooks to browse, filled with photographs that show the town as it looks today as well as way back when. Nearby, an impressive diorama features Temecula in about 1914. Temecula's favorite son was Erle Stanley Gardner, author of the famous Perry Mason stories popularized on television, who lived in Temecula from 1937 until his death in 1970. The museum exhibits a sampling of Gardner's 185 mystery novels and a collection of memorabilia about the prolific author. (Open Wednesday through Sunday from 11:00 A.M. to 4:00 P.M.; donations accepted.) A Visitor Information Center is here too.

Dinner: **Temecula Creek Inn,** 44501 Rainbow Canyon Road, Temecula. (800) 962–7335; (909) 676–5631. Intimate dining room with cathedral ceiling overlooks the golf course and features wine country cuisine. Varied appetizers highlight spoonleaf spinach with fennel, mushrooms, toasted walnuts, and Gorgonzola cheese. Traditional osso buco with basil fettuccine is a grill favorite as is roasted salmon with spinach, served with shitake mushrooms and red wine sauces. The wines are from local vineyards and elsewhere.

Lodging: Temecula Creek Inn, 44501 Rainbow Canyon Road, Temecula, CA 92593. (800) 962–7335; (909) 676–5631. Centered atop 300 acres, eighty large, well-furnished rooms in soft colors, each with sitting area and all with fairway views, are tucked into five low-rise lodges. Honor bar, minirefrigerator, coffeemaker, hair dryer, cable TV, compartmented bathroom, two phones; three 9-hole golf courses, putting green, driving range, two tennis courts, heated swimming pool with hydro spa; dining room, lounge with nightly entertainment; conference facilities. Dinners and breakfasts included in two-night golf packages; outstanding Sunday Champagne buffet brunch.

Day 2

Morning

Breakfast: At the Inn. Full breakfast is included in the golf package and is served in the sunny dining room overlooking green fairways and energetic golfers. Try the scrambled eggs with smoked salmon and toasted bagel with cream cheese or the avocado-and-green-chili burrito with scrambled eggs and salsa, covered with melted cheese and served with refried black beans and excellent coffee.

After breakfast golfers will want to get out on any of Temecula Creek Inn's three challenging 9-hole **golf** courses: the Creek, the Oaks, or the Stone House. Wine lovers will want to visit the nearby wineries, about 4 miles east of the city.

Temecula Valley is a prime Southern California wine-growing area. Its soil and climate, in addition to the vintners' skill, produce award-winning wines served in the White House as well as to the Queen of England and the rest of us. **Temecula wine country** was first discovered in the 1840s by the legendary wine master Jean Louis Vignes and was rediscovered in the 1960s. The first vines were planted in 1967.

Obtain a "Wine Country Tour Map" from the hotel. Take I–5 north to the first exit and follow the circular wine trail along Rancho California Road (about 4 miles east of the city). Continue past Palomar Village, follow the sign TEMECULA WINE COUNTRY straight ahead, pass a golf course on the left, and you'll soon see the vineyards and hilly terrain on both sides of the highway.

The twelve wineries and vineyards that cover about 4,000 acres in the rolling hills of the valley's eastern region are close together on a scenic road and easily visited in a day or half-day outing. Most offer daily or weekend tasting and tours; hours and days vary; some charge a small tasting fee.

Be sure to check the winery guide and map for the days and hours each winery is open, to avoid disappointment after long uphill drives (some wineries are on dirt roads). Frequently, fast traffic behind you may not allow you sufficient time to slow down and turn into the narrow winery driveways. In that case, it may be better to continue along the road and catch that one as you circle back. Learn to speak Chardonnay as you sample the wines and talk to the proprietors or winemakers about the various wines. Attractive giftshops feature gift-packs and mementos; some have cheese and deli items to purchase for an impromptu picnic beneath fragrant grape arbors.

Your first stop on the left side of the road is **Callaway Vineyard and Winery** (32720 Rancho California Road; 909–676–4001). Atop 750 acres, it's the largest premium Southern California winery. On the long uphill drive, vines and flags frame the road. White wine is all they make—Queen Elizabeth favors the White Riesling. Visitor center, picnic area/giftshop; informative hourly tours given Monday through Friday from 11:00 A.M. to 3:00 P.M. and Saturday and Sunday until 4:00 P.M. Large tasting room open daily from 10:30 A.M. to 5:00 P.M. $3.00 tasting fee includes winery logo glass.

Continue on the same side of the road, to **Mount Palomar Winery** (33820 Rancho California Road; 909–676–5047). Daily tasting and tours, 9:00 A.M. to 5:00 P.M.; tasting bar, $2.00 for four samples. Riesling and White Cabernet are the most popular wines. This is the only winery in Temecula making Cream Sherry. Giftshop. Purchase bread, cheese, and deli fare and enjoy a picnic under the grape arbor.

Further on is **Temecula Crest Winery** (40620 Calle Contento (a small road on the left; 909–676–8231), which has been here since 1994 on a twenty-acre spread and specializes in white and red wines. Its Sauvignon Blanc is reputed to be one of the best in the valley; the most popular is the Cabernet Blanc, like a White Zinfandel. Tasting daily, 10:00 A.M. to 5:00 P.M.; group tours and tasting by appointment. The fee for tasting six white wines is $2.25—and you get to keep the glass; the fee for tasting the three reds is $4.00 and is applied toward your purchase. The lovely shaded picnic area offers marvelous views of the valley.

Go back and across the road to **Thornton Winery** (32575 Rancho California Road; 909–699–0099). Attractive Mediterranean-style buildings with a wide courtyard and a large fountain overlook the sweet valley of vineyards. Six award-winning sparkling wines are produced in the *methode champenoise.* Twenty-minute tours and tasting Saturday and Sunday at 10:00 A.M., 4:00 P.M. and 6:00 P.M. Champagne bar tasting weekdays from noon to 4:00 P.M. and Sunday from 11:00 A.M. to 5:00 P.M.; $6.00 for four Champagne tastings. Pretty giftshop.

Lunch: **Cafe Champagne,** in the courtyard of the Thornton Winery. Intimate, with open kitchen; overlooks vineyards. A popular luncheon destination, offering California cuisine of mesquite-grilled steaks, salads, and sandwiches enhanced with fresh herbs grown in the herb garden (reservations, 909–699–0099).

Afternoon

Continue along the route de vin to **Maurice Car'rie Winery** (34225 Rancho California Road; 909–676–1711). The large white Victorian-style tasting building set back on a broad lawn is bordered with roses. Patio tables and chairs and a little gazebo are inviting for picnics. Good-looking interior has a large chandelier and a ceiling skylight. Tasting 10:00 A.M. to 5:00 P.M. daily. The most popular wine of their fourteen varietals is Sara Bella Cabernet. Giftshop, deli items.

Continue along the quiet road to the white windmill that marks the entrance to wine country's newest addition, **Van Roekel Vineyards & Winery** (34567 Rancho California Road, 909–699–6961). It opened in 1994 with attractive tasting bar and showroom featuring merlot among many other wines. There's a gourmet deli, spacious giftshop displays glassware, aprons, logo cups, and small split bottles of wine that are perfect gifts or souvenirs. Open daily 10:00 A.M. to 5:00 P.M.

Back down the road again is **Baily Tasting and Sales Room** (33833 Rancho California Road; 909–676–1896). A wonderfully scenic hilltop location for wine sampling, with panoramic view of vineyards and Mount Palomar from the veranda. Tasting daily 10:00 A.M. to 5:00 P.M.; fee includes winery logo glass. Cabernet Blanc is the most popular wine here. Picnic area; giftshop.

Dinner: Temecula Creek Inn. If you enjoy music with dinner, the lounge presents nightly entertainment, and the food service is good. The filet mignon is delicious, with green peppercorn béarnaise and roasted red bliss potatoes. Linger over brandy and dessert—a surprisingly good bread pudding or ice cream sundaes.

Lodging: Temecula Creek Inn.

Day 3

Morning

Breakfast: At the inn.

After breakfast lounge around the pool, play another round of golf on the uncrowded courses, hit some tennis balls, visit more wineries, or return to Old Town Temecula.

To visit more of the valley's fine wineries, start with **Hart Winery** (32500 Rancho California Road; 909–676–6300). This hospitable winery in a red, barnlike building offers tasting daily of red and white wines from 9:00 A.M. to 4:30 P.M.; the tasting fee starts your winery logo glass collection.

Continue to **Cilurzo Vineyard and Winery** (41220 Calle Contento; 909–676–5250). This family-run operation was the first vineyard in Temecula and specializes in red wines, with Petite Sirah heading the list. Tasting and tours daily from 9:30 A.M. to 5:00 P.M.; tasting fee is refunded with wine purchase. Lakeside picnic area.

Drop in at **Keyways Vineyard and Winery** (37338 De Portola Road; 909–676–1451). Ten acres of this three-year-old winery are planted in varietal grapes; the most popular wines are Chardonnay and Muscat Canelli. This eclectic winery has llamas out in the pasture, a miniature train running through the property, antiques, antique cars, a giftshop, and a picnic area. Tasting room open daily from 10:00 A.M. to 5:00 P.M. Fee to sample six wines.

A bit farther along is **Filsinger Vineyard and Winery** (39050 De Portola Road; 909–676–4594). The white stucco building with red-tile cupola is adorned with a colorful flower-bordered gazebo. Here since 1980, the vineyard consists of twenty-five acres planted in varietals producing seven wines and three Champagnes. Most popular are the Gewurztraminer and Blanc de Blanc Champagne. Tasting and tours weekends from 10:30 A.M. to 5:00 P.M., and weekdays by appointment; $1.00 to taste five wines is refunded on purchase. Gift items, picnic area.

Lunch: Pick up some lunch fixings along the way and snack on Filsinger's pretty picnic patio.

Afternoon

Retrace your route from Old Town Temecula back to Los Angeles.

There's More

Lake Skinner, off Rancho California Road, 10 miles northeast of Temecula. (909) 926–1541. For year-round family fun, this beautiful recreation area offers fishing, boating, hiking (about 300 campsites, many with full hookups), cafe, equestrian trails. Site of the annual Balloon and Wine Festival.

Temecula Stampede, 28721 Front Street, between 1st and 2nd streets, Old Town Temecula. (909) 695–1760. Temecula's Country-Western nightclub, features 4,000 square feet of dance floor, plus mechanical bull. After 6:00 P.M. here's where the action is. No reason to stay in your hotel room when you can join the fun here. Live bands, special concerts, dance lessons.

Sam Hicks Park, Mercedes and Moreno streets, at the north end of Old Town. This small, historic park features Temecula's Monument Rock, a massive (twenty-ton) granite marker with fifty-six names of pioneers sandblasted on its surface, in tribute to former settlers.

Hot air balloon rides. DAE Flights, P.O. Box 1671, Temecula, CA 92390. (800) 221–4905; (909) 676–3902. Soar over the valley in an eight-stories-high balloon. Daily one-hour flights begin at 6:30 A.M., with preflight continental breakfast. Brunch with Champagne ceremony served after the flight. Phone for reservations.

Temecula Shuttle, 28657 Front Street, Suite A, Temecula. (909) 695–9999. Narrated tours and tastings of wine country, souvenir wineglass, appetizer party tray, Culbertson Champagne toast; $30.00 per person, in luxury air-conditioned vans. Advance reservations required. Senior discount.

Santa Margerita Winery, 33490 Madera del Playa (just past Cilurzo Winery). (909) 676–8431. Turn right on Madera del Playa for this winery, which opened in 1991. No-charge tasting and touring, on weekends from 11:00 A.M. to 4:30 P.M. and on weekdays by appointment, for its aged Cabernet Sauvignon.

Special Events

Farmer's market. Every Saturday in Old Town.

First weekend in February. Annual Barrel Tasting, all wineries. Sample wines, festive foods; meet the winemakers as you tour the wineries.

Last weekend in February. Early Times Mid-Winter Road Run, Old Town Temecula.

Last weekend in April. Temecula Valley Annual Two-Day Balloon and Wine Festival. (909) 676–4713. Two days. Daily liftoff, entertainment, wine tasting, children's fair at beautiful Lake Skinner.

Last weekend in April and last weekend in August. Semiannual Western Days, Old Town Temecula. (909) 676–4718.

Fourth of July. Parade, Old Town Temecula. Greek Festival.

September. Harvest Festival, all wineries.

First weekend in October. Annual Great Temecula Tractor Race. (800) 800–4038; (909) 676–4718. Temecula Showgrounds. Three days; mudboggin' obstacle course for kids, pig race, fair, country-western music and Chili Cook-Off.

Fourth weekend in October. PRCA Rodeo and ICS Chili Cook-Off, Temecula Showgrounds. (800) 800–4038.

Last Saturday in October. Pumpkin Run 5K and 10K, Old Town Temecula. (909) 676–4718. Costumes, children's events.

November and December. An Old Town Christmas.

Other Recommended Restaurants and Lodgings

Baily Wine Country Cafe, 27644 Ynez Road, Temecula. (909) 676–9567. Located in the bustling, commercial, newer shopping-dining center of the town (where you'll find many other restaurants to try). Enjoy lunch and dinner on the pretty patio or inside this upscale, busy cafe where bins of wine are stacked in the entrance foyer. California/continental cuisine includes southwestern-style grilled-cheese three-layer sandwich for lunch; dinner features salmon Wellington, grilled New York strip steak, and shrimp with smoky apricot BBQ sauce, plus salads, soups, sandwiches, and a large selection of Temecula valley wines, including those from Baily Vineyard and Winery.

Rosa's Cantina, 28636 Front Street, corner of Main, Old Town. (909) 695–2468. Popular for good Mexican food; serve-yourself, casual dining inside or on patio. Moderate-priced specialties include tacos, burritos, chimichanga, nachos, tostados, and *combinaciones*.

Texas Lil's Mesquite Grill, 28495C Front Street, Old Town. (909) 699–5457. A lively local favorite for steak, ribs, hefty sandwiches, and the hottest Texas chili this side of the Alamo.

Swing Inn Cafe, 28676 Front Street, Old Town. (909) 676–2321. Popular since the cowboys and ranch days; cozy and busy. Home-style cooking—spaghettis, soups, sandwiches, and daily specials.

Embassy Suites, 29345 Rancho California Road and I–15. (800) 362–2779; (909) 676–5656. Lake setting of 136 luxurious suites with wetbar, refrigerator, microwave, TV, VCR, stereo, heated swimming pool, spa, fitness center, restaurant, lounge. Complimentary full, cooked-to-order breakfast; complimentary evening beverage.

Loma Vista Bed and Breakfast, 33350 La Serena Way, Temecula. (909) 676–7047. Set high on a hilltop, the B&B overlooks citrus groves and vineyards. All rooms have air-conditioning and private baths with tubs/showers. Rates include a Champagne breakfast, served in the spacious dining room, and wine and cheese in the afternoon. Guestrooms are named after wines—Champagne, Chardonnay, and so forth—and individually furnished. Packages offered with hot air balloon companies.

For More Information

Old Town Temecula Mainstreet Association, 28636 Front Street, Suite 106, Temecula, CA 92590. (909) 699–8138.

Temecula Valley Chamber of Commerce, 27450 Ynez Road Suite 10, Temecula, CA 92391. (909) 676–5090.

Temecula Valley Vintners Association, P.O. Box 1601, Temecula, CA 92390. (909) 699–3626.

Fallbrook

Uncrowded scenic golf fairways abound at Pala Mesa Resort.

Rural Getaway

2 NIGHTS

Golf • Tennis • Avocado and orange groves • Rural countryside
Mission • Scenic drives • Galleries • Antiques
Indian mission school and cultural center

This relaxing three-day excursion takes you far off the beaten path to a tranquil, small country village where you'll discover a part of the world you thought didn't exist anymore. In Fallbrook, the "Friendly

Village," set in a quiet valley surrounded by farms and rocky foothills, you are deep in a rural countryside of open space, huge old sycamores, and ancient oaks shading meandering silver streams. Everything is so natural and undisturbed that you may feel you've stumbled back into time and half-expect a stagecoach to rattle past. But what rattles past turns out to be just a golf cart instead.

This sleepy pioneer town is an ideal place to unwind for a few days. Enroute you'll visit the "King" of Southern California missions (in Oceanside), then overnight in Fallbrook at a first-rate resort that boasts one of the most beautiful championship golf courses in Southern California, play tennis alongside orange trees, swim, and relax. Downtown you'll browse an old-fashioned Main Street that's as sedate as a dowager aunt, enjoy hearty small-town cooking, shop for antiques and fine art, visit avocado packing plants in season, stop at a macadamia nut orchard, explore an 1816 Indian mission school, and pan for gemstones direct from a nearby mine.

Fallbrook was settled in 1869 and became a town in 1885. Dubbed the "Avocado Capital of the World" with its favorable climate of long, warm, dry summers and cool, crisp nights, it is a primary avocado-growing area. Wherever you look, the fertile land is covered with Fallbrook's *green gold;* its multimillion-dollar avocado crop that keeps packing plants busy receiving, sorting, and shipping the fruit as fast as the local growers keep trucking it in. Other flourishing local crops include citrus, macadamia nuts, strawberries, tomatoes, kiwi, subtropical fruit, and flowers. Wine grapes are still cultivated here.

Day 1

Morning

Drive south from Los Angeles on I–5 to Fallbrook, about a two-hour drive, stopping en route to visit Mission San Luis Rey in Oceanside. At Oceanside take Highway 76/Mission Avenue exit; go east for about 4 miles, past El Camino Real, to the mission, and turn north.

Mission San Luis Rey de Francia, 4050 Mission Avenue in San Luis Rey (619–757–3651), is the majestic "King of Missions," founded in 1798 by the Spanish Franciscans. The eighteenth and the largest of California's twenty-one missions, it has been splendidly restored, from its beautifully landscaped gardens to its cerulean dome. The mission flourished, with property extending over a 15-mile radius, until secularization during Mexico's occupation of California but then deteriorated. After President Lincoln returned all the missions to the

Catholic churches in 1865 (a month before his assassination), restoration began.

Pick up a map for a self-guided tour, then walk along the foyer from the museum to the old church, where small glass-walled room displays depict mission life in the nineteenth century: the Friar's Bedroom; the Weavery, with large spinning wheel and fabrics; and other interesting scenes. The church, with its 6-foot-thick adobe walls built in 1811, decorative turquoise pillars, and distinctive high-domed skylight, opens to a serene courtyard and the Sacred Gardens and Bells.

The mission church is still used for regular services. Artifacts relating to the mission's history are housed in the museum, and the gift-shop sells religious artifacts, books, and souvenirs. San Luis Rey Mission, a National Historic Landmark, is an impressive setting for year-round concerts, fiestas, and gala events. The museum and gift-shop are open Monday through Saturday from 10:00 A.M. to 4:30 P.M. and Sunday from noon to 4:30 P.M. Admission.

When you leave Mission San Luis Rey, continue east on Highway 76 toward Fallbrook. After San Luis Rey Downs Golf Course, take S13/Mission Road to the left at the fork past Bonsall Shopping Center/River Village, and follow this quiet two-lane country road past a string of antiques shops tucked into small cottages you might note for later attention. At the first traffic light, bear right at the Y onto Main Street, the heart of downtown **Fallbrook,** for lunch and a brief look around the small central business section before going on to your hotel.

Lunch: **The Packing House Restaurant,** 115 South Main Street (between Fallbrook and Alvarado streets), Fallbrook. (619) 728–5458. This popular local hangout opened in 1976 in a brick building that had been first a meat market and then, in the 1930s, a prominent hotel. Head for the convivial bar at the rear and have a cool drink in the "Judge's Chambers," with its lazy ceiling fans and soft music. The restaurant's comfy leather booths are surrounded by shelves of books and photos on the walls. The salad bar features plenty of extra fixin's; the Packing House cheeseburger is served with good french fries or baked potato. There are also a choice of charbroiled steaks and a selection of chicken dishes. Lunch and dinner, Sunday brunch.

Afternoon

After lunch golfers may want to drive directly to **Pala Mesa Resort** for a round or two of golf, but those with a later starting time will enjoy a stroll around sleepy old **Main Street,** with its relaxed, turn-of-the-century flavor. It's quiet. There aren't any parking meters, but there's hardly any traffic. Around here two or three cars at the traffic light is called congestion. Residents strive to preserve the village atmosphere, and a few restored pioneer storefronts of the 1800s reflect a vigorous past and add to its charm and authenticity.

Main Street welcomes you with large terra-cotta planters filled with colorful plants and flowers in front of stores; wooden benches invite you to sit awhile; and tall, leafy trees provide shade and beauty. You'll want to linger, browsing the small antiques shops, boutiques, and art galleries.

Your first stop should be the **Westerner,** a large, wonderfully old-fashioned general store that's been anchored here on Main Street forever. This is the real thing—you don't find many of these around anymore. In addition to top clothing lines for men and women, you can buy saddles and leathergoods for horses, boots for the family, childrenswear, straw hats, genuine Stetson cowboy hats, and T-shirts. Atop the glass counters at the front of the store are old-time large glass jars filled with penny candy, marked 1¢ Of particular interest is the large display of prize Indian jewelry, in silver and turquoise, from rings, belt buckles, and bracelets to elaborate Squash necklaces, all collected by the owner on frequent trips to Indian reservations in New Mexico.

The 7-mile route to your hotel is a scenic introduction to Fallbrook's countryside—plenty of open space and the air still as pure and clear as when the first avocado trees were planted in 1913. On the hilly rural road, you'll pass many churches, small farms, and nurseries. From downtown, take Fallbrook Street west to Stagecoach Lane, turn right, and continue until it ends at Reche Road (named for Fallbrook's first settlers). Turn left on Reche to Old Highway 395, turn right, and follow 395 around to the Pala Mesa Resort entrance.

After check-in, golfers and tennis players should arrange their game times. Most golfers won't want to waste any time getting out on Pala Mesa's stunning course. Nongolfers will have fun tooling around the well-manicured fairways in a golf cart or cooling off at the swimming pool. Others can drive out across the valley to historic Mission San Antonio de Pala and nearby attractions, about an 8-mile (half-hour) drive.

Turn right from Pala Mesa Resort on Old Highway 395 to the traffic light at Highway 76 and turn left. Continue east to **Mission San Antonio de Pala.** After the sign for the mission, turn off on Pala Mission Road, where you'll easily see the 50-foot gleaming white bell tower of the mission. It's an enjoyable drive along a hilly backcountry road of miles of citrus and avocado groves in all directions; horses and cattle graze in sunny open meadows in this broad fertile valley strewn with boulders and rocks. Pala's granite-ribbed hills are well known to rockhounds, as they are rich in semiprecious stones and gems.

Mission San Antonio de Pala, Box 70, Pala, CA 92059 (619–742–3317) was founded by the Franciscan Fathers in 1816 on the 12,000-acre Pala Reservation as an *assistencia* to the larger Mission San Luis Rey. It is the only one of the original Spanish California missions still serving the Native American; the mission school, newly named the Virginia Banks Elementary School, has an enrollment of about 175 students from neighboring reservations and villages.

Pala has survived despite the adversity of secularization, earthquakes, and floods. The chapel, with its 42-inch-thick adobe walls, and the west wing were partially restored in 1903. Heavy winter floods of 1916 further destroyed much of the little mission, and it lay in ruins until restoration began in 1948. Its tall, graceful bell tower with its crowning cross was rebuilt to stand apart from the main structure; the campanile's two bells are the original ones from 1816. Visitors are welcome to tour the grounds, giftshop/museum, and small chapel.

The rambling low building with red-tile roof, a fine example of Mission architecture, is beautifully situated amid informal gardens of flowers and citrus and palm trees. Inside, the long narrow chapel, with original sloping worn tile floor, displays primitive Indian paintings on its walls. The giftshop museum houses a rich collection of old Indian-carved statues and relics as well as Indian jewelry, turquoise rings, copper bracelets, pottery, and beaded moccasins crafted by Indians. The large gems and mineral-rock specimens displayed were found in the area and elsewhere.

Take time to wander around the quiet grounds, seeing the ruins of the old, still-producing olive garden, the sacred shrines, the courtyard, and the old cemetery, where hundreds of Spanish pioneers and Indians are buried beneath ancient pepper trees. Museum and giftshop open Tuesday through Sunday from 10:00 A.M. to 3:00 P.M. Admission.

Around the corner in a white adobe building on Pala-Temecula Road, only a few hundred feet from the mission, are the **Cupa Cultural Center and Museum** (619–742–1590), established in 1971 to preserve the culture and heritage of the Cupeño Indians. The small museum shows restored artifacts, baskets, games, and exhibits of mission life and the history of the Indian era in early California. Other displays reflect the establishment of **Pala Reservation** in 1875 as home for Luiseño Indians, later joined by the Cupeños in 1903. A forty-five-minute video depicts the eviction of the Cupeños in 1903 from their tribal lands in Warner Springs to the Pala Reservation. Open Monday through Friday, 8:00 A.M. to 5:00 P.M.

For the fun and thrill of panning and discovering your own gemstones, continue east from the Cupa Cultural Center on Highway 76 about 1 mile, to Magee Road, and turn left to **Gems of Pala,** Highway 76 at Magee Road (P.O. Box 382) Pala, CA 92059. (619–743–1356). The hills around Pala are historically known for their semiprecious minerals, with huge deposits of pegmatic minerals, including the rare and valuable pink tourmalines, quartz, lapidulite, topaz, and other rare species.

Since 1890 the **Stewart Mine** has been producing some of the finest natural pink tourmalines for jewelry and museums. Tourmaline has more variety of color than any other gem, with pink, blue, green, and bicolor being the most prized. This rural country store is a bonanza for rockhounds, mineralogists, hobbyists, and your average fun-loving treasure seeker.

Buckets of underground mine gravel are brought up from the mine in three sizes, priced at $10, $25 and $50. A five-minute instructional video gets you started on finding the gems by using screens to shake out the dirt, then washing the gravel (like panning for gold). Then comes the excitement as you watch for the colored stones to stand out from the gravel. You get to keep whatever gemstones you find in your bucket. There's a kid's table, plus large mineral specimens, carvings, gemstones, and gifts for sale. Open Thursday through Sunday from 10:00 A.M. to 4:00 P.M.; from December to March 15, call ahead, as hours are subject to change. To return to your hotel, go west on Highway 76 to Old Highway 395, then turn right to the resort.

Dinner: **Alexander's,** Pala Mesa Resort, Fallbrook. The tall-ceilinged, handsome dining room edging the green fairways offers views of nearby foothills framing the golf course. The chef's California Casual Cuisine menu selections change weekly. Lively appetizers, such as vegetable spring roll with Thai peanut sauce, and various salads are great starters, followed by specialty pizzas and pasta dishes. From the grill, New York strip has brandy tarragon demiglaze. Sunday brunch is from 10:30 A.M. to 2:00 P.M. Reservations are recommended. J.P.'s Bar & Grill is cozy for cocktails and sandwiches, with live entertainment weekends.

Lodging: **Pala Mesa Resort,** 2001 Old Highway 395, Fallbrook, CA 92028. (800) 722–4700; (619) 728–5881. Framed by avocado groves and sprawling across 205 rolling acres of majestic old sycamore and oak trees. Accommodations are set in clusters of two-story ranch-style buildings and feature 133 large, well-furnished guestrooms and suites in California ranch decor, overlooking lush fairways or stunning mountain vistas. Minirefrigerator and honor bar, large walk-in closet, writing desk, color cable TV tucked in a gleaming armoire, private scenic balcony; 18-hole championship golf course, driving range, putting greens, practice sand bunker, pro shop, four night-lighted tennis courts, volleyball court, jogging trails; heated swimming pool, Jacuzzi, exercise and weight room, conference center. Various golf packages are combined with dining and other amenities.

Day 2

Morning

Breakfast: Alexander's, Pala Mesa Resort. The sunny, glass-walled dining room overlooking the velvety green fairways is a lovely place to begin your second day in Fallbrook, and you can watch golfers tee off while you are sipping your morning coffee and enjoying breakfast. The Tex-Mex omelet, combining grilled diced chicken breast with chili, scallions, and Jack cheese, is served with breakfast potatoes— baby red potatoes, sautéed and roasted.

After breakfast golfers will head for the front nine of this well-manicured course with its panoramic views of avocado trees blanketing hillsides and citrus trees blooming alongside rolling fairways, where jackrabbits and squirrels scamper freely about, keeping an eye on the ball. Or, why not drive around to see more of Fallbrook's beautiful pastoral countryside before going downtown to have lunch and browse. Follow a curved, quiet tree-lined road past shady orchards, drowsy ponds, and farmhouses where children ride chestnut ponies around sunlit corrals. You can also enjoy the dramatic views of orange and avocado trees beneath deep blue skies across green hillside and canyons.

You'll find a more glamorous scene at **The Collector,** 912 Live Oak Park Road (800–854–1598; 619–728–9121), a fine jewelry shop tucked away on a narrow country lane. Turn left on Old Highway 395 to Reche Road. Just past rustic Live Oak Park, with its shaded picnic tables, playground, and stately old trees, turn right on Live Oak Park Road for about 2 blocks. Look for the sign in front of a rambling brown house.

Established in 1968 by its owners, The Collector is noted for custom-designed, high-quality gemstone jewelry and loose colored stones, on display in the glittering showroom. Among the loose gemstones are tourmalines in various colors, primarily the valuable pink, green, bicolor, and watermelon. Gift ideas range from small animal carvings, fossils, minerals, and amethyst, quartz, and other large specimen stones to books on gemstones. Open Monday through Friday, 10:00 A.M. to 5:00 P.M. (A sister store is in La Jolla.)

Head back to downtown Fallbrook for lunch by driving north on Live Oak Park Road about 1 or 2 blocks to Alvarado Street and turn left (west), to Main Street, where you turn left again. Just past the Y in the road where Main Street becomes Mission Road, look for Vince's in the large Colony Shopping Center, across the street from Thrifty Drugs.

Lunch: **Vince's Italian Restaurant,** 1331 South Mission Road, Fallbrook. (619) 728–1221. This cheery local favorite, here since 1985, has added a sparkling Italian grocery with a bakery and deli. It's an attractive restaurant, where ceiling fans twirl above tables set with red-and-white-checked cloths. The moderately priced, extensive luncheon menu highlights pizzas, lasagna with soup or salad, and many other delicious Italian specialties. Since the restaurant is noted for serving large portions, you may want to share. The Torpedo, an enormous, tasty submarine sandwich filled with salami, ham, mortadella, and cheese, can feed the whole family, as can the side order of spaghetti with excellent meat sauce. There's a good wine selection. Browse the adjoining small grocery for pastas, olive oils, balsam vinegars, wines, olives, and gourmet cooking accessories. The bakery has luscious pastries, focaccia, and other Italian breads; an appealing deli counter is stocked with a fine variety of cheeses, salads, and meats plus it prepares food to take out. Closed Monday.

Afternoon

Fallbrook's bustling avocado packing plants in the downtown section are highlights to visit. At **Del Rey Avocado Company** (1260 South Main Street; 619–728–8325), during harvest season, visitors can usually watch the packing of avocados for shipping and/or buy some to tote home or have sent as gifts. There aren't too many places where you can see really huge cartons filled with deep green, glossy avocados forklifted off the trucks onto conveyor belts in the packing house, where they are sorted as they go down the production line and are finally boxed for delivery. Open Monday through Friday, 8:00 A.M. to 5:00 P.M. (closed from noon to 1:00 P.M.).

Practically around the corner, **McDaniel Fruit Company** (965 East Mission Road; 619–728–8438) is another large packing house where you might watch hundreds of avocados rolling down the assembly line to be boxed for shipment. McDaniel is not always open to visitors, but you might take a chance as long as you're nearby and drop in. Open Monday through Friday, 8:00 A.M. to 5:00 P.M. (closed from noon to 1:00 P.M.).

This is a good time to continue exploring sleepy Main Street's boutiques, antiques shops, and art galleries. Heading the list are Antique Mall, at 205 North Main; and Kitty's Korner, for gifts and collectibles, at 223. Look too for Ruthy's, Begin Again, and Granny's Antiques. Christel's Mercantile, at 127 Main, shows dressy and casual women's clothing. Valentina's Sportswear is another fashionable boutique. Wander through the trendy shops of Jackson Square's charming flower-and-plant-filled brick courtyard, have a snack at Bistro Cafe, and view current exhibitions at Brandon Art Gallery, here for some fifteen years and showing fine contemporary and traditional art. Village Stationers, on the corner of Alvarado, is great for gifts, stuffed animals, pottery, and the like. Across Main Street, the landmark Harrison Drugs, a sleek, lovely store with upscale merchandise, features fine perfumes, cosmetics, gift items, toys, and lots of other irresistibles.

To return to Pala Mesa Resort from downtown, take Fallbrook Street or Alvarado Street east to Stagecoach Lane; turn right on Stagecoach to Reche Road, turn left, and continue to Old Highway 395. Then turn right and follow 395 around to your hotel—or you can cut off 395 by turning right on little Tecalote Drive, just past the trailer park, and following Tecalote the back way to the hotel parking area.

Dinner: **Alexander's,** Pala Mesa Resort. Tonight you can start with smoked salmon with radicchio, spinach and arugula with roasted peppers and balsamic vinegars, or black and white linguine with sautéed fresh clams, Chardonnay, and herbs, then go on to the blackened breast of chicken with a tequila tomato sauce. Save room for dessert of apple crumb cake topped with ice cream.

Lodging: Pala Mesa Resort.

Day 3

Morning

Breakfast: **Alexander's,** Pala Mesa Resort. "The Healthy Start" of scrambled Eggbeaters or an omelet with sliced tomatoes, cottage cheese, and toasted bagel is a good option, as is *huevos rancheros—* corn tortilla topped with refried beans, fried egg, salsa, avocado, and cheese, served with breakfast potatoes.

Before leaving, golfers may want to play another round or half-round on the fairways of this picturesque course, zero-in on their putting, or hit a bucket of balls on the driving range.

Afternoon

On your return to Los Angeles driving through Fallbrook, try to stop at some of the small antiques shops clustered together in small pioneer cottages near Valley Fort at the **Stage Stop Antique Shops,** 3137 South Mission Road, Fallbrook. All are open Thursday through Saturday, 10:00 A.M. to 5:00 P.M., and Sunday from noon to 5:00 P.M.

Tin Barn Antiques. (619) 723–1609. Early American and Victorian antiques and memorabilia, country primitives, farm equipment, old stoves, and more.

Millie's Antiques 'N Old Lace. (619) 728–9206. Vintage clothing, fancy labels, and antique costume rental.
    Country Elegance Antiques and Collectibles. (619) 723–3417. Jewelry and estate sales.
    Ivy House Consignments and Antiques. (619) 728–7038. Estate sales and appraisals. Retrace your way back to Los Angeles via Highway 76 west to I–5 north.

There's More

Open market, at Village Square, Main and Alvarado, Fallbrook. Lively Farmer's Market with arts and crafts, fresh produce from local growers. Open Friday and Saturday from 9:00 A.M. 1:00 P.M.
    Golf. Fallbrook Country Club, 2757 Gird Road. (619) 728–8334. An 18-hole public golf course beneath beautiful old oaks and sycamores. Pro shop, driving range. Clubhouse restaurant.
    Atkin's Nursery, 3129 Reche Road, Fallbrook. (619) 728–1610. Here's where to purchase young avocado and citrus trees and start your own groves at home.
    Cooper's Nut House, 1378 Willow Glen Road, Fallbrook. (619) 728–6409. A friendly source for macadamia nuts, candies, crackers, and giftpacks—topped off with a tour of the macadamia grove. Fallbrook is a major grower of macadamia nuts.
    Coyote Hill Farms, 1517 Macadamia Nut Drive, Fallbrook. (619) 723–3564. All-occasion gift baskets, avocados, fruit, vegetables, fresh and dried flowers and arrangements. Special Guacamole Kit features freshly picked Hass avocados from the owner's grove, dip mix, chips, literature, recipes. By appointment only during business hours.
    The Jewelry Connection, 855 South Main Street, Fallbrook. Fine estate jewelry; Lladro, Doulton, Hummel items; old watches and other collectibles.
    Kirk's Antiques, 321 North Orange Street (2 blocks east of Main Street) (619) 728–6333. One of the oldest antiques shops in town, housed in a vintage one-hundred-year-old cottage. Hours vary; phone ahead.
    The Last Straw Feed Store & Petting Zoo, 2762 South Mission Road. (619) 728–6482. Get a real feel of country atmosphere. You'll spot the big windmill on the hill. The feed store opens to a large pasture where you can pet the goats, cows, llama, camel, turkeys, lambs, sheep, and other domestic animals. Excellent photo opportunities here and lots of appeal for children who enjoy the open space. Open Monday through Saturday, 9:00 A.M. to 5:00 P.M.; closed Sunday.

This Old House, 30158 Mission Road, Bonsall. (619) 631–2888. En route to Oceanside, this new and unique antiques mall of about fifty dealers is located in a fine old building. Large selection of glassware, dolls, oak and Victorian furniture, toys, clocks, jewelry, primitives, and collectibles, plus lots of western items.

Special Events

Note: Call for admission fees.

Beginning of April. Easter Sunday Easter Egg Hunt, Community Center, Heald and Fallbrook streets.

April 21. Annual Avocado Festival. One-day Street Faire, 8:00 A.M. to 5:00 P.M., on Main Street. Some 250 arts and crafts booths, beer gardens, farmers market, nursery section, entertainment, bike rides. Fallbrook Chamber of Commerce, (619) 723–4058.

Last weekend in May. Annual Antique Automobile Club vintage auto show, Fallbrook High School.

Beginning of summer. Mission San Luis Rey annual fiesta commemorating founding of the mission. Arts and crafts booths, food, entertainment, carnival rides. Oceanside. (619) 757–3659.

Third week in August. Annual Concert on the Green, at the lakeside gazebo of Grand Tradition, 1602 South Mission Road, Fallbrook (bring picnic dinner). Antique Show and Sale, Soroptomist Club, Fallbrook High School.

End of summer. Heritage Ball annual gala, Mission San Luis Rey. Dinner and dancing. Oceanside. (619) 757–3659.

October 1. Annual Harvest Hoedown. One-day Street Faire, 8:00 A.M. to 5:00 P.M. Crafts, gift and food booths, entertainment, beer garden. Fallbrook Chamber of Commerce, (619) 723–4058.

Mid-November. Holiday Craft Fair, Community Center, Heald and Fallbrook streets. Indoor/outdoor; Christmas gifts.

First Saturday in December. Christmas Parade, downtown Main Street. Floats, marching bands.

Other Recommended Restaurants and Lodgings

Bistro Cafe, 119 North Main Street, in Jackson Square. (619) 723–3559. Follow the narrow, brick-paved courtyard of trees, flowers, and small boutiques to the cafe in the rear, where umbrella'd tables provide a cool haven for lunch of gourmet pizza, sandwiches, stuffed potatoes, and such. Le Bistro, perched upstairs, is noted for fine dining selections, such as pepper steak, duck l'orange, and rack of lamb.

La Caseta Mexican Restaurant, 111 North Vine Street, corner of East Alvarado, near the Sheriff's station. (619) 728–4041. Perennial favorite for its variety of selections, such as chicken and enchilada *especialidades,* burritos, and *chimichangas,* served with rice, beans, and assorted garnishes. Closed Sunday.

Main Street Cafe, 1309 South Mission Road, in Colony Shopping Center. (619) 728–8120. This attractive restaurant features a fresh salad bar, sandwiches, daily specials.

Village Inn Restaurant, 1415 South Mission Road. (619) 731–0007. Known for family-style dining, salad bar; seafood, chicken, cocktails; Sunday brunch.

El Jardin Mexican Restaurant, 1581 South Mission Road. (619) 728–4556. A pretty place with hanging plants and comfortable booths; longtime local favorite for homemade chili, beef and chicken *fajitas,* and other tasty specialties. Sunday brunch.

Mesquite Broiler, 1019 South Mission Road. (619) 728–8008. In the old firehouse; well recommended by residents for fragrant, delicious BBQ ribs, beef, chicken, steak.

La Estancia Inn, 3535 Highway 395, South Fallbrook. (619) 723–2888. Spanish-style villa with southwestern decor; forty-one deluxe rooms, some with sitting area, spa, kitchenettes; in-room safes; ice vending machines, swimming pool, and heated spa. Poolside dining cabana, restaurant. Continental cuisine features broiled Maine lobster, fish, chicken dishes. Early-bird menu, Sunday Champagne buffet brunch.

Travelodge, 1608 South Main Street. (619) 723–1527; (800) 255–3050 (reservations). Thirty-six air-conditioned guestrooms, with refrigerator or kitchenette, double beds, TV with remote control, satellite TV movies, AM/FM clock radio. Nonsmoker rooms; Jacuzzi; courtesy coffee in lobby.

Franciscan Inn, 1635 South Mission Road. (619) 723–1127. Fifty-one deluxe air-conditioned rooms, king and queen beds, kitchenettes, cable TV, heated swimming pool, courtesy coffee.

For More Information

Fallbrook Chamber of Commerce, 233-A East Mission Road, Fallbrook, CA 92028. (619) 728–5845.

Escondido/Lake San Marcos

Visitors on safari at Wild Animal Park meet a Ugandan giraffe.

Wine, Pontoons, and Safari

1 NIGHT

Wild animal park • Wineries • Antique cars • Lake
Ethnic and gourmet dining • Resorts • Boating

This varied two-day itinerary takes you on new adventures, with plenty of change of pace and scene. Using Escondido as a convenient hub to explore the rural area, you visit and taste-tour local wineries, see a marvelous collection of classic restored antique cars, go on a safari through an 1,800-acre wildlife preserve, view a historic battlefield, and go boating on a peaceful, secluded lake.

Day 1

Morning

Drive south from Los Angeles on I–5 to Oceanside. Take Highway 78 east to I–15 north. Exit at Mountain Meadow Road; turn right to the stop sign and left on the frontage road, Champagne Boulevard, proceeding for about 2.5 miles to the Welk Resort Center.

Lunch: **Welk Resort Center,** 8860 Lawrence Welk Drive, Escondido. (800) 932–9355. The enticing Buffet du Chef in the resort's large dining room overlooking the inviting golf fairways features carved-to-order roast beef, roast chicken, or fish fillets, plus another entree as well as an extensive salad bar assortment. The buffet is served Sunday, Tuesday, Wednesday, and Thursday from 11:15 A.M. to 1:15 P.M. Regular popular luncheon menu is also available daily.

Afternoon

Continue along the frontage road, Champagne Boulevard, a very short distance to the **Deer Park Wine Tasting Car Museum,** 29013 Champagne Boulevard (760–749–1666). This place is perfect for car nostalgia buffs and for wine enthusiasts, who can taste wines from the surrounding vineyard and from the Napa Valley at this family-owned and -operated winery tasting room. As you tour the winery, you can view the large collection of antique cars and convertibles.

The Market Deli, giftshop, wine-tasting room, and a dozen classic cars share space in the large Market Building. After sampling the wines guests take a self-guided tour of the winery (tours offered daily from 10:00 A.M. to 5:00 P.M.). The gourmet Market Deli's sandwiches are named for cars: the Ford is roast beef, the Chevy is ham, the Edsel is turkey, and so forth. Order a sandwich, buy some wine, and picnic in the winery's beautiful fifteen-acre park (the deli closes at 3:00 P.M.). The giftshop's selection includes car models, books, posters, wine accessories, and wineglasses, plus T-shirts and other items. The Wine Boutique offers California premium wines from limited-production wineries.

The gleaming cars on display include a 1928 Ford that sold for $550, a 1935 Packard, and a 1931 Chrysler Deluxe that sold for $1,545. Each car is fully identified. In the new Mission-style Winery Building, with a collection of autos of the 1950s, the prize is the triple black, 1953 Cadillac Eldorado. The Car Museum, in another building, displays open roadsters, touring cars, and nostalgic convertibles, resembling everyone's dream car (the Car Museum closes at 4:00 P.M.).

Leave Deer Park and drive back past the Welk Resort Center, go up the hill to the four-way stop, and turn right on I–15 south to Highway 78, about 7 miles. Stay on Highway 78 to the Rancho Santa Fe exit. Turn left and continue for about 2 miles to Lake San Marcos Drive; turn left and go downhill to the end of the street to your hotel, **Quails Inn,** in **Lake San Marcos,** a small, exclusive, nontouristy city in a rural resort setting.

After checking into your lakefront hotel, you'll have time for a refreshing **boat ride** on Lake San Marcos. Ask the desk clerk to arrange a ride for you, and walk or drive to the boathouse, just past Quails Dinnerhouse. Here a small lawn tapers down to the lovely lake, where swans pose elegantly and ducks quack as they paddle around close to shore. After receiving easy instructions to operate the electric gondolas or open-air pontoon boat, you'll soon be out on the cool, secluded, 1.25-mile-long lake, gliding around the little inlets to the dam and back. (Hourly boat fee.)

Dinner: **Quails Dinnerhouse at Quails Inn,** Lake San Marcos Resort, Lake San Marcos. (760) 744–2455. Overlooking the lake, the restaurant is a town favorite for the spectacular seafood/salad bar and other entrees. For faster service take the stairway down to the convivial Lakeside Lounge, which also overlooks the water. Happy Hour, Monday through Friday from 4:00 to 7:00 P.M. with lower-priced drinks, features an extensive variety of hot and cold complimentary hors d'oeuvres. The regular dinner menu offers fish-and-chips, Cajun chicken, cheeseburgers with terrific cross-fries (basket-weave), and different nightly specials.

Lodging: **The Quails Inn Hotel,** Lake San Marcos Resort, 1025 La Bonita Drive, Lake San Marcos, CA 92069. Reservations: (800) 447–6556; (760) 744–0120. You'll appreciate this quiet and romantic lakeside setting of 142 nicely appointed large rooms, plus suites and apartments, some with patio overlooking the private lake. In-room coffeemaker, separate bathroom pullman counters with roomy storage, bathtub and stall shower, fresh flowers, and daily newspaper. Three restaurants; cocktail lounge with entertainment nightly. Boating on the lake; 18-hole Championship Country Club golf course and access to 18-hole executive course; volleyball area, four tennis courts, four paddle-tennis courts; four heated swimming pools; fitness center; large conference center. Theater, Sunday brunch.

Day 2

Morning

Breakfast: **Lake San Marcos Country Club Dining Room,** 1950 San Pablo Drive, Lake San Marcos. (760) 744–9385. The pretty dining rooms overlook the lush fairways. You don't have to be Jack Nicklaus to enjoy the Golfer's Tee-Off breakfast of eggs with ham or bacon, potatoes, and muffins; other options include waffles and buttermilk pancakes. Also open to the public for lunch and dinner.

Investigate the good-looking **Village Center** across from the hotel, with coffeeshop, small market, liquor store, pharmacy, and shops; hotel guests may charge purchases to their rooms. Then walk down to the lake and enjoy a quiet stroll alongside the tranquil water. Relax and watch the ducks and the swans and the little children who chase the ducks across the lawn and into the water as they offer them food. If you have time, go for another sail around Lake San Marcos—it's a wonderful experience. You may want to have lunch early today, since lots of activities are scheduled for the afternoon.

Drive up San Marino Drive to Rancho Santa Fe Road, turn right to San Marcos Boulevard, and turn right again several blocks later to San Marcos's famous **Restaurant Row,** on the left. Here's an exciting variety of twelve fine restaurants in one convenient location (see "Other Recommended Restaurants and Lodgings").

Lunch: **Bruno's Italian Restaurant & Pizzeria,** 1020 San Marcos Boulevard, San Marcos. (760) 744–7700. Recommended enthusiastically by fussy diners, the lunch buffet, served Monday through Saturday, features ten items, including veal parmigiana, several pizzas, seafood, and pasta. Other menu selections are hearty sandwiches and a salad bar.

Afternoon

To visit the San Diego Wild Animal Park, take San Marcos Boulevard past Restaurant Row to Freeway 78; go east to I–15, then south to the Via Rancho Parkway exit. Turn left onto San Pasqual Road, and follow it until it becomes Highway 78, leading to the Wild Animal Park (about 6 miles).

San Diego Wild Animal Park, 15600 San Pasqual Valley Road (Highway 78) in Escondido (760–747–8702). It's almost a culture shock on the Wgasa Bush Line Monorail's fifty-minute narrated safari, where you skirt the 5-mile perimeter of Asian and African animal habitats. As your guide describes many of the 2,500 animals living in the 2,100-acre preserve—a haven for vanishing wildlife species—you may feel as though you've been deposited in Africa, as you see animals roaming freely in dramatic open plains.

In addition to Asian and African elephants, you'll see giraffes, Persian gazelles, flamingos, zebras, ostriches, Arabian oryx, Sumatran tigers, wild horses, 4,000-pound white rhinos, many species of antelope, and numerous other wild animals and birds. You won't always see the tigers and other animals that sleep throughout the day, and many are too far away. A zoom lens for your camera is useful, as are binoculars. The right-hand side of the monorail affords better viewing.

When your safari ends, visit the 17-acre Nairobi African Village, with its restaurants, snackbars, and shops. Check the map you received at entry for schedules of the engaging bird, elephant, and other daily shows. Youngsters adore the Petting Kraal and Animal Care Center, where they can cuddle the koalas and watch nursery feedings. Lush botanical gardens, a wooden bridge, a waterfall cascading down boulders, a treehouse, and large, colorful macaws all enhance your exit (if you can find it) from the park. (Open daily from 9:00 A.M. to dusk; seasonal events and special exhibits; admission and parking fee; entry ticket includes monorail, animal shows, and exhibits.)

To get to the Orfila Vineyards & Winery, turn left on San Pasqual Road; go 3 miles, passing a large produce stand, Old San Pasqual Road, and a Christmas tree farm. Look for vineyards on the low hillside at the left of the road, and continue to the large ORFILA VINEYARDS & WINERY sign, turning left through the gates past a picnic lawn to the wine-tasting room.

In the deliciously cool, flag-decorated tasting room of **Orfila Vineyards & Winery** (formerly the Thomas Jaeger Winery), 13455 San Pasqual Road, Escondido (760–738–6500), you'll sample a variety of multi-award-winning wines of San Diego's largest premium winery, then enjoy self-guided tours through the vineyard and winery (or you can join a guided tour at 2:00 P.M.). Orfila's seventy acres of vineyards in San Diego County include thirty acres of estate vineyards planted in new and upcoming varieties of Syrah and Sangiovese, plus forty-five acres in Fallbrook growing Merlot, Chardonnay, and other grapes. Many visitors purchase luncheon snack foods—cheese, crackers, individual pizza or smoked salmon—and a bottle of wine and then picnic on the patio beneath the shady grape arbor overlooking the vineyards and the beautiful San Pasqual Valley. The Winery Gift Shop is stocked with wine, T-shirts, glasses, corkscrews, coasters, cookbooks, beribboned gift baskets, and fascinating food- and wine-related items you won't find elsewhere. Wine tasting is offered daily from 10:00 A.M. to 6:00 P.M.

To reach I–15 north to Los Angeles, go west on San Pasqual Road to San Pasqual Valley Road/Highway 78. Stay on 78 west for 7 to 10 miles until you come to I–15. From I–15, take Beach Cities/Riverside 91 exit to the left. Then look for I–5 north just past Anaheim and take it into downtown Los Angeles.

There's More

Ferrara Winery, 1120 West 15th Avenue Escondido. (760) 745–7632. San Diego County's oldest grape-growing winery is a designated State Historical Point of Interest. If you enjoy the challenge of finding Ferrara, the tasting room offers a selection of premium wine, Monday through Friday from 9:00 A.M. to 5:30 P.M. and Saturday and Sunday from 10:00 A.M. The deli makes sandwiches to enjoy in the hundred-year-old vineyard. Enter the winery, with its two red-brick pillars and machinery out front, from the parking lot next to number 1160 in a residential street.

Palomar Observatory, forty-five minutes northeast of Escondido on Palomar Mountain. (760) 742–2119. The home of the 200-inch Hale Telescope offers two kinds of tours. On the third Saturday of each month, four one-hour free tours are given on a reserved basis for groups; call or write for reservation forms. Additionally, the Reuben H. Fleet Space Theater and Science Center in San Diego offers six tours yearly, May through October; reserve through them at (760) 238–1233. Fee.

The observatory is open daily, except Christmas, from 8:00 A.M. to 4:30 P.M. Visitors can take a free self-guided tour and view the Hale Telescope from the gallery in the dome; there is no viewing through the telescope. The giftshop is open daily during July and August and otherwise only on weekends. Take Highway 76 to County Road S6 and wind up the mountain to the observatory gate.

San Pasqual State Historic Park and Museum, east of the San Diego Wild Animal Park on Highway 78, 115808 San Pasqual Valley Road, Escondido. (760) 489–0076. For history buffs; the fifty-acre hillside park overlooks the site of the **Battle of San Pasqual,** December 6, 1846, between U.S. forces and Mexico, during the Mexican-American War. This battle was a small conflict but the most severe fought in California. You can travel back into California history at the modern Visitor Center and Museum, which presents the story of the battle in a short video, along with maps, displays, and artifacts. Open Saturday and Sunday from 10:00 A.M. to 5:00 P.M. Other exhibits highlight the history of the pastoral San Pasqual Valley. Outdoors, visitors can follow easy pathways and nature trails through the park, perhaps even spot an animal or two roaming through the nearby San Diego Wild Animal Park.

An annual reenactment of the Battle of San Pasqual is presented on the Sunday closest to December 6. In a colorful presentation dragoons, Californios, Marines, and horsemen dressed in period attire use muskets, cannons, and horse charges to provide a lively, memorable event.

Heritage Walk Museum Complex, Grape Day Park, 321 North Broadway, Escondido. (760) 743–8207. For a quick glimpse into Escondido's past, take Highway 78 east, turning left on Washington to Grape Day Park, with tall, beautiful shade trees. Heritage Walk museum complex includes buildings preserved from Escondido's beginnings in 1888. Stroll around to see the town's first library, a little 1894 yellow cottage with brown trim, the 1900s Red Barn with wagon and windmill, a two-story 1790 country house, a blacksmith shop currently used for restoring stagecoaches, and the 1888 Santa Fe Railroad Depot, which ended passenger service in 1945 and is at present used by the local historical society. Buildings are open Thursday through Saturday from 1:00 to 4:00 P.M. but can be viewed at any time.

Bates Nut Farm, 15954 Woods Valley Road, Valley Center. (760) 749–3333. About fifteen minutes northeast of Escondido, here's where to stock up on packages of dried fruits, candies, and fresh-roasted nuts from all over the world. Kids get to feed ducks and geese and pet the sheep and goats. Gift boutique; freshly ground peanut butter; special festive events during the year. Open daily, 8:00 A.M. to 5:00 P.M.

California Center for the Arts, at 340 North Escondido Boulevard, Escondido. (760) 738–4120. This stunning new $80 million center opened in 1994 on twelve Village Green acres adjoining Grape Day Park. The 1,500-seat Concert Hall and 400-seat Center Theatre for Performing Arts present hundreds of performances each season. The Art Museum, with sculpture court, showcases three major exhibitions yearly of contemporary California and international artists. Museum hours: Tuesday through Saturday from 10:00 A.M. to 5:00 P.M. and Sunday from noon to 5:00 P.M.

Golf. The Vineyard at Escondido, 925 San Pasqual Road (before Orfila Vineyards and on the way to San Diego Wild Animal Park). (760) 735–9545. Recently opened, the lush, well-maintained 18-hole golf course has a lighted practice range and a pro shop. Open to the public.

Farmer's market, on Grand Avenue between Calmia and Broadway, Escondido. (760) 745–8877. Tuesdays from 3:00 P.M. to dusk; call for special winter hours and location.

San Diego North County Factory Outlet Center, 1050 Vallecitos Boulevard, San Marcos. (760) 471–1500. This sparkling air-conditioned mall showcases twenty-five outlets of factory-direct shops offering discounts of 25 to 75 percent on men's, women's, and children's clothing; shoes and leathergoods; perfume, jewelry; and books and kitchenware.

Special Events

Mid-April, early August, middle to the end of October, mid-November, late November, and mid-December. Bates Nut Farm Fairs and Shows, Valley Center.

May 19. Escondido Street Faire, downtown Escondido. Third largest Street Faire in California; 600 booths, crafts, live entertainment on several stages, farmer's market, pancake breakfast, food from around the world. From 9:00 A.M. to 5:00 P.M.

Early June, mid-to-late June, early August, and late December. San Pasqual Battlefield events, Escondido.

Early September. Chili Cook-Off, Walnut Grove Park, San Marcos. (760) 744–1270.

End of September. Annual Harvest Festival, Escondido Historical Society, at Grape Day Park, Escondido. From 9:00 A.M. to 4:00 P.M. (760) 741–8207.

Sunday closest to December 6. Battle Day, San Pasqual State Historic Park. Starts at 10:00 A.M. (760) 489–0076.

Mid-December. Christmas Parade, 1500 North Broadway to Grand Avenue, Escondido. Starts at 10:00 A.M.

Other Recommended Restaurants and Lodgings

San Marcos

Fish House Vera Cruz and Rancho Vera Cruz. In Restaurant Row. (760) 744–8000. The two restaurants share the same building, with separate entrances and dining rooms. The Fish House is popular for tasty, fresh, mesquite-broiled seafood. Rancho Vera Cruz is equally popular for fine steaks.

Acapulco Mexican Restaurant and Cantina. (760) 471–2150. A local hangout for its variety of Mexican dishes, lively Happy Hour with complimentary hors d'oeuvres, and Sunday brunch.

Escondido

The Brigantine Restaurant, 421 West Felicita Avenue. (760) 743–4718. South of Grape Day Park. Another reliable choice for seafood entrees.

Cocina del Charro, 625 North Quince. (760) 745–1382. Serves authentic Mexican specialties, *carne asada* burritos, and enchiladas for lunch and dinner; Sunday brunch.

Welk Resort Center, 8860 Lawrence Welk Drive. (800) 932–9355; (760) 749–3000. Sprawling, 1,000-acre resort with three 18-hole golf courses established by the late orchestra leader has 132 spacious rooms, 6 suites, and two-bedroom villas, all with views of the golf course, with patios or balconies. In-room coffeemaker and TV; giftshops, market/deli, beauty shop; three swimming pools with spas. Restaurant and lounge; karaoke five nights a week. Conference facilities; live theater performances.

Rancho Santa Fe.

The Inn at Rancho Santa Fe, 5951 Linea del Cielo, Rancho Santa Fe. (800) 654–2928; (760) 756–1131. American-California cuisine offered in the Vintage Room, a cozy, romantic spot with glowing fireplace, for lunch and dinner and on summer weekends; Garden Room, overlooking the gardens and pool, serves brunch.

For More Information

San Diego North County Convention and Visitors Bureau, 720 North Broadway, Escondido, CA 92025. (800) 848–3336; (760) 745–4741.

San Marcos Chamber of Commerce, 144 West Mission Road, San Marcos, CA 92069. (760) 744–1270.

Julian/Anza Borrego/ Borrego Springs

Julian's Town Hall is a center for year-round events.

Gold Rush and Desert Grandeur

_____ 1 NIGHT _____

Fruit orchards • Gold-mining town • Museum • Horse-and-buggy ride
Country shopping • Desert state park • Historic trails and nature walks
Wildflowers • Bighorn sheep

There's plenty of change in this two-day itinerary that gets you off the fast track. It takes you high up in the mountains of north San Diego County to a small historic gold-mining town still reflecting its aura of the 1870 Gold Rush days, then down to the mighty Anza Borrego Desert to explore the natural wonders of the nation's second largest state park. You'll also stay overnight in a luxurious, desert-oasis resort and browse a small, upscale resort community surrounded by spring wildflowers.

Day 1

Morning

Leave Los Angeles via I–5 south through Oceanside, then head east on Highway 78 into Escondido, continuing on 78 up the mountains to Julian, about a three-hour drive. Following Highway 78 on the scenic drive up to Julian, the backcountry road borders a woodsy stream as it climbs and weaves through broad rolling plains where cattle graze in sunny pastures. In fall the open fields tumbled with fat golden pumpkins are bucolic treats for city dwellers. Look for roadside stands selling eggs, cider, pears, and apples (in fall) and buy as you go along. Better yet, wait until the return trip to purchase fresh produce to take home. About 7 miles from Julian, you'll pass **Dudley's Bakery and Restaurant** on the left near Highway 79, noted for baking twenty varieties of bread daily and for its long lines. It's so popular that it has a toll-free number so customers can call in a pickup order: (800) 225-3348, 8:00 A.M. to 5:00 P.M. (Closed Monday and Tuesday.)

Julian, a former Gold Rush mining town and a National Historic Site, is a sleepy, 4-block-square rural community. At 4,235 feet high in the oak-and-pine hills, Julian's apples and cider lure thousands of visitors to its Fall Harvest Festival in October and November. The town celebrates other seasons too, with festivals and arts and crafts shows. Cafes and restaurants feature fresh apple pie year-round by the slice, or you can lasso a whole pie.

In our harried, computerized age, visitors come to Julian for more than apples. They come for its atmosphere and nostalgic reminders of simpler times and for the romance of an exciting, lusty era they missed.

Julian has about 1,000 residents; adding in the surrounding suburbs, the population hits 2,000. There are no movie houses, glitz, or shopping malls in this rustic, pint-size village that dozes all week and hums with tourists on the weekend. Most stores close between 5:00 and 6:00 P.M., and all are open weekends.

Lunch: **Romano's Dodge House,** 2718 B Street, Julian. (760) 765-1003. Around the corner from Julian Lodge. Considered the best

Italian food in town; they treat you like one of the family, except you don't have to help with the dishes. Sample the lasagna, pizza, and veal and pasta selections. (Sorry, no apple pie here.) There's a small bar. Closed Tuesday and Wednesday.

Afternoon

Julian is a true success story, one that began in 1869, when miners found placer gold in a nearby stream. Searching farther upstream, they discovered gold ore in 1870. As claims were staked out and mines multiplied, the exciting Gold Rush began. One of the local residents, Mike Julian, helped record and lay out the town site, and the towns-people named it after him.

In a dizzying boom, gold seekers, prospectors, and miners showed up from all over the West, by sea from Northern California and by stage from San Diego. Within a month nearly 1,000 gold hunters arrived to work the town's mines. Julian expanded rapidly, as buildings sprang up along bustling Main Street. In its prime the town had four general stores, fifteen hotels, a dozen saloons, two livery stables, and two stage lines to San Diego.

The bonanza ended ten years later, when the rich veins of gold in the mines were exhausted after producing millions of dollars worth of gold. The stampede ended when the migrant miners rushed off to a new boom in Tombstone, Arizona, in 1880.

Julian didn't become a ghost town, as did so many others. Farmers found the rich soil and pleasant mountain climate ideal for growing apples and pears. A ragtag bunch stayed on and homesteaded the fertile valley and hills. Julian soon became an active farming-trading community.

Drop in at the **Town Hall,** at the corner of Washington and Main, in a historic 1913 building—it's the center of all year-round activities. Take a look at its historic photos and pick up a list of special events. The Chamber of Commerce is located here (see "For More Information").

Around the corner, **Julian Pioneer Museum,** 2811 Washington Street (760–765–0227), is the city's oldest building. Built in 1875, it was originally the town's brewery and later a blacksmith shop. Restored and enlarged, the museum is called "Julian's Attic" by the townsfolk. It's filled with a jumble of old furniture, photos and historical records, mining equipment, a gleaming old square Weber grand piano, a Victorian carriage, and many other items depicting the city's life in the Gold Rush days of 1869. Open Tuesday through Sunday April through November; and weekends and holidays December through March; 10:00 A.M. to 4:00 P.M. Donation.

Among the shops and cafes at this historic part of **Main Street** near the site of the Washington Mine around the Fire Station are several antiques stores tucked in small cottages. Mosey down Main Street, with its wooden 1800s buildings, to Mom's Cafe, where you can watch the bakers making hundreds of apple pies daily. Next door the **Warm Hearth** is a treasure to browse, with its perky country music and old-fashioned but trendy country-style antique items, like Coca-Cola signs, baskets, and tins of Lipton's tea. Check out the great-looking Indian pottery, baskets, kachinas, and jewelry in the rear of the store, all authentic and rather expensive. Near the end of Main Street, Julian Cider Mill, a family-owned local institution, offers welcome cups of its hot cider in winter and sips of cold boysenberry-apple cider in summer. From about October through March, you can watch apples being pressed into cider. Additionally, you'll always find a nice assortment of dried fruit, honey, nuts, candy, and popcorn.

Across the way on B Street, take time to browse **K. O. Corral's rustic courtyard shops.** To tour Julian's only remaining 1897 operating gold mine, drive up hilly C Street about 6 blocks to the **Eagle and High Peak Gold Mines** (760–765–0036). Take the hour-and-forty-five-minute guided tour through 1,000 feet of underground tunnels, and relive the gold-fever days. Daily tours start at 10:00 A.M.; the last tour is at 2:30 P.M.; the site is closed before 10:00 A.M. and after 4:00 P.M. (Picnic area, closed Christmas and Easter; fee.)

Among the two dozen or more remaining historic structures in town, the 1869 **Julian Hotel,** 2032 Main Street (800–734–5854; 760–765–0201), on the National Register of Historic Places and the sole survivor of the town's fifteen hotels in its heyday, began as a restaurant owned by a freed Georgia slave whose wife's delectable southern cooking attracted hungry travelers on the Butterfield Stage. They built a successful hotel around it, and it's now a popular B&B with sixteen rooms, most with baths down the hall, and a separate honeymoon cottage.

When you have explored Julian, drive through to the end of Main Street for the 2-mile, one-hour drive down the mountainside to Borrego Springs and Anza Borrego Desert State Park. Be advised to leave in daylight, as this is a very curvy, very dangerous mountain road. The road is cut right through the low mountains, with pure desolation on both sides toward the flat desert plains below. It's a hair-raising ride down Banner Grade, with many curves as the road descends to the desert floor where the vast, 600,000-acre park stretches to the soft, sensuous foothills, as you wind and twist through Yaqui Pass. Just after Rams Hill you arrive at La Casa del Zorro Desert Resort Hotel, a welcome oasis of palm trees, lush green grass, and fountains.

Check into your hotel, and if there's time and daylight, get back on S3, Borrego Springs Road, to explore the little town of **Borrego Springs,** and plan to visit the huge state park tomorrow. Follow the green Christmas Circle turnaround along Palm Canyon Drive to the

good-looking, smartly landscaped mall of shops and restaurants—
Kendall's Cafe, Pot Luck, Borrego Goldsmith Jewelers, Union Bank,
and others. Across the street a smaller shopping complex includes the
Live Theater, a restaurant, and a gas station. The library and the Borrego Springs Chamber of Commerce are 1 block farther along (see
"For More Information"), if you need any information or brochures. All
stores close between 5:00 and 6:00 P.M., earlier in summer.

Borrego Springs's population of 3,000 increases in winter to about
8,000. This peaceful community is often compared with Palm Springs
of the 1930s. But residents know there is no danger of urban sprawl
or crowding, as the city is completely surrounded by the magnificent
desert park.

Its enviable lifestyle of peace and quiet in the warm, clean desert
air includes golf, tennis, swimming, and other good-life amenities.
Temperatures can rise in the summer from 107 degrees to around 124
degrees, but evenings are cooler. Accommodations range from luxury
resorts to smaller hotels.

Dinner: **La Casa del Zorro,** 3845 Yaqui Pass Road, Borrego
Springs. (800) 824–1884; (760) 767–5323. Two dining rooms feature
varying Early Bird Special entrees from 4:00 to 6:00 P.M. Weekday
Happy Hour from 3:00 to 7:00 P.M. includes complimentary hors
d'oeuvres.

Lodging: La Casa del Zorro, 3845 Yaqui Pass Road, Borrego Springs,
CA 92004. (800) 824–1884; (760) 767–5323. This luxury desert hideaway, a *Mobil Travel Guide* four-star and a AAA four-diamond resort,
offers seventy-seven elegantly decorated rooms, deluxe suites, and casitas on thirty-eight acres of lush desert landscaping. Rooms feature
alarm clock, coffeemaker, hair dryer, daily newspaper, terry robes,
large fireplace, TV, comfortable lounge chairs, and good lighting.
Complimentary coffee in the lobby; three swimming pools and spas,
six night-lighted tennis courts, tennis pro shop, putting green, fitness
room; salon, giftshop; two restaurants, bar and lounge, Saturday and
Sunday buffet brunch, jazz weekends. Seasonal rates, special events,
and conference center. Country club golf nearby.

Day 2

Morning

Breakfast: At the hotel. In two dining rooms, elegantly served continental breakfast includes a generous bowl of fresh fruit or yogurt plus
muffins, toast, or croissants, juice, and coffee. Full breakfast features
Belgian waffles and egg specialties.

Drive to Borrego Springs and, following the green Christmas Circle turnaround on Palm Canyon Drive, continue on S22 to the state park, past the shopping village, about a 7-mile drive through the vast, serene desert. In spring, after the winter rains, thousands of tourists arrive from early March through mid-April to marvel at the spectacular view of wildflowers carpeting the arid desert floor and hillsides.

Anza Borrego Desert State Park, the largest park in California and the second largest in the United States covering more than a half-million acres, attracts close to a million visitors in the winter season, from October through May. These visitors explore and experience the park's open wilderness beauty, taking self-guided auto tours to many points of interest and hiking, camping, mountain biking, and back-packing amid the palm-studded canyons, plains, and desolate bad-lands. Elevations range from 15 feet to more than 7,000 feet of the towering Santa Rosa Mountains.

The park is named for Spanish explorer Juan Bautista de Anza, who led an expedition for Spain from Mexico through Cahuilla Indian territory in 1774 and discovered the first overland route to California. Markers commemorate the historic event. *Borrego* is the Spanish name for the elusive peninsular bighorn sheep that take refuge here.

The area resembles a surreal desert moonscape and is as natural and rugged as when the Spaniards first arrived hundreds of years ago. Surrounded by the tall cinnamon mountains, it is a scene of desolation and solitude, absolutely haunting in its stark, lonely beauty and grandeur. Park rangers advise visitors to carry plenty of water and to wear a hat and sunblock. It can be very hot.

Drive up to the Visitor Center. The entrance is not visible from the road, in its underground building sheltered beneath a low hillside with a desert sand roof dotted with low native plants. The center provides slide shows on the hour and the half-hour; these explain the desert's history and its variety of more than 600 species of plants and 300 species of reptiles and birds, including the fast little roadrunner. Among native animals are the bobcat, coyote, and kangaroo rat.

The center offers naturalist talks, guided walks, hikes, and tours and provides brochures and maps of the most scenic places. *Note:* The Visitor Center (760–767–4205) is open daily only from October through May, from 9:00 A.M. to 5:00 P.M., and open only on weekends and holidays from June through September. The Administration Office (760–767–5311) has opposite hours, open weekdays from 8:00 A.M. to 5:00 P.M. and closed weekends and holidays.

The favorite and most scenic hike is the Palm Canyon Nature Trail, a 1.5-mile hike up through the hills to an oasis of a grove of about 1,000 palm trees thriving in the rocky canyon. Other trails cover the historic routes traveled in the 1840s and 1850s by Kit Carson, the Mormon Batallion, adventurers, gold seekers the first transcontinental mail service, and the famous Butterfield Overland Stage traveling from St. Louis to San Francisco, a twenty-four-day journey of extreme hardships wherein passengers frequently had to get out and help push the stagecoach over steep mountain passes. Today's visitors on self-guided auto tours can follow the deep wagon-wheel ruts along the road, look across the incredible shimmering desert, and reclaim a bit of history in the Old West for themselves.

To return to Los Angeles, you need to retrace your way, driving back up the mountain and through Julian and down Highway 78. From Anza Borrego Park go back on the road to Casa del Zorro, following the curve to the right on S3. This is the same very winding and curvy road you drove down from Julian, only now it winds sharply up and up around the mountains. The spectacular views make up for all the curves, with the mountains covered in various shades of green.

Afternoon

You can spend time browsing again in Julian, have lunch or more apple pie, or continue through town on Main Street, turning left on Washington and on to Highway 78, a rolling pleasant road. You'll pass many fruit orchards on the way (see "There's More"). Continue on Highway 78 to I–5 north to Los Angeles.

There's More

Country Carriages, available in front of Julian Drug. (760) 765–1471. Offers romantic, old-fashioned buggy rides. Fee.

If you like to buy fresh fruit, look for apple and pear orchards located throughout Julian. Pears are available in different seasons, with a good crop in September; apples are usually harvested in October, and peaches in August.

The following **fruit markets** are on Highway 78, 3 miles west of Julian just past Wynola Road (on the right). They're usually open daily from 9:00 A.M. to 5:00 P.M. and sell, depending on the season, apples, pears, peaches, cider, jams and jellies, and other items.

Farmers Mountain Vale Ranch, 4510 Highway 78, Julian. (760) 765–0188. In addition to the fresh fruits, this ranch also bakes and sells delicious apple pies.

Manzanita Ranch, 4470 Highway 78, Julian. (760) 765–0102. Apples, pears, cider, winter vegetables.

Meyers Orchard, 3962 Highway 78, Julian. (760) 765–0233. Apples, pears, peaches.

The Apple Store, Julian Orchard, 1255 Julian Orchards Drive, Julian. (760) 765–2959. Apples only; no cider. You can pick your own apples here or buy those already bagged. Jonathan, McIntosh, Golden and Red Delicious, Rome Beauty, and others.

Apple Lane Orchard, 2641 Apple Lane, Julian. (760) 765–2645. Here's where you can watch cider pressing on Thursday mornings, and apple slicing during "Apple Days."

Julian Apple Mountain Orchard, 1125 Farmer Road, Julian. (760) 765–1906. Here's where you can actually rent a tree (fees vary), which entitles you to all the produce for the harvest season. Come up and pick your own apples. Additionally, you'll find cider presses, a country giftstore with gourmet goodies, and family recreational activities.

Wineries. Menghini Winery, 1150 Julian Orchards Drive, Julian. (760) 765–2072. Enjoy wine tasting and a guided tour of this family-run winery with picnic area. Open Friday, Saturday, and Sunday from 10:00 A.M. to 4:00 P.M.; open weekdays by appointment.

Witch Creek Winery, on B Street in K.O. Corral, Julian. (760) 765–2023. Drop by for wine tasting Wednesday through Saturday, from 10:00 A.M. to 6:00 P.M.

Julian Donkey Treks, P.O. Box 1884. (760) 765–1182. Fun and discovery of Julian's wilderness by leading a miniature donkey on a nature walk.

Julian Gold Mining Company, 1921 Main Street. (760) 765–3106. Relive the pioneer days—pan for gold right on Main Street.

Old Time Photo. Dress up in old-fashioned western clothes and pose for photos inside the Warm Hearth Building on Main Street.

Special Events

Note: All events take place in Julian Town Hall unless otherwise noted.

January through mid-December. Art shows and crafts shows. Contact Chamber of Commerce for schedule.

February, March, and end of April. Spring wildflowers, Borrego Springs.

Late March to early April. Grapefruit Festival. Arts and Crafts Show, Borrego Springs.

Early May. Spinning and Weaving Show.

Early to mid-May. Annual Wildflower Show.

Late June to early July. Annual Heritage Quilt Show.

Fourth of July. Annual Deep-Pit Barbecue Dinner, American Legion Hall, Second and Washington streets.

Late August to early September. Annual Weed Show.

Mid-September. Lions Club Banjo/Fiddle Contest. Annual Wood-turners Show and Sale.

Mid-September through November. Julian Apple Harvest time.

Every weekend in October. Triangle Club Melodrama.

Last weekend in October to early November. Desert Festival, street parade. Borrego Springs.

Late November. Christmas Craft Show.

Other Recommended
Restaurants and Lodgings

Julian

Rongbranch Restaurant and Boar's Head Saloon, 2722 Washington Street. (760) 765–2265. This perennial favorite is well known for hearty sandwiches, charbroiled burgers—also buffalo burgers made of lean ground buffalo meat. Variety of pies, convivial saloon, and attractive giftshop.

Julian Pie Company, 1921 Main Street. (760) 765–3330. Dine in the front yard on salads, soups, sandwiches, and a new-shaped pie.

Kendall's Korner, 3rd and B Street. (760) 765–1560. Specializes in omelets and pancakes for breakfast and lunch. Open daily: Monday through Friday from 6:00 A.M. to 3:00 P.M. and Saturday and Sunday to 7:30 P.M. Patio dining.

Bar-B-Q Dinner Theatre, Pine Hills Lodge, P.O. Box 701, Julian, CA 92036. (760) 765–1100. Join the fun Friday and Saturday evenings. Bar-B-Q at 7:00 P.M.; curtain at 8:00 P.M. Enjoy baby back pork ribs, chicken, zesty beans, salads, Dudley's bread.

Julian Lodge Bed and Breakfast, 4th and C Street. (800) 542–1420; (760) 765–1420. Two-story, modern; twenty-three rooms with bath, cable TV, air conditioning, and heat. Continental breakfast served in homey lobby.

Borrego Springs

Note: Summer hours and days are subject to change.

George and Ernie's Little Italy, The Center. (760) 767–3938. Open Wednesday through Sunday, 11:00 A.M. to 2:00 P.M. and 5:00 to 9:00 P.M. Closed Monday and Tuesday.

Kendall's Cafe, The Mall. (760) 767–3938. Open Monday through Wednesday from 6:00 A.M. to 2:00 P.M. and Thursday through Saturday until 8:00 P.M.; Mexican food served Thursday through Sunday, from 11:30 A.M. to 8:00 P.M.

Rams Hill Country Club Restaurant, Yaqui Pass Road. (760) 767–5000. Lunch Monday through Saturday from noon to 2:00 P.M.; dinner nightly from 6:00 P.M.; Sunday minibrunch from 8:00 A.M. to 2:00 P.M.

Palm Canyon Resort, 22 Palm Canyon Drive. (800) 242–0044; (760) 767–5341. Fourteen-acre complex includes forty-four-room hotel, deluxe RV park, two swimming pools and spas, restaurant, lounge, minimarket, bike rentals.

Rams Hill, 4343 Yaqui Pass Road, P.O. Box 2190. (760) 767–5028. Rentals of privately owned, well-furnished homes, with weekly, monthly, and group rates. Championship 18-hole golf course, pro shop; swimming pool, Jacuzzi; restaurant, lounge.

Villas Borrego, P.O. Box 185. (760) 767–5371. One- and two-bedroom villas with patios, swimming pool.

Road Runner Golf and Country Club, 1010 Palm Canyon Drive, P.O. Box 3081. (760) 767–5374. Family-owned, luxury mobile home retirement community, with 18-hole executive golf course, clubhouse, tennis courts, and large therapeutic swimming pool.

For More Information

Julian Chamber of Commerce, Town Hall, P.O. Box 413, Washington and Main streets, Julian, CA 92036. (760) 765–1857. Open daily from 10:00 A.M. to 4:00 or 5:00 P.M.

Julian Historical Society. (760) 765–0436.

Borrego Springs Chamber of Commerce, P.O. Box 66, 622 Palm Canyon Drive, Borrego Springs, CA 92004. (760) 767–5565.

Anza Borrego Desert State Park, P.O. Box 299, Borrego Springs, CA 92004. (760) 767–5311. Reservations: MISTIX, (800) 444–PARK.

Santa Catalina Island

Beautiful Santa Catalina Island's Avalon Bay.

Island Getaway

—————————————— 1 NIGHT ——————————————

Ocean cruise to island • Beach • Pier • Scuba/snorkel diving
Boating and fishing • Hiking • Island and harbor tours • Glass-bottom boat
Wilderness • Dance casino • Horseback riding

On your two-day Santa Catalina Island escape, which begins with a
brisk ocean voyage, you'll soon be seduced by an entirely different
environment.

The island air, surrounded by the sea, is clearer, the sun is brighter, and there are no automobiles. Sunbathe and swim in a small protected beach area; scuba and snorkel in translucent waters; go sailing, fishing, or biking; and join a variety of scenic tours around the island, from the peaceful sparkling harbor to the undeveloped wilderness interior where buffalo and deer roam freely. Enjoy a glass-bottom boat trip; visit the world-famous Casino Building, which hosted many of the Big Bands of the 1930s and 1940s; (Harry James, Woody Herman, Jimmy Dorsey were just a few), and dine in fine style at water's edge.

Day 1

Morning

From Los Angeles the fastest way to get to Catalina by boat (about one hour) is from Long Beach via the Catalina Express boats, which make frequent daily departures year-round from the *Queen Mary* port alongside the legendary ocean liner whose celebrity passengers included royalty, Hollywood stars, and millionaires.

Head south on Santa Anna Freeway I–5 to Long Beach Freeway 710 south to Long Beach. Follow signs to the *Queen Mary,* which lead you to the Catalina Express Port and parking lot: it's advisable to arrive twenty minutes or more before departure time. Lock up your car (daily rates) and board the *Catalina Express,* a double-deck, one-hundred-passenger cruiser. It's best to keep your luggage light or in small bags that you can stow in the ship's hold as you board or can carry on with you to place under your airline-style seat. This saves waiting for your luggage when you arrive in Catalina.

The 21.8-mile crossing may be a bit rough in a few spots but on the whole is fairly smooth sailing, as the fast boat seems to skim across the waves. Pretty soon you spot the tall jagged hills of **Catalina Island** rising dramatically out of the limitless ocean; then you see the tall, graceful round Casino Building in the blue bay encircled by small boats, and you're disembarking in **Avalon.**

Beginning in the 1920s and through its heyday of the 1930s and early 1940s, visitors sailed to Catalina Island from Los Angeles aboard either of two Great White steamers, the S.S. *Avalon* and the S.S. *Catalina,* which carried 2,000 passengers on a never-to-be forgotten adventure. Orchestras played for dancing, and there were food, romance, and the thrill of a two-and-a-half-hour ocean voyage, even though the crossing was frequently rough. (The *Avalon* retired in 1956, and the *Catalina* discontinued its sailings in 1976. Both stopped service during World War II, when they were commandeered by U.S. forces.)

The big ships were welcomed at the pier in Avalon by entertaining, costumed mariachis, as well as by island residents and visitors, since meeting the boat was a high spot of the day. When you left the island on the Great White steamer, your departure was sentimentally serenaded by the mariachis, and folks lined up waving good-bye. During the glamorous Big Band era, all the famous names—Benny Goodman Count Basie, Harry James, Freddy Martin, Ray Noble, Tommy Dorsey, Jan Garber, Jimmy Dorsey, and others—played nightly for thousands of enthusiastic dancers at the elegant Casino overlooking Catalina Bay. The Casino made history in May 1940, when 6,200 people came to swing and sway to the lilting music of Kay Kyser and his orchestra.

Nowadays high-speed cruisers make multiple sailings to and from Catalina Island daily. Four boat companies service the island, with departures from Long Beach and San Pedro harbors, Huntington Harbor, and the Balboa Pavilion at Newport Beach. You can also reach Catalina by helicopter service, from both San Pedro and Long Beach.

Most hotels arrange to meet their guests at the pier and transport them to the hotel via golf cart or taxi as a courtesy service. Upon arrival you may as well check in if your room is ready. You should inquire about check-out time, which is usually quite early, around 10:30 or 11:00 A.M.

Investigate **Crescent Avenue,** Avalon's main street, with its shops and cafes, palm trees, and postage-stamp-size beach that could probably fit in your backyard. The population in Avalon—the only city on the 21-mile-long, 8-mile-wide island—is about 3,000. Summertime visitors increase this to 6,000, and on weekends up to 10,000 visitors crowd the tiny, 1-square-mile city, feeling lucky to find a place to stand on the beach, let alone sprawl on the warm sand.

You'll soon be aware of the pleasant absence of cars, as automobile use is limited. There are no rental cars on Catalina Island. Vehicle permits are tightly restricted by the city, and the waiting list is said to be about eight years. In Avalon you mostly walk, ride a bike, use a golf cart, or board a tram.

There are no traffic, no noise or congestion, no smog, and no freeways here—truly an island paradise. You'll really feel on vacation in this happy-go-lucky little seaside resort. There's a vague European Riviera feeling in its compactness, tall palm trees, and jumble of cottages covered with flaming bougainvillea climbing up the steep hillsides. Bells chime from a hilltop; small boats rock in the sunny bay. The air is soft, and the fragrant, caressing breeze is balmy. It's a bit funky, a bit scruffy—and relaxed, friendly, romantic, carefree, and disarming.

Lunch: **Antonio's Pizzeria and Cabaret,** 230 Crescent Avenue Avalon. (310) 510–0008. Select a window table overlooking the blue postcard bay or sit out on the deck in this large, casual local hangout with 1950s decor and sawdust and peanut shells on the floor. Made-to-order thick-crust pizza with four cheeses is served hot and tasty. There are also pasta, steaks, and chicken. Individual jukeboxes at each table are where all the good 1950s music is coming from.

Afternoon

Crescent Avenue, sometimes called Front Street, is made for leisurely window shopping or relaxing on a bench watching the action in the yacht-filled harbor. As the only offshore mooring for Southern California yachtsmen, Catalina originally gained popularity as a yacht haven and sportfishing mecca and is still a prestigious yachting anchorage. John Wayne and other celebrity outdoorsmen used to sail their yachts over to fish for swordfish and marlin. Author Zane Grey, who lived up in the hills for many years, was an ardent fisherman as well.

The tall, stately Casino Building dominates the far side of the bay. Shops and restaurants line both sides of the busy, broad, red-bricked street. Stores feature beachwear, casual attire, souvenirs, T-shirts, and kitsch you never dreamed of. Catalina Island Department Store carries active sportswear; good-looking Sugarloaf Books has magazines, gifts, and postcards. The staff at the Visitors Information Center, across from the green Pleasure Pier, will be happy to help you line up sightseeing tours convenient to your busy schedule.

A leading island attraction is the twelve-story, landmark art deco **Casino Building,** which opened in 1929 and is where all the Big Bands played during the swinging years. During the 1930s the famous Casino Ballroom vibrated with 3,000 to 5,000 dancers on an average night. During a forty-minute guided tour of the historic Casino Building, you're waltzed out on the circular dance floor for a nostalgic twirl, then onto the broad terrace for photogenic views of the harbor, city, and mountains. This tour also includes the **Avalon Theater,** the **Catalina Island Museum,** and the **Catalina Art Association Gallery** in the building (fee for tour).

Dinner: **Cafe Prego,** 403 Crescent Avenue, Avalon. (310) 510–1218. Considered Avalon's finest Italian cuisine. Try to snag a streetside window table or one facing the water so you can watch the lights twinkling in the harbor. You could be in a small, romantic seaside cafe in Portofino. Dinners include soup, crisp salad, and a basket of bread. Try the richly flavored pasta combo: manicotti and cannelloni with *aglio e olio* linguine. Dinner only; casual dress; best to reserve.

Lodging: **Pavilion Lodge** on Crescent Avenue, Avalon, CA 90704. (800) 414–2754 (from California, 8:00 A.M. to 5:00 P.M.); (310)

510–1788 (twenty-four-hour service). Opposite the beachfront, seventy-one rooms cluster around a sunny, grassy courtyard. Newly remodeled and refurbished, the lodge is sparkling clean, with cable TV, minirefrigerator, in-room coffeemaker, complimentary coffee in the lobby, and courtesy baggage service to and from the boat terminal (no in-room telephone). Two-person, two-night packages from Sunday to Wednesday include round-trip boat transportation and choice of two island tours.

Day 2

Morning

Breakfast: **The Busy Bee,** 306 Crescent Avenue, Avalon (310) 510–1983. If the sun's shining, you'll want breakfast outdoors at one of Catalina's oldest restaurants. At a deckside table over the shining water, you can savor pancakes and eggs, New Orleans Scramble with Cajun sausage, and other specialties.

In summer Avalon is a splendid place to lounge on the beach or go for a swim. But after breakfast you'll probably have to check out of your room. The Pavilion Lodge will store your luggage and transport it to the boat in time for your departure. (Not all hotels include this courtesy service.)

To see more of Santa Catalina Island than just the downtown area, opt for the **Avalon Scenic Tour,** which takes you on a 9-mile, fifty-minute narrated tour from the waterfront up into the hills high above the harbor. Your driver tells the history of Catalina Island, which was discovered in 1542 by Juan Cabrillo, a Portuguese explorer, who named it San Salvador. It was rediscovered sixty years later by Spanish explorer Sebastian Viscaino, who renamed it Santa Catalina in honor of St. Catherine's Feast Day. Both explorers claimed the island for Spain, which did not attempt to colonize it.

During the 1880s Yankee sailors and Russian fur traders from Alaska began a thriving, illegal sea-otter fur trade. Additionally, there were cattle and sheep raising, smuggling, and a gold stampede, all of which ended during the Civil War, when U.S. Army (Union) troops arrived and took possession of the island. Their barracks building, which remains in the small village of Two Harbors at the other end of the island, is now the home of the Isthmus Yacht Club.

The tour-guide driver then fills you in about the island's many owners. At the end of the Mexican War in 1848, Pio Pico, California's last Mexican governor, allegedly deeded the island to an American,

Thomas Robbins, in exchange for a horse and silver-trimmed saddle. There was a succession of private American owners before the island was sold to the Banning Brothers, who formed Santa Catalina Island Company to develop the island as a pleasure and fishing resort.

Outside of Avalon the rest of the island's 74 square miles are largely uninhabitable and pretty much the same as they were when the island was discovered 450 years ago, thanks to the foresight of William Wrigley, Jr., the chewing-gum magnate who purchased Catalina Island in 1919 and began improvements and conservation programs to preserve its natural beauty. In 1972 the Wrigley family established the Santa Catalina Island Conservancy to protect and preserve Catalina for future generations. The conservancy now owns about 86 percent of the island's 76 square miles.

Among other high spots brought to passengers' attention is Zane Grey's "Pueblo Hotel." Built in 1926, it is the former hillside home of the prolific author of eighty-nine books, including *Riders of the Purple Sage, Call of the Canyon,* and other western novels. Also pointed out is the former Wrigley estate, now a popular four-star country inn. The bus winds up around the hills, and you have passed absolutely no other car on the road, which overlooks Catalina's 9-hole golf course, tennis courts, stables, and the baseball field where, from 1921, Wrigley's Chicago Cubs held their annual spring baseball training for about twenty-six years. View stops and photo opportunities are plentiful on this tour (tour fee).

Lunch: **Armstrong's Fish Market and Seafood Restaurant,** 306 Crescent Avenue, Avalon. (310) 510–0113. Sit inside the small, cheery dining room with blue-and-white checkered tablecloths or out on the broad deck over Avalon Bay. Lunch favorites are mesquite-charbroiled fresh swordfish and seafood specialties that include rice pilaf, cole slaw, or steamed vegetable.

Afternoon

Stroll the green **Pleasure Pier,** where the Chamber of Commerce can answer any questions and make suggestions. Along the pier you'll find boat rentals and Catalina Diver's Supply Shop. Eric's is known for burgers, sandwiches, and ice cream. At the end of the pier where the seagulls convene, Earl & Rosie's Seafood snack bar has, since 1967, been dispensing burgers, fries, and its specialty abalone burgers with tartar sauce and melted cheese.

About midway along this pier, board the **Glass Bottom Boat,** where you can see through Catalina's crystalline waters below the surface of the sea to a marine preserve of brightly hued fish and giant beds of kelp. This cruise is best on a sunny day when visibility is generally 70 to 80 percent. The iridescent orange Garibaldi, California's state marine fish, is easy to spot. Sleek baby California sea lions do somersaults beneath the glass floor, so close you can count their whiskers. Occasionally you might see a cormorant, a large feathered bird that swims underwater, greedily feasting on fish as fast as it can catch them in its long beak. Night trips are also available (trip fee).

If there's time before you leave the island, browse Avalon's fascinating side streets. **Catalina Design Center,** 125 Sumner Avenue, is a stunning shop, with contemporary handmade jewelry, mobiles, art objects, and T-shirts. On Metropole Street are Von's grocery and the multilevel **Metropole Market Place and Hotel,** a rambling complex of small shops and restaurants around a pretty courtyard.

Head for the boat pier about fifteen to twenty minutes before departing the storybook island to claim your luggage, if it's been forwarded by your hotel. The cruise back to the mainland is frequently smoother sailing than coming over. Disembarking in Long Beach, pick up your car and head for the 710 Freeway north to Los Angeles.

There's More

Santa Catalina Island Company Discovery Tours, P.O. Box 737, Avalon, CA 90704. (310) 510–2500. This company offers a variety of island tours. The extremely popular Inland Motor Tour is a three-and-three-quarter-hour scenic adventure that includes an Arabian horse show and visits the rugged and unspoiled wilderness interior, where you can see rare native plants and free, roaming buffalo herds, descendants of those brought over in 1924 for the filming of Zane Grey's book *The Vanishing American.* Inquire about other exciting island tours.

Wrigley Memorial and Botanical Garden, 1400 Avalon Canyon Road, honors William Wrigley, Jr.'s, lifework in preservation of the island. The huge memorial is an almost forty-acre showcase of Catalina native plants. Open daily, 8:00 A.M. to 5:00 P.M. Tram service from Island Plaza.

Two Harbors at the Isthmus is a casual, secluded small village for camping and hiking; it has swimming beaches and a B&B as well. Among many movies filmed in this scenic area are *Hurricane, Mutiny on the Bounty,* and *MacArthur.* For information call (313) 510–0303.

Catalina Safari Bus, located in the Plaza, along Crescent Avenue (310) 510–2525 supplies daily scheduled transportation between Avalon and Two Harbors, with stops throughout the island. Call (310) 510–7265.

West End Divers offers daily scuba and snorkeling trips. Call (310) 510–0303.

Brown's Bike Rentals and Sales, 107 Pebbly Beach Road, Avalon. (310) 510–0986. Across from the basketball court. Open 9:00 A.M. to 5:00 P.M. Permit required outside of Avalon or Two Harbors.

Boats to Catalina from different ports. Catalina Express, from both Long Beach and San Pedro harbors. (800) 995–4386; (310) 519–1212.

Catalina Cruises, from Long Beach and San Pedro harbors. (800) 228–2546.

Catalina Flyer, from Newport Beach's historic Balboa Pavilion. (714) 673–5245.

Sail Catalina, the newest cross-channel passenger service, departs from Huntington Harbor, (310) 592–5790.

Island Express Helicopter Service departs from both Long Beach and San Pedro. (310) 510–2525.

Special Events

January. Benefit 50-mile Run, Avalon to Two Harbors. (310) 510–0787.

March. Catalina Island benefit marathon and 5K and 10K runs. Catalina Country Dance Celebration, Casino Ballroom, nonstop dancing to top-notch country dance bands.

June. Swing Camp Catalina. Classes and performances by leading swing dancers from around the world, with 1940s-style Big Band Dance. (818) 799–5689. Silent Film Benefit in historic Avalon Theater in the Casino Building; reception follows.

July 4. Parade and fireworks display, dinner dancing in Casino Ballroom, golf cart parade.

September. Annual Catalina Festival of Art, outdoors on Crescent Avenue. (310) 510–0808.

October. Annual three-day, two-weekend Catalina Jazz Trax Festival, in the legendary Casino Ballroom. Ticket information, (800) 866–TRAX. Catalina Country Music Festival, (619) 458–9586. Catalina Island Halloween Mardi Gras Music & Comedy Festival, Avalon, (619) 458–9586. Halloween at the Isthmus, carnival, dinner and dancing at Two Harbors Reef Restaurant & Saloon.

November. Catalina Island Triathlon, premier end-of-season event. All participants must be a Tri-Fed member. Information: Pacific Sports, (818) 357–9699. Annual Plein Air Painters of America Festival (date subject to change), dinner and art sale at Casino Ballroom, Saturday evening; luncheon on Sunday. (310) 510–1552.

December 31. Annual New Year's Eve Celebration, Casino Ballroom. (310) 510–1520. New Year's Eve Celebration with dinner, dancing, and gala party at Two Harbors.

Other Recommended
Restaurants and Lodgings

Avalon

Note: Catalina Island hotels offer various midweek and seasonal rates and packages. The high-rate summer season is mid-June to mid-September. Some packages include round-trip boat passage, island tours, a courtesy taxi to and from the boat dock, and continental breakfast. It's best to inquire when making reservations.

Channel House, 205 Crescent Avenue. (310) 510–1617. Noted for savory European cuisine. Lunch and dinner specialties feature schnitzel, chicken pasta Cabo San Lucas; Sunday brunch.

Ristorante Villa Portofino, 111 Crescent Avenue. (310) 510–0508. This classy dining room with flowers on white tablecloths opens to the beachfront street. A dinner favorite for northern Italian dishes of homemade pastas, lasagna, ravioli filled with pheasant, Penne Arrabiata. Reservations recommended.

Sally's Waffle Shop, on the beachfront opposite the green Pleasure Pier. (310) 510–0355. Breakfast headquarters for islanders and visitors who fancy its variety of omelets and waffles.

Casa Mariquita, 229 Metropole Avenue. (800) 545–1182; (310) 510–1192. AAA, new Spanish-style hotel, 3/4 block from the beach, with nineteen rooms, cable TV, minifridge, and complimentary coffee, tea, and hot chocolate. Two-night, midweek packages include boat trip and tours.

Hotel Metropole, 123 Crescent Avenue. (800) 300–8528 California; (800) 541–8528 (United States); (310) 510–1884. Opened in 1990 in attractive Metropole Market Place; entrance is on Whitley Avenue. Forty-seven custom rooms, cable TV, complimentary continental breakfast in the lobby, welcome bottle of house wine. Various two-night, midweek seasonal rates and packages include round-trip boat passage.

Seacrest Inn, 201 Clarissa (P.O. Box 128), Avalon, CA 90704. (310) 510–0800. A small, romantic retreat with Victorian decor themed for honeymoons, weddings, and anniversaries. Fresh, non-smoking rooms; in-room whirlpool for two in most rooms and suites; air-conditioned; remote-control TV, HBO, VCR; refrigerator; complimentary continental breakfast. Sundeck with view; 1 block to beach. Complimentary luggage service to and from boats. Special romance and wedding packages.

For More Information

Catalina Island Chamber of Commerce and Visitors Bureau, P.O. Box 217, Avalon, CA 90704. (310) 510–1520.

Baja Cruise

Cruiseship *Viking Serenade* will take you to paradise.

Bon Voyage, Amigos

——————————— 4 NIGHTS ———————————

Ocean voyage • Entertainment • Casino gaming • Lavish buffets
Children's playroom/teen nightclub • Fine dining • Ports of call • Duty-free
shopping • Shore excursions • Swimming/sunning

This is an exciting, different excursion that takes you on a luxurious
four-day ocean voyage to Catalina Island and Ensenada, Mexico,

aboard Royal Caribbean Cruise's 1,512-passenger *Viking Serenade,* for a romantic and affordable escape.

The ship's "breakthrough rates" (at this writing) are from approximately $324/person for four days and $292 for the three-day weekend cruise, which calls only at Ensenada. In the competitive cruise ship climate, look for special and seniors' discounts and also bookings where additional passengers can cabin-share free or for very low fares or port charges only.

Royal Caribbean Cruises, Ltd. has had this highly popular cruise since June 1991, when actress and comedienne Whoopi Goldberg christened the *Viking Serenade* with a traditional Champagne splash. The ship sails from Los Angeles every Monday and Friday night year-round.

While the cruise on this big floating resort may be short, the scope of attractions, shipboard activities, and amenities is equal to that featured on longer cruises: clear, invigorating ocean air; round-the-clock service and pampering; nightly Las Vegas–style lounge shows, casino gaming, and Bingo; shore excursions, ports of call; swimming, poolside music, children's activities, and disco and other diversions—not to mention lavish buffets offering up to eight hearty meals and snacks a day.

What's more, you don't need an elaborate wardrobe and hopefully you won't gain much weight—though, early on, the cruise director warns you you're liable to gain a pound or so a day.

It's a happy, comfortable, well-planned cruise. Service is excellent; the food is abundant but rather standard fare, yet the capable dining room staff makes it seem better. Actually, how can you serve gourmet food to more than 1,000 people?

Day 1

Morning

From Los Angeles take the Harbor Freeway south until the freeway ends and becomes Gaffey, a surface street. Stay on Gaffey until 1st Street, the first traffic signal. Turn left on 1st Street to Harbor Boulevard (several blocks). Turn left on Harbor Boulevard to the cruiseship parking lot, then turn right for your ship's berth.

After paying the parking fee, find a parking spot, unload your luggage, and wait a few minutes for the shuttle to pick you up and drive you to the ship, where porters will take your luggage to your cabin while you check in. Be sure luggage tags are attached, listing your name and cabin number. (Incidentally, alcohol cannot be brought aboard the ship for consumption aboard, a dubious practice to keep bars and lounges busy, particularly since prices on bar drinks are quite high.)

You go through a security check similar to airport procedures. It's wise to keep your camera film in a clear plastic bag for a hand-check—same for your camera, if it's already loaded—rather than submit both to Xray, which is damaging to film. To check in with the cruiseline, show your passport and photo ID (or a copy of the first two pages of your passport). You're up the gangway to start your adventure, welcomed aboard, and a porter leads you to your stateroom. Be sure your luggage has arrived.

Well, let's face it—it's not the *Love Boat* on television. The cabin is rather cramped, and the narrow twin beds were probably designed for Ken and Barbie. Still, how much time do you really spend in your room? The large window helps expand your space, and there are a color television for in-room movies, a radio, phone, a desk, plenty of unremovable hangers in the closets, and storage drawers. Don't expect much from the bed lamps. A tiny bathroom with shower has convenient shelves for toiletries and cosmetics.

Lunch: In the glass-enclosed **Windjammer Cafe,** which opens to the sundeck for indoor/outdoor dining. The ship sails at 5:00 P.M.; Embarkation Buffet is from 12:30 to 4:00 P.M. It's pleasant self-service for hot dogs, pasta, fresh fruit, coffee, tea, and attractive pastries. Already shipboard food hospitality has begun as you make your selections.

Afternoon

Be sure to read the ship's daily activity sheet so you won't miss anything. At 3:30 P.M. a "Shopping and Port Information" talk about shore excursions on Catalina and Ensenada also discusses duty and customs allowances (all U.S. citizens may bring back $400 worth of duty-free purchases and one liter of alcohol per adult). This is followed by a compulsory lifeboat drill. Then it's bon voyage to Los Angeles as the ship sets sail, with lively poolside music, for Catalina Island. This is a good time to explore the ship to find out where the different lounges and venues are located.

It's exciting! There's something going on constantly all over the ship, and people wander about at all hours on different decks in different lounges. Hot music wails from the late-night disco. Slot machines chirp and clink in the casino; couples gather round a cozy piano bar; sun-worshipers lie motionless around the pool. Solo travelers don't feel lonely, with more than 1,000 shipmates to chat with and discussions and classes to join.

Dinner: There are two equally attractive dining rooms, both named after operas—*Aida* and *The Magic Flute*—and two breakfast, lunch, and dinner seatings. The main dinner seating is at 6:15 P.M.; the second seating is at 8:30 P.M. The nightly lounge shows follow each seating. If you decide you want to change your seating time, talk to the maître d' as soon as possible. Nobody dresses for dinner this first night out—most people stay in their traveling clothes, as it's been a long day.

You're seated at a table for six or eight passengers, the best way to make new friends right away. Tonight's international dinner theme is Italian, reflected in such menu specialties as Buffalo Mozzarella antipasti, minestrone Genovese *zuppe,* spaghetti *Bolognese,* scampi *oreganata* (shrimp in basil-oregano sauce, accompanied by risotto), veal parmigiana, and grilled tenderloin with fresh tomato pizza sauce. The waiters gather round the tables to serenade you with "O Sole Mio" as you order tiramisù, ice cream, or both for dessert.

After dinner passengers head for the *Welcome Aboard Show,* a musical revue in the Hello Dolly Lounge, or for dancing in other lounges. The Welcome Aboard Midnight Buffet in the Magic Flute dining room is a beautiful presentation of exotic tropical fruit platters, pasta, cold meats, a huge carved turkey carved to order, and heavenly desserts, including pastries and ice cream.

Day 2

Morning

The *Viking Serenade* is anchored in the beautiful blue **Catalina Harbor.** Nearby, a flotilla of white yachts pirouette around the landmark round Casino Building, where all the famous Big Bands played for thousands of dancers during Catalina's heyday of the 1930s and 1940s. It's a sunny, sparkling setting that beckons you ashore.

To accommodate passengers' shore activities when the ship is in port, both seatings for the dining room are rescheduled, with full-service breakfast from 7:30 to 9:30 A.M. and buffet luncheon from noon to 2:30 P.M.

Breakfast: Additionally, you can order room service continental breakfast of coffee, pastry, and croissant. And, if you're in a hurry to go ashore, the Windjammer Cafe offers self-service limited breakfast from 7:30 to 10:00 A.M. of juice, ham or bacon, eggs, potatoes, and coffee.

Passengers are tendered ashore in the ship's launch to tiny Avalon, the only city in the 1-square-mile storybook island, where they disperse for various shore tours. The popular Glass Bottom Boat tour, with views below the water's surface of brightly hued fish and frolicking baby sea lions, leaves from the green Pleasure Pier. On the narrated island tours, you'll learn some of the island's history and visit the unspoiled wilderness interior, where the buffalo and deer roam free, and see other popular Catalina attractions. Stroll and windowshop the sun-washed oceanfront along lovely Crescent Avenue, the city's main street, with its colorful flowers, fountains, tall palms, boutiques, and inviting sidewalk and seaside cafes. Bathers and sun lovers sprawl on a golden, palm-treed, vest pocket-size beach. C. C. Gallagher's, a small espresso-dessert bar, also sells pottery, spices, and cards. Browse Sugarloaf Bookstore for its wide selection of books, magazines, and cards, and wander through the charming Metropole Marketplace complex of shops and galleries.

You're soon pleasantly aware of the absence of cars. Automobile use is limited, and no traffic, noise, or congestion mars California's tropical island paradise. On casual Catalina you mostly walk, ride a bike, pilot a golf cart, or hop on the open-air tram. A romantic, Mediterranean flavor and allure are in the brilliant sunshine, narrow curving streets, and bougainvillea-covered hillside cottages.

Lunch: Board the tender back to the ship for a delightful buffet luncheon in the dining room. The beautifully presented foods include hot and cold dishes, salads, cold cuts, fruits, and a variety of desserts.

Afternoon

You can explore Avalon until the last tender to the ship leaves at 4:30 P.M. If you've missed lunch, be sure that you're back in time for the afternoon snack of ice cream, cookies, and sandwiches in the Windjammer Cafe. Then relax poolside for the rest of the afternoon, listening to the steel band's calypso and reggae rhythms as the ship sails out of the harbor.

Passengers dress up for the captain's formal cocktail party this second night of the cruise. "Welcome to our world," sings genial Scandinavian captain Kent Ringborn, in a melodious greeting. The orchestra plays dreamy music as you have your photo taken with the captain, sip his Champagne and nibble hors d'oeuvres, make new friends, then join others on the dance floor.

Dinner: For French dinner tonight the menu highlights such Gallic specialties as escargot *Bourguignone,* onion soup, and classic *coq au vins.* Heading the dessert list are Napoleons and chocolate soufflé.

After dinner it's fun to explore the string of attractive ship boutiques, which feature perfume, jewelry, Lladro porcelains, Baccarat and Lalique crystal, baby gifts, logo items, and liquor and sundries.

You can try your luck in the casino, then watch the revue in the Hello Dolly Lounge and perhaps attend the late-night adults-only comedy show. Take the elevator to the snug Viking Crown Lounge atop the ship, where people dance to loud disco music and laser lights. Though a large ship with eleven passenger decks, the *Viking Serenade* has a good layout, and it's easy to find your way around to the different lounges and bars. The foyers are hung with good-looking fine art, and corridors are lined with colorful photographs of round-the-world scenes.

The Italian Buffet at midnight, served in The Magic Flute dining room, is a feast of pasta, fresh tropical fruits, pizza, hand-carved turkey, desserts, and ice cream. Aboard ship the policy is never to go to sleep hungry!

Day 3

Morning

On the third lovely day of your cruise, the ship is docked in *Bahia de Todos Santos* (All Saints Bay) in Ensenada, Mexico, a duty-free port made for shoppers.

Breakfast: Before going ashore, take time for breakfast in the dining room. Start with chilled melon, then the cheese or ham omelette with hash browned potatoes, and perhaps a bit of tasty smoked salmon and cream cheese. Passengers disperse for selected shore excursions; some board the shuttle to downtown Ensenada, where the shops are lower-priced than in the Cruise Terminal Building.

Ensenada is a great contrast to laid-back Catalina. You're south of the border, where lively music pours from cafes, cars, and shops. Bustling Avenida Lopez Mateos, the main tourist shopping street, is a small, animated bazaar of boutiques, cantinas, patio cafes, and exotic sights. Street vendors sell jewelry, windchimes, and souvenirs; handsomely costumed mariachis stroll along, carrying guitars and trumpets to serenade diners in cafes; corner food stands do a brisk business in local specialties.

Good news for bargain hunters is the recent devaluation of the Mexican peso, an event that has nearly doubled the dollar's buying power. At this writing the dollar is worth more than seven pesos. Look for good values in Mexican handicrafts, pottery, sterling silver jewelry (stamped 925), ironwood sculptures, straw hats, and leather items—belts, handbags, and cowboy boots. There are many other reliable shops than those the ship recommends. Some offer discounts or are open to negotiation—be sure to brush up on your bargaining skills as well as on your Spanish. Sara's is a popular, upscale boutique; Mario's Silver Shop sells designer jewelry and also fine guitars. Some liquor prices, especially for Kahlua, are irresistibly low; but perfumes seem better priced in the ship boutiques. Savvy cruisers purchase prescription medication over the counter at prices lower than those in the United States.

Though it's featured on ship tours, you can walk down along Avenida Lopez Mateos to the **Riviera del Pacifico,** the city's cultural events center and showpiece. This handsome, sprawling complex, of beautiful gardens and a museum, was a glamorous 1930s gambling casino and resort with a celebrity clientele (including Hollywood film stars and gangster Al Capone) until the Mexican government outlawed gambling in 1936. Mexican *folklorico* entertainment is presented on the Patio Bougambilia during ship tour visits.

Grab a taxi back up Avenida Lopez Mateos to the busy corner of Ruiz and follow the music pouring from Papas and Beer, the local hot spot, for the cafe's tasty french fries (papas), washed down with cool Mexican beer. (To avoid stomach upsets, don't drink tap water or use ice in your drinks while in port.)

You don't want to miss Hussong's Cantina. Remember in the movie *Casablanca,* where "everybody goes to Rick's"? well, here, everybody who visits Ensenada goes to legendary Hussong's, the unattractive, noisy, and crowded saloon with sawdust on the floor and an awesome noise decibel; it's been the town's top watering hole and hangout since it opened in 1892.

Lunch: Ensenada has many fine restaurants, but any taxi will whisk you back to the ship in time for the buffet luncheon. If you're having too much fun sightseeing ashore, you can catch the Sun Worshipper's Snack Lunch 'til 4:00 P.M. in the Windjammer Cafe or the afternoon snack served from 4:00 to 5:00 P.M. Better yet, if you're starving, why not order sandwiches from room service to tide you over till dinner.

Afternoon

Among diverse shipboard activities to join as the *Viking Serenade* sails out of Ensenada's harbor are the line dance class, deck games, and cruise crafts, where you can learn the fine art of napkin folding. Best of all, however, is lounging in a sunny deck chair listening to the rhythmic poolside music, loafing away the rest of the afternoon.

Dinner: The waiters' ruffled shirts are festive for Mexican specialties tonight. Starters include chicken enchilada and guacamole with nachos appetizers, then popular *huachinango a la Vera Cruzana* (sautéed red snapper fillet). Desserts include Kalúha cream brulee and banana cream pie. But save some room for the not-to-be-missed Gala Buffet later tonight.

It's worth staying up late for the Gala Buffet, held in the Magic Flute dining room. It begins at 12:30 A.M., and passengers are invited in earlier to take photographs. This is a highspot of the cruise—an extravaganza of gorgeous, imaginatively presented foods. A long, long table is arrayed with ice sculptures; lacy, chocolate Eiffel towers; dinosaur-shaped breads; mangoes, papayas, and other gleaming tropical fruits; cold meats, turkey breast, lobster, chicken, shrimp, caviar, and smoked salmon; various imported cheeses; and fabulous desserts, including *croquembouche* pyramids (caramel-coated creampuffs), a bevy of cakes, tiramisù, petits fours, and much more. The tables are beautifully set, and the whole ship turns out for this stunning event. What a wonderful goodnight snack!

Day 4

Morning

Breakfast: Make your last day at sea a leisurely one. There's plenty of time for a full breakfast in the dining room if you've been missing it so far. After juice or fresh fruit, try delicious eggs Benedict. You can add blueberry or banana pancakes and French toast to get the day started just right.

Be sure to attend the morning "Debarkation" talk, where the cruise director briefs passengers on tipping, immigration, and baggage-handling procedures for your arrival in Los Angeles tomorrow.

Lunch: Today's dining room menu features Maryland corn chowder, salads, cold fruit entrees, then spaghetti Bolognese, bouillabaisse Provençale, osso buco, and other hearty ethnic specialties.

Afternoon

You probably missed the early morning cooking demo, but the ice-carving demo is extremely popular. Afterward, why not remain poolside listening to the steel band's seductive music, relax watching the Santa Barbara Islands drift by on your way back to Los Angeles, and perhaps doze in the warm sun before you even think about packing?

Dinner: For the **America the Beautiful dinner** your last night aboard ship, waiters are attired in straw boaters, red-and-white striped vests, red jackets, and black slacks. Go for the shrimp cocktail, prime rib, or turkey and all the trimmings. Then, in farewell dinner tradition and drama, lights are dimmed and waiters troop in carrying blazing Baked Alaska, a spectacular dessert of layer cake topped with ice cream and meringue. After serving guests, the dining staff of twenty-seven nationalities gather around to sing a sentimental chorus of "America the Beautiful."

Farewell Show Time in the Hello Dolly Lounge, dancing in other lounges, and a final hearty midnight Farewell Buffet round out the evening in fine style. You should be all packed for debarkation tomorrow and your tips distributed. When you put your luggage in the corridor, be sure to keep overnight sleeping attire and toiletries as well as clothing for tomorrow's trip home: You don't want to be the passenger in another cruise director story who packed all his or her clothes and had to straggle ashore barefoot, wrapped in the bedspread!

Day 5

Morning

Breakfast: There's time for breakfast, in the Windjammer Cafe, of eggs, hash brown potatoes, pancakes, and such, after which you wait for your luggage-tag color to be called. Debarkation is fast and efficient. You may find a surprise at the foot of the gangway—Captain Kent, saying good-bye personally, shaking hands to departing guests. "Thank you for joining us," he says. "Come back soon."

After zipping through customs, the shuttle returns you to your car. Exit the parking lot, turning right, and continue to the first signal, where you turn left for the Harbor Freeway back to Los Angeles.

There's More

Viking Serenade, a large ship, is considered midsize by cruise industry standards: 40,130 tons, 623 feet long, and 89 feet wide, with eleven passenger decks, five elevators, and two stabilizers: 1,512 passengers double occupancy, 1,863 passengers total capacity, 612 crew. Service is exemplary throughout the ship. There are 756 staterooms (478 outside and 278 inside, including 5 outside staterooms with balconies and 4 handicapped-accessible staterooms). Ship facilities include two dining rooms, Hello Dolly Lounge, Bali Hai Lounge, Casino Royale, Schooner Bar, Windjammer Cafe, Teen Center, and children's playroom. Among amenities are ShipShape Fitness Center, sauna and massage rooms, Serenade boutiques, photo gallery, outdoor pool with retractable glass roof, sunshine pool, beauty and barber shop, medical center, shuffleboard area, jogging track, video-game room, card room, and conference center. Designated smoking and nonsmoking areas.

Interior decor is contemporary combination of California casual, European elegant, and Scandinavian functional.

Other Recommended Baja Cruiseships

Carnival Cruise Line's SuperLiner *Holiday* began its three- and four-day Baja cruise schedule in June 1995 and sails year-round, following the same itinerary as the *Viking Serenade*. Good-size stateroom is larger than on the *Viking Serenade* and has narrow twin beds, window, desk, and storage drawers; closet has convenient wall safe. Closed-circuit TV, telephone, good headboard lighting for reading in bed, stack tables and chair, tiny bathroom with shower and storage shelves. Nine passenger decks, eight elevators, dual stabilizers; 46,052 tons, 727 feet long, 92-foot beam; 1,452 passengers double occupancy, 1,800 passengers total capacity; 660 officers (Italian) and crew (international). 726 staterooms: (447 outside and 279 inside, including 10 outside suites with balconies and 15 handicapped-accessible staterooms). Ship facilities include two dining rooms, eight nightclubs and lounges, gaming Club Casino, children's playroom, children's pool with kiddie slide, teen center, electronic game room, and circular pool. Amenities include room service; health club with whirlpools, massage and sauna rooms, exercise weight room; infirmary; beauty salon, barber shop, Galleria shopping mall, photo gallery; shuffleboard. Main swimming pool has 114-foot-long, 15-foot-high water slide. No smoking in dining rooms or main show lounge. Service is fair; food abundant but standard cruise cuisine. Distinctive interiors showcase individualized themes for different public spaces, from laser lights to casual and intimate.

How they stack up:

Holiday passengers are mostly younger, livelier, and more boisterous, and they include more children. *Viking Serenade* guests are both young and mature, slightly more sedate, and upscale.

Cabin accommodations: *Holiday* cabins are larger, though beds are just as narrow.

Cuisine: A varied abundance of food is served on both ships, not quite gourmet, with so many passengers. *Viking Serenade* food is a notch better, plus the cruise offers superior dining-room staff and service; superior service throughout.

Entertainment: *Holiday* leads, with more sophisticated, Las Vegas–style lounge shows and elaborate costumes. Better dance orchestra; better poolside steel-band music.

Viking Serenade has a slight overall edge; however, both are enjoyable cruises—convenient and well priced. Both ships follow the same itinerary on this Baja tango, departing year-round from Los Angeles every Monday for the four-day cruise to Ensenada and Catalina Island; departing every Friday for the three-day cruise to Ensenada. *Bon voyage!*

For More Information

Royal Caribbean Cruises, Ltd., 1050 Caribbean Way, Miami, FL 33132–2096. (305) 539–6000.

Carnival Cruise Lines, Carnival Place, 3655 N.W. 87th Avenue, Miami, FL 33178–2428. (800) 327–9501.

Northern Escapes

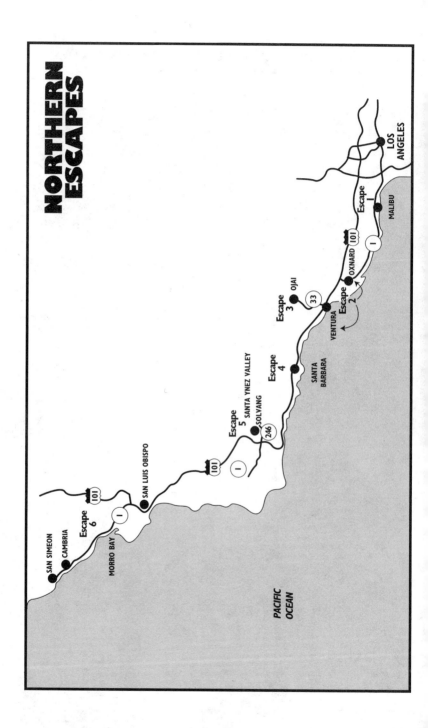

NORTHERN ESCAPES

LOS ANGELES

MALIBU

Escape 1

OXNARD 101

1

Escape 2

VENTURA

OJAI 33

Escape 3

SANTA BARBARA

Escape 4

SANTA YNEZ VALLEY

Escape 5

SOLVANG 246

101

1

SAN LUIS OBISPO

MORRO BAY

1

Escape 6

CAMBRIA

SAN SIMEON

PACIFIC OCEAN

Malibu

Classic pool at entrance of J. Paul Getty Villa Museum.

Surf and Celebrities

1 NIGHT

Beaches • Watersports • Celebrities • Museums
Shopping • Parks • Hiking • Horseback riding

Malibu is a magical name forever identified with the romance and glamour of movie stars and celebrities, golden beaches, bronzed sunbathers and surfers, partying, and rich, famous, and beautiful people

with extravagant beach houses and fancy, expensive cars—the epit-
ome of everything the California good life stands for.

In reality, Malibu is a small, unpretentious, and informal residential community, situated on a stunningly expensive and scenic
beachfront that stretches 27 miles up the Gold Coast to the Ventura
County line.

In a two-day outing to the seductive beach kingdom, you'll soak up
the same sun on soft, sandy beaches as the Academy Award winners
who live nearby; stroll the water's frothy edge; and watch sportfishing
boats set out and anglers cast their lines; follow the fearless, easy-
riding surfers as the big rollers overtake them; goggle for celebrities
(check the markets, bookstores, and cafes); visit the world's richest
museum; go surfing at a world-famous surfing beach; and go scuba
and skin diving. Learn to speak Malibu, the most beautiful word in
Southern California.

Day 1

Morning

Drive out Sunset Boulevard west of San Diego Freeway 405 for a
scenic, curving drive past Bel Air, Brentwood, Mandeville Canyon, the
Riviera (with all Italian street names), the Riviera Country Club, and
beautiful estates and lush landscaping along the way.

Sunset Boulevard winds down and curves past Rustic and Sullivan
canyons, and tall eucalyptus trees grace the scenic road, adding to its
rural look. On weekends there's another look: one of traffic and slow-
moving cars going to and from the beaches, as Sunset is the main
thoroughfare. Try to visit Malibu during the week, when traffic is light
and you'll find more parking spaces at the beach.

You pass **Will Rogers State Historic Park,** formerly the ranch of
the American humorist and movie star. His 137-acre estate, with a
polo field and a picnic area, is open for tours.

Drive through the Pacific Palisades area, where former President
Reagan used to live; it has the only business section on Sunset
Boulevard. Continue past Temescal Canyon and Marquez Knolls,
winding down again as you approach the ocean around the Self-
Realization complex and its small lake. You arrive at the beach at Pacific Coast Highway, where you can see the blue bay and the surfers
dotting the water.

You're at your first stop as you turn into the driveway for the **J. Paul
Getty Villa Museum,** 17985 Pacific Coast Highway (310–458–2003),
nestled in a canyon on a sixty-five-acre estate, a half-mile past Sunset

Boulevard. Admission and parking are free, but you must phone ahead for a parking reservation. There is no drop-in visiting.

Follow through the wide stone arches up the hill to "Visitor Parking" in the underground garage. Take the elevator to the second floor, turn left, walk up a few marble steps, and you're viewing the long, serene pool and main peristyle garden, with its formal plantings leading to the vestibule entrance and the museum. Plan to spend several hours touring the Getty's treasures.

The Getty, a private museum founded in 1954 and located in a Roman-style villa built in 1974, is said to be the richest museum in the world. The building is a re-creation of an ancient Roman country villa that was buried, along with Pompeii, in the eruption of Mount Vesuvius in A.D. 79. Archaeologists rediscovered the villa, 60 feet below the earth, during the eighteenth century. Their notes and copies of its floor plan were the basis for the design of the museum.

Its prestigious permanent collections include Greek and Roman antiquities, found on the main level. Upper galleries house pre-twentieth-century drawings, European paintings, sculpture, rare illuminated medieval manuscripts, decorative arts made for French nobility and the high bourgeoisie, and American and European photographs from the 1830s to the present. The small, busy bookstore, on the main level, just to the left as you enter the vestibule, contains many art publications, books, posters, postcards, and color slides. The Garden Tea Room, through the vestibule and to the left, offers moderately priced cafeteria-style lunches of sandwiches, salads, soups, and desserts from 11:00 A.M. to 2:30 P.M. and light refreshments from 9:30 A.M. to 4:30 P.M. Changing exhibitions, lectures, courses, and programs are part of the museum's ongoing offerings. (Open Tuesday through Sunday, 10:00 A.M. to 5:00 P.M.; closed Monday and all major holidays.)

Note: When the new J. Paul Getty Center is completed in West Los Angeles in the fall of 1997, all collections except antiquities will be moved there. The villa in Malibu will close in summer 1997 for a period of renovation and will open in the year 2000 as a museum and study center devoted exclusively to Roman and Greek art.

Leaving the museum, you see the ocean glittering through the trees. Turn left to Pacific Coast Highway and then turn right, past Topanga Canyon and the beginning of Malibu, past the Reel Inn Restaurant (18661), noted for fresh fish. Continue along past Big Rock Beach, Las Flores Beach, and Surfriders State Beach to the famous storm damaged **Malibu Pier** and hope for some roadside parking.

Lunch: **Alice's Restaurant,** 23000 Pacific Coast Highway, Malibu. (310) 456–6646. Tucked alongside Malibu Pier, this congenial, casual, and elegant landmark offers windows facing the beach and ocean. The door at the left of the bar is open to the pier, and everywhere you look are beach and ocean. The rather high-priced California cuisine menu includes smoked chicken quesadillas, a good Cobb salad, and daily lunch specials of fresh fish, pastas, sandwiches, and hamburgers.

Afternoon

Drift onto the sand at **Surfriders Beach,** considered the best surfing beach in Southern California, to watch the surfers riding the long rollers in to shore. This beach is also excellent for swimming; restrooms and showers are here too.

You're at Malibu Lagoon State Park and the **Adamson House and Malibu Lagoon Museum,** 23200 Pacific Coast Highway (310–456–8432; giftshop, 310–456–9378). The small museum is part of the Adamson House built in 1929 for the Rindge family's daughter and her husband. Any Malibu buff will tell you that the house has always been here on the surfers' beach. May and Frederick Rindge originally bought the entire 13,000-acre Malibu Rancho in 1891 for around $10 an acre. Years later, during the 1920s, May Rindge fought winning battles to keep Southern Pacific from running tracks through her backyard. Finally, in 1925, the state of California built the Pacific Coast Highway through Malibu. The Adamson House has been designated a National Historic Site, as well as a California landmark.

The small house is furnished with beautiful old Spanish Colonial Revival–style pieces with lead-framed bottle glass windows, hand-carved teakwood doors and hand-painted murals. At first glance the seashore seems a strange place for an elaborate fringed Persian carpet. But after a careful second look, you realize that the floor is made entirely of the once-renowned "Malibu Potteries" ceramic tiles of the 1920s, in the intricate, floral design of a Persian carpet, complete with fringe. The clear orange, bright yellow, and jade green colors have not lost their jewel-like richness after so many years. (Open Wednesday through Saturday, 11:00 A.M. to 3:00 P.M.)

Movie stars began arriving in Malibu in the early 1920s and established an exclusive private enclave. **Malibu Colony** is still home to many celebrities, including Johnny Carson, Barbra Streisand, Cher, Ali McGraw, Burgess Meredith, Carroll O'Connor, and a roster of directors, producers, writers, and other creative people who live, work, and cherish their privacy in the area where Chumash Indians lived for 4,000 years.

You can't really see the stars' homes, because they front on the beach. With their closed garage doors facing the road, you can't check out the Mercedes, BMWs, and Rolls-Royces or even the Land Rovers. With a scarcity of beachfront property, all of it extremely expensive, houses are packed tightly together.

Unfortunately, Malibu is periodically subjected to nature's terrible rampages and destructive forces, with raging fires sweeping through the area, fueled by heavy winds. Disastrous landslides and flooding during a heavy rainy season cause lavish beachfront homes to slide and wash partly away into the roaring sea, and million-dollar profiles are seen on the late news piling sandbags around their homes, attempting to protect them from damage. Residents seem to accept nature's ravages, and many consider it a small price to pay for the privilege of living in beautiful exclusive Malibu.

Hikers and equestrians explore richly scenic canyons and parks in the Santa Monica Mountains, where many movies and TV series are filmed. Most of these areas provide overlooks for exceptional panoramic coastline viewing.

Back on Pacific Coast Highway, drive to the 23700 block to Malibu Colony, where most of the stars reside. Turn left at the signal on Webb Way to Malibu Road and **Malibu Colony Plaza.** This attractive, sprawling complex of coral buildings with red-tile roofs is surrounded by a tropical landscape of hanging flower baskets, a fountain, and benches. Besides popular restaurant hangouts—Coogie's, Granita—among the numerous trendy shops are Theodore Beach chic sportswear, Theodore Kids, handsome SavOn Drug, Hughes Market and Deli, and Nikki's clothing store. To drive along the famed Malibu Beach colony road to see where the stars live, turn left on Webb Way and left again at Malibu Road and drive until you come to the gatehouse, where the rest is a private road. Public-access stairways to the beaches are between 24300 and 24700 Malibu Road.

As you continue along Pacific Coast Highway, you pass the unobtrusive **Pepperdine University campus** on the inland side and also Mulholland Road to the valley and Freeway 101/Calabasas. Traffic is fast and can be relentless behind you, allowing little time to pause and look around as you drive. You go past the Malibu Fish/Seafood restaurant, then past Corral and Latigo Canyon, where huge boulders loom in the waters close offshore. At **Malibu Bluffs Community Park,** the emerald grass leads to playground equipment, a soccer field, and groups of active youngsters. You curve down toward several beautiful bays along this scenic highway under a blue Malibu sky, and—who needs the French Riviera?

Drive past Paradise Cove, where they filmed *Gilligan's Island* and some of the *Rockford Files* series. At **Point Dume State Beach,** you'll find a big beautiful beach that has volleyball facilities and is excellent for swimming, diving, and fishing. Point Dume was named by English explorer George Vancouver, sent by King George III to explore America's West Coast in 1792. The explorer named the point after Father Dumetz, a padre he met at San Buenaventura to the north (now Ventura).

After Point Dume you come to **Zuma Beach,** the most popular beach in the area, covering 105 acres and offering a volleyball court and playground. It's a broad, clean expanse of sand, and there's a strong surf with high waves. Zuma has good swimming but also has dangerous riptides in the summer, though there's plenty of skin diving and good fishing. Street parking is available, and you can step from the busy roadside onto the soft warm sand.

Next is **Trancas Beach,** at about 31800 Pacific Coast Highway, where many celebrities live. Drive along rural Broad Beach Road, noting its expensive beachfront homes; here tall sand dunes act as windbreaks. Public-access stairways to beaches are in the 31200 to 31300 block.

After Encinal Beach continue around the curving bay past Nicholas Beach, with its dramatic ocean bluffs, to the very popular **Leo Carrillo Beach State Park,** practically at the Ventura County line. There's good skin and scuba diving here as well as good swimming. Sailboarders love it, and you'll sometimes see about 200 of them out on the water at one time. This state park has two campgrounds; for information call (818) 706–1310.

Returning from Leo Carrillo Beach, drive back toward Malibu Pier. Turn off the highway and drive down some of the quiet oceanside streets to the water and prowl the uncrowded beaches.

Continuing east, turn left, inland across the highway, at **Cross Creek Road and Malibu Creek Plaza,** 3800 Cross Creek Road, to a large shopping and dining center that includes Wherehouse, Crown Books, Super Care Drugs, Malibu Theatre, and other shops and eateries.

There's more across the narrow street at **Malibu Country Shops,** on Civic Center Way, and at **Malibu Country Mart,** 335 Cross Creek Road, an upscale, inviting shopping-dining complex that rambles around lawns, pathways, and a children's play area. Browsers especially like to explore the bakery, clothing and jewelry stores, Siblings and Treasure Estate Sale antiques shops, Discovery and J. K. Mining Co. for gifts and accessories, and Cosentino's Nursery.

Dinner: **Allegria Restaurant and Pizzeria,** 22821 Pacific Coast Highway, Malibu. (310) 456–3132. Country Italian cooking offered in rustic Venetian decor, with artwork on the walls (Carnival masks, scenes of Venice), comfortable booths with velvet cushions, and pleasant service. Popular antipasti is tasty cold seafood salad of calamari, shrimp, and clams; there's a long list of about three dozen thincrust pizzas to select from. For a hot, fragrant entree, *pollo erborato,* a boneless marinated chicken roasted with herbs, is served with asparagus and roast potatoes. Closed Monday.

Lodging: **Malibu Beach Inn,** 22878 Pacific Coast Highway, Malibu, CA 90265. (800) 4–MALIBU; (310) 456–6445. Steps from Malibu Pier, fairly new, handsome Spanish-style hotel on the beach features forty-seven rooms, including three suites, all with beachfront balconies and panoramic views right on to Hawaii, wetbar, refrigerator, fireplace, TV and VCR, clock radio, coffeemaker, hair dryer, personal safe, and nightly turndown service. Complimentary California continental breakfast is served in the hotel lobby, on the oceanfront patio, or in your room. On weekends there is a two-night minimum stay, though there's the occasional exception.

Day 2

Morning

Breakfast: At the inn. Festive complimentary continental breakfast served in the lobby includes bagels, muffins, English muffins, assorted fresh melons and fruits, cereal, and tea, coffee, and hot chocolate.

This is going to be a beach day. Malibu's beaches are clean and beautiful, and you'll welcome the chance to enjoy them at a relaxed pace. Swim, sunbathe, or stroll along the water's edge and watch the lively action in the surf.

Lunch: **Malibu Inn Restaurant,** 22969 Pacific Coast Highway, Malibu. (310) 456–6106. Across from Malibu Pier; a local hangout, with wooden floor, booths, old-fashioned glass, mirrors, and photos decor. Southwestern specialties include *fajitas* and tacos; pizza, pasta, and hamburgers served as well. Funky bar in adjacent room.

Afternoon

Enjoy the rest of the day at sunny and peaceful Malibu beach. Retrace your route back to Los Angeles.

There's More

Golf. Malibu Golf Course, 901 Encinal Canyon Road and Mulholland Highway. (818) 889–6680. Privately owned 18-hole course but visitors welcome.

Horseback riding. Arabians for rent. (310) 456–2173. Red Barn Stables. (818) 707–9395.

Pepperdine Equestrian Center. (310) 456–4367. Trail-riding lessons.

K.C.'s Malibu Stables & White Cloud Ranch, 400 Kanan Dume Road and Mulholland Highway. (818) 735–0619.

The Stables at Calamigos Ranch, Kanan Dume Road and Mulholland Highway. (818) 991–2767.

Tennis. Malibu Racquet Club, 23847 Stuart Ranch Road. (310) 456–3313. Extends privileges to guests of Malibu Beach Inn and Casa Malibu.

Malibu Riding & Tennis Club, 33905 Pacific Coast Highway. (310) 457–9783.

Surf fishing. Wylie's Bait & Tackle, 18757 Pacific Coast Highway. (310) 456–2321.

Nursery. Cosentino's Nursery, 21201 Pacific Coast Highway. (310) 456–6707.

Camping, RV parks. State of California Department of Parks and Recreation, 1925 Las Virgenes Road, Calabasas, CA 91302–1909. (818) 880–0350.

Malibu Beach RV Park, 25801 Pacific Coast Highway. (310) 456–6052.

Surfboard rentals. Zuma Jay's, 22775 Pacific Coast Highway. (310) 456–8044. Rents surfboards, wetsuits, fins, boogie boards. Lessons available.

National Progression Surfboards, 22935.5 Pacific Coast Highway. (310) 456–6302. Kayak rentals, wetsuits, and longboards (9 feet) for rent.

Kayaking. Malibu Makos Surf Club at Point Dume. (310) 456–8409. Experienced lifeguards teach ocean kayaking.

Mountain biking. Cycle Design, 3900 Cross Creek Road. (310) 456–1685. Rental bikes to get you up into the canyons.

Pepperdine University, 24255 Pacific Coast Highway, Malibu. (310) 456–4851. The lovely campus sprawls across 830 acres and is open for visitors to enjoy its beautiful parks and range of athletic and cultural events. Center for the Arts features three theaters and an art museum, with a variety of concerts, lectures, and ballet, theater, and music performances. Frederick Weisman Museum of Art, opened in 1992, features 3,000 square feet of exhibition space; the series of changing exhibitions is augmented with selections from the prestigious modern and contemporary collection of Frederick R. Weisman.

Special Events

Last full weekend in July. Art Festival.

Last weekend in November and three full weekends in December. County Christmas Village, Calamigos Ranch, 327 Latigo Canyon Road.

Other Recommended
Restaurants and Lodgings

Malibu

Granita, 23725 West Malibu Road, Malibu Colony Plaza. (310) 456–0488. More discreet than an unlisted phone number, this place has no name sign identifying it as Wolfgang Puck's posh restaurant, but its expensive decor is a giveaway, from the glass-screened patio to the marble entrance. The trademark open kitchen features scallops appetizers, entrees such as roast Sonoma lamb with artichoke mousse, and, for dessert, pecan tart.

Geoffrey's Restaurant, 27400 Pacific Coast Highway. (310) 457–4519. On an ocean bluff, with terrific views and attractive gardens. Expensive, regional American cuisine favors grilled steak, creative gourmet salads, and fresh fish.

Beaurivage, 26025 Pacific Coast Highway. (310) 456–5733. Across from the ocean; the red-tiled roof makes it easy to spot. Recently remodeled, light and flowery decor feels just right in this Mediterranean restaurant. Menu offers Italian, Greek, and Spanish foods as well as porterhouse steaks. Dinner only, plus Sunday Champagne brunch. Good service, expensive, dressy.

Coogie's Beach Cafe, 23755 West Malibu Road, Malibu Colony Plaza. (310) 317–1444. High-tech decor, large, bright, casual family place where, along with salads and charbroiled hamburgers, specialties include Szechuan-style mahi-mahi and linguine with shrimp.

Charley Brown's, Malibu Sea Lion, 21150 Pacific Coast Highway. (310) 456–2810. The original Sea Lion has been long-gone but the same tables overlook the broad expanse of ocean. Green Grocer salad bar is an extensive array of cold appetizers, a meal in itself or an addition to entrees. Sunday Champagne brunch.

Bambu Malibu, 3835 Cross Creek Road, Suite #8, Malibu Country Mart. (310) 456–5464. Here is California cuisine together with a full sushi/sashimi bar. Pleasant garden patio dining. Lunch and dinner.

Guido's Malibu, 3874 Cross Creek Road. (310) 456–1979. Noted for hearty food and portions, they prepare Caesar salad tableside, as it should be; romantic views of Malibu Creek and nearby foothills.

Moonshadows Malibu, 20356 West Pacific Highway. (310) 456–3010. A landmark facing the ocean; serves steaks, seafood, and pasta and features a handsome salad bar.

Tra Di Noi Ristorante, 3835 Cross Creek Road. (310) 456–0169. *The* place for Italian country fare, paper-thin pizza, and Mama's lasagna. Patio dining; lunch and dinner.

Theodore's Shoppe & Tea Room, 29169 Heathcliff Road, Suite #189. (310) 457–9276. Breakfast, lunch, and tea daily. English favorites, salads, homemade soups, sandwiches, pastries. High teas, coffee specialty drinks. Shop features teddy bears, all-occasion cards, giftwrap, toys, books, crystal, bone china, other gift items. Open Monday through Saturday, 10:00 A.M. to 6:00 P.M., and Sunday, 11:00 A.M. to 6:00 P.M.

Casa Malibu Inn on the Beach, 22752 Pacific Coast Highway. (800) 831–0858; (310) 456–2219. Twenty-one rooms around a sunny courtyard, some with beachfront decks, all with coffeemaker, refrigerator, cable TV, clock radio. You'll need to book a month in advance for summer weekends.

Malibu Shores Motel, 23033 Pacific Coast Highway. (310) 456–6559. On the inland side; two-story typical motel, small bedroom, small bath.

For More Information

Malibu Chamber of Commerce, 23805 Stuart Ranch Road (extension of Webb Way), Suite 100, Malibu, CA 90265–4897. (310) 456–9025.

The Santa Monica Mountains Conservancy. (800) 533–PARK. Provides park and hiking information.

Malibu Creek State Park. (818) 706–1310. Provides campsite, hiking, and fishing information.

Surf/tide reports. (310) 457–9701.

Ventura/Oxnard

Lighthouse at Oxnard's Channel Island Harbor

Harbor Hopping

_____ 1 NIGHT _____

Historic sites • Beaches • Waterfront dining • Local produce
Harbor and island cruises • Whale-watching • Antiques • Watersports

_____

This two-day, one-night escape to a nearby pair of small, friendly coastal cities offers refreshing harbor and marina activities and lifestyles, a famous mission, historical sites, museums, and adventure cruises to scenic offshore islands. You'll shop, dine, and snack at the bubbling waterfronts; purchase fresh produce at its source; and stretch out on splendid, sunny, uncrowded beaches.

Day 1

Morning

Drive north on Ventura Freeway 101 through the San Fernando Valley. Along the Conejo Grade you can see the flat valley spread out to the foothills. Though much of the time the air is misty, you can still see across acres of citrus groves and farms and frequently spot workers in the fields picking the strawberries for which the area is famous—like a painting by Millet. Ventura County is a leading producer of lemons and strawberries and has a great deal of open space. In Oxnard, from the freeway and along roads leading to the ocean and beaches, are miles of lemon groves and fields of strawberries and celery, which flourish in the rich soil of the Oxnard Plain. After passing Oxnard, continue a short distance north to Ventura, alongside richly cultivated farms. Ancient, leafy eucalyptus trees with trunks as thick as a barn door stand tall astride the freeway.

In **Ventura** exit the freeway at California Street, turning right on California Street and then left on Main for the historic downtown area. The city's noted **San Buenaventura Mission,** 211 East Main Street (805–643–4318), where the city of Ventura began, is a few blocks farther along Main, between Junipero and Palm.

You enter the mission a few doors away, through its giftshop, at 225 East Main Street, which sells religious artifacts and cards. The giftshop leads to the small Museum of Vestments, which displays clothing worn by the missionary fathers over a 200-year period. Walk through the pleasant mission garden, with its Spanish-style fountain and tall shady trees. The small church, graced by a tall beamed ceiling, wrought-iron chandeliers, wall paintings, and lighted candles at the altar, holds services every Sunday. San Buenaventura Mission, founded in 1782, was the ninth of twenty-one California missions built during Spain's occupation of California, and it was the last mission founded by Father Junípero Serra. The mission, open from 10:00 A.M. to 5:00 P.M. daily, offers self-guided tours (50-cent admission fee).

Next door to the church, the red-tile-roofed **Albinger Archaeological Museum,** 113 East Main Street, (805–648–5823), exhibits some of the 30,000 artifacts discovered in a 1974–75 dig. The oldest treasure is a bowl dating back 2,500 years. (Open Tuesday through Sunday from 10:00 A.M. to 4:00 P.M.; free.)

Across the street the **Ventura County Museum of History and Art,** 100 East Main Street (805–653–0323), houses three galleries. The Smith Gallery features the George Stuart Historical Figures Collection of some 197 miniature figures in rotating exhibits. Authentically detailed and elaborately costumed, the figures represent leading historical persons, including Abraham Lincoln, Queen Victoria, Marie Antoinette, and Louis XIV. The Native American Room displays Chumash Indian pottery and a small, glass-enclosed statue of Father Junípero Serra. The Hoffman Gallery's changing exhibitions range from fine arts to local history. The giftshop is nicely stocked with ethnic jewelry as well as a variety of art, travel, and local history books. (Open Tuesday through Sunday from 10:00 A.M. to 5:00 P.M.; docent-led tours Sunday at 1:30 P.M.; free.)

About 5 blocks from the mission, **Ortega Adobe,** 100 West Main Street (805–654–7837), is the last of the downtown area's small adobes. Built in 1857, this is the site where Emilio Ortega began fire-roasting his chiles and started the popular Pioneer Ortega Chili Company, said to be the first commercial food manufacturing venture in California. The furnishings and interior of this small, red-tile-roofed home offer insight into family living during the era.

Before driving down to the waterfront for lunch and sightseeing, check out some of Ventura's noted **antiques dealers** on Main Street. Heirloom Antiques, 494 East Main Street (805–643–6050), ensconced on the corner in what formerly was the First National Bank of 1926, claims to have the largest selection of French antique furniture in the tricounties. My Last Hurrah, at 451 East Main, shows California pottery, vintage clothing, china, and primitives. (Open Tuesday through Saturday from noon to 4:30 P.M. and Sunday till 4:00 P.M.). Nicholby Antiques, 404 East Main, is a group of forty dealers of glass, toys, furniture, and collectibles.

To get to the waterfront and Ventura Harbor Village, turn right on California Street and continue to Harbor Boulevard; then turn left for approximately 2 miles, until you see the harbor entrance.

Lunch: **Milano's Italian Restaurant,** 1559 Spinnaker Drive, Ventura. (805) 658–0388. Practically an institution for home-style family cooking and dining at waterside, with cozy red-and-white checked tablecloths and friendly service. Favorite Luncheon Specialties, served with hot garlic bread and your choice of soup or salad, include baked lasagna layered with rich meat sauce and ricotta, parmesan, and mozzarella cheeses; flavorful eggplant parmesan is served with pasta.

Afternoon

Ventura Harbor Village, spread along thirty-three waterfront acres, is the area's largest harborside dining-shopping-entertainment showcase. Tall, red-roofed spires and arches envelop shops, galleries, restaurants, theater, and a carousel, amid bright flowers, colorful sail-boats, and yachts swaying in the sparkling marina. For a spin across the water, board the *Bay Queen* for forty-minute **cruises,** which leave hourly Tuesday through Sunday, from 1567 Spinnaker Drive, Slip 14 (805–642–7753).

Drop by the gray, weathered, three-story **Channel Islands National Park Headquarters and Visitors Center,** 1901 Spinnaker Drive (805–644–8262). Park rangers offer information on what you'll see on trips to the five rugged, primeval Channel Islands, lying just 14 miles off Ventura's coast. Tidepool displays and topographic island ex-hibits point out the characteristics of each island. The elevator whisks you to the top-floor deck tower for a tremendous panoramic view of the harbor, the mountains, and the Channel Islands out in the Pacific. (Open daily from 8:00 A.M. to 5:00 P.M., later in summer; free). For more detailed and firsthand information on year-round excursions to the islands, visit Island Packers, the only commercial charter permitted to land on the Channel Islands (1867 Spinnaker Drive. Information: 805–642–7688).

If you want to get out on the sand and in the water, practically next door to the Channel Island National Park Headquarters is **Marina Cove Beach,** the city's safest swimming beach, protected by a break-water and offering a children's play area and restrooms. **Surfer's Point,** at Seaside Park, is one of the most popular surfing and sail-boarding beaches. Closer by, the 1,500-foot-long **Ventura Pier,** com-pleted in 1872, had its heyday when the harbor was filled with steamships whose passengers and cargoes waited to be loaded and unloaded. Nowadays visitors strolling the long, peaceful pier can watch fishermen casting their lines for bass and bonita.

Dinner: **Alexander's Restaurant** in Harbortown Marina Resort, 1050 Schooner Drive, Ventura. (805) 658–2000. Alongside the boat-filled marina, it's a sleek scene for such specialties as oven-roasted rack of lamb, prime rib, and baby back pork chops, served with choice of soup or salad, baked potato or rice pilaf. Sunday brunch. Genial Happy Hour in the adjacent Dockside Lounge features compli-mentary hors d'oeuvres.

Lodging: **Harbortown Marina Resort,** 1050 Schooner Drive, Ven-tura, CA 93001. Reservations, (800) 229–3732 (in California); (805) 658–1212. An AAA, four-diamond resort 1 block from the beach and edging the marina. The dynamic, rambling architecture was designed by the Frank Lloyd Wright Foundation. Offers views from each of its 160 rooms and suites, cable TV, heated swimming pool, three tennis courts, spa, and nearby golf. Suite rates include breakfast buffet in Alexander's Restaurant.

Day 2

Morning

Breakfast: At the resort. Breakfast buffet in **Alexander's Restaurant** offers ample selections, from omelets, any-style eggs, and cold cereal to bagels and lox.

Oxnard, 60 miles from Los Angeles and the "Strawberry Capital of the United States," is just minutes away along the scenic Gold Coast. Follow Harbor Boulevard south along the beautiful stretches of pale, near-deserted beaches from San Buenaventura State Beach, which begins at Ventura Pier, passing McGrath State Beach, with its sand dunes and lagoons, and Mandalay Beach to Channel Islands Boulevard and Channel Islands Harbor, a lively waterfront resort, recreation, and dining marketplace. Chumash Indians fished and hunted here in the dramatic, lonely marshes you can see from the highway.

The horseshoe-shaped **Channel Islands Harbor** complex comprises **Harbor Landing,** the **Marine Emporium,** and **Fisherman's Wharf,** flagged by its white lighthouse and home to the **Ventura County Maritime Museum.** In this bustling area a variety of specialty shops, restaurants, and sidewalk cafes add to the appeal of the special and sunny seaside setting.

Channel Islands Harbor, considered one of California's finest full-service facilities, has 2,600 boat slips, four yacht clubs, and nine full-service marinas. It also offers beautifully landscaped parks with attractive picnic areas and barbecues.

Stroll around the terra-cotta-colored buildings of **Harbor Landing Promenade** (2800 South Harbor Boulevard), with its cheery waterfront restaurants and chic shops, and watch the masts of boats and small craft bobbing in the pristine harbor. Along here you can buy a yacht, charter a sportfishing or cruise boat, take sailing lessons, rent a bike or a boat, and go whale-watching from December through March, when the Pacific gray whales pass through the channel on their annual migration from Alaska to Baja. For a change of scene, board the **Harbor Hopper ferry** for a tour of the harbor. Hours are seasonal; call for a schedule (805–985–4677).

From Harbor Landing drive or walk alongside the water a few blocks to the Marine Emporium, 3600 South Harbor Boulevard (805–984–3677), a gray-and-white-trimmed waterfront shopping-dining complex of New England–style clapboard architecture. Among the numerous shops, **Coast Chandlery** features traditional nautical items and supplies that are in sharp contrast to the unique clothing and gift boutique in the **Dress Canvas Loft** upstairs.

Fisherman's Wharf, just across the water, is your next destination. To get there, turn right on Channel Islands Boulevard, go across the bridge to Victoria Avenue, turn right, and park.

Lunch: **Pier 17** in Fisherman's Wharf, 3910 West Channel Islands Boulevard at Victoria Avenue, Oxnard. (805) 985–3922. Casual and popular seafood specialty house, in the shadow of the picturesque lighthouse. The lunch bunch goes for the salad bar, sandwiches, salmon, or deep-fried fish-and-chips or beer-battered shrimp; all are equally delicious on the sunny cobblestone patio or in the attractive dining room overlooking the sparkling water. Happy Hour 3:00 to 7:00 P.M. with complimentary hors d'oeuvres; Sunday brunch.

Afternoon

On Fisherman's Wharf, the striking white lighthouse stores icing equipment for the commercial fishing boats that unload their catch at the dock. Pleasureboats also tie up here for provisioning.

Walk along the boardwalk to the Ventura County Maritime Museum, 2731 South Victoria Boulevard (805–984–6260), located in a large square behind the small waterfront buildings. This new museum is a seafarer's Valhalla. On display are twenty-four models of historic ships, including the *Golden Hinde, Old Ironsides,* the *Mayflower,* and the *Bounty,* as well as antique ship models and many other sailing exhibits and artifacts. (Open Thursday through Monday, 11:00 A.M. to 5:00 P.M.; donation).

En route back to Los Angeles, visit the **Seabee Museum,** Ventura Road and Sunkist; (805–982–5163), in the Naval Construction Battalion Center in Port Hueneme, a commercial and military port. (Drive east on Channel Islands Boulevard to Ventura Road, turning right on Sunkist, to reach the museum.) The Seabees is the branch of the U.S. Navy that goes overseas and builds bridges, runways, and other immediate needs for the armed forces. The museum was established in 1947 to preserve its history and achievements.

Among the museum's exhibits of U.S. and foreign military memorabilia—from World War II and the Korean and Vietnam wars—collected by the Seabees on foreign shores and donated to the museum are unusual musical instruments, coins, weapons, uniforms, and posters. Dioramas feature Seabee major construction jobs throughout the world; a giftshop sells logo Seabee T-shirts, caps, and souvenirs. (Open daily until 4:30 P.M., weekdays from 8:00 A.M., Saturday from 9:00 A.M., and Sunday from 2:30 P.M., closed holidays; free).

When you leave the museum, follow Ventura Road to Surfside Drive and **Port Hueneme Beach Park,** a beautiful quiet beach ideal for swimming and surfing, with palm trees, a playground, a fishing pier, barbecue pits, picnic areas, and restrooms. **Port Hueneme Historical Museum,** nearby at 220 Market and Hueneme Road (805–480–2023), displays the early days of the historic port (open Monday through Friday, 10:00 A.M. to 3:00 P.M.). Port Hueneme is the only deep-water facility between Los Angeles and San Francisco, a thriving international port where, among other goods, imported automobiles are unloaded for U.S. distribution.

To return to Los Angeles, take Fourth Street to Pleasant Valley Road, turn right, and follow Pleasant Valley Road as it angles up toward Highway 34; turn right (south) on 34 until it intersects Freeway 101 south to Los Angeles.

There's More

Olivas Adobe, 4200 Olivas Park Drive, Ventura. (805) 644–4346. Built in 1847 by wealthy Don Raimundo Olivas for his family on his 4,700-acre rancho, when early California life revolved around working farms and ranches. Listed on the National Register of Historic Places, the spacious, two-story, Monterey-style home is furnished with antiques of the period. Grounds open daily, 9:00 A.M. to 4:00 P.M.; house open weekends, 10:00 A.M. to 4:00 P.M. A major portion of adjacent land is now Olivas Park Golf Course.

Ventura Certified Farmers' Markets. (805) 529–6266. Held twice weekly, these fairly small markets offer good prices on fresh fruits and vegetables, eggs, seafood, plants, and flowers. Two outdoor locations: Montgomery Ward Parking Lot, Mills Road and Main Street, Wednesday, 10:00 A.M. to 1:00 P.M., and corner of Santa Clara and Figueroa streets, Saturday, 8:30 A.M. to noon. For more information call (805) 654–7846.

Amtrak. Since 1992 Ventura has been an Amtrak stop for trains traveling between San Diego and Santa Barbara, with four stops daily at the platform located on Harbor Boulevard near the Ventura County Fairgrounds. For information call Ventura Commerce and Visitor's Bureau, (800) 333–2981. In Oxnard, Metrolink stops twice daily, Monday through Friday, at Oxnard Transportation Center (800–487–8787).

Golf. Olivas Park Golf Course, 3750 Olivas Park Drive, Ventura. (805) 642–4303. Next to Olivas Adobe; 18-hole golf course, driving range (night-lighted), pro shop, restaurant, and lounge.

Buenaventura Golf Course, 5882 Olivas Park Drive, Ventura. (805) 642–2231. Public 18-hole golf course, pro shop, restaurant, and lounge.

Jim Hall Kart Racing Schools, 1555G Morse Avenue, Ventura. (805) 642–1329.

Ventura Sportsfishing, 1516 Anchors Way, Ventura. (805) 650–1255.

Oxnard Carnegie Art Museum, 424 South C Street, Oxnard. (805) 385–8157. On the National Register of Historic Places and built in 1907 as a Carnegie Library, this neoclassical-style museum, with stately pillars, houses a permanent collection of more than 200 paintings and sculptures focusing on California painters from the 1920s to the present; important changing exhibits. Open Tuesday through Friday, 10:00 A.M. to 5:00 P.M.; Saturday and Sunday, 1:00 to 5:00 P.M. Admission.

Gull Wings Children's Museum, 418 West Fourth Street, Oxnard. (805) 483–3005. Alongside the art museum. Children love the hands-on, touchable exhibits and activities. Giftshop. Open Wednesday through Friday from 1:00 to 5:00 P.M., Saturday from 10:00 A.M., and Sunday from noon. Admission.

Farmers' markets and produce stands. Experience Oxnard's wonderful agricultural bounties with visits to the farmers' markets and the many produce stands in the area. You'll find a large variety of local vegetables, fruits, and flowers. Farmers Market Downtown, in Plaza Park, 300 West 5th Street, Oxnard. Every Thursday rain or shine from 10:00 A.M. to 1:00 P.M., you'll find more than a hundred items on sale fresh from the farm.

Farmers Market Harbor Landing, 2810 South Harbor Boulevard, Channel Islands Harbor, Oxnard. (805) 985–4853. Every Sunday, 10:00 A.M. to 2:00 P.M., for seasonal fresh produce, cut flowers, bakery goods, seafood, and gourmet items.

Independently owned produce stands are located throughout Oxnard. Here are three areas: Olivas Park Drive and Telephone Road, along Victoria south of Gonzales, and south of Olivas Park Drive.

Heritage Square. 715 South A Street, Oxnard. (805) 483–7960. A look at early Oxnard history in a docent- or self-guided tour of lovely old Victorian mansions and farmhouses restored or replicated. Summertime Friday-evening concerts.

Oxnard Factory Outlet, 2251 Outlet Center Drive. (805) 485–2244. From the 101 Freeway, exit Rice to Gonzales; turn right to the shops and restaurants. The stores feature discounts on name brands in home furnishings, accessories, designer fashions, childrenswear, and other merchandise. Open Monday through Saturday from 10:00 A.M. to 8:00 P.M., Sunday from 11:00 A.M. to 6:00 P.M.

Special Events

December through March. Whale-watching, Ventura.

Mid-April. Taste of Ventura County, annual food and wine festival at Channel Islands Harbor, Oxnard.

End of April. Annual California Beach Party. Food, entertainment, crafts, Ventura.

Cinco de Mayo, Oxnard. Festival, College Park, Oxnard.

Mid-May. Fiesta Del Sol, Harbor Village. Weekend activities, Ventura.

May 19–29. Annual California Strawberry Festival. A statewide food event at Channel Islands Harbor. Gourmet strawberry foods, contests, entertainment, Oxnard.

End of May. Earth Day. Kite Festival, Ventura.

July. Oxnard Sports Festival.

July 4. Street Fair. Dawn's Early Light Fireworks, Ventura. Fireworks Street Fair. Music Extravaganza, Oxnard.

August 19–20. Ventura County Fair, Seaside Park. Salsa Festival, Plaza Park, Oxnard.

Early September. Oxnard Air Show, Oxnard Airport.

Mid-September. Ventura Music Celebration. Fiestas Patrias Parade and Celebration, Oxnard.

End of September. Annual California Beach Party, Ventura. Food, entertainment, crafts. Official Power Boat races, Ventura.

Early October. Annual Maritime Days, Channel Islands Harbor. Nautical celebration, classic yacht races, exhibits, food, entertainment, Oxnard. Port Hueneme Harbor Days, Hueneme Park. Point Mugee Air Show, Point Mugee Naval Air Test Center.

Early December. Holiday Street Festival. Food, entertainment, arts and crafts, Ventura.

December 8. Parade of Lights and Harborfest, Channel Islands Harbor. Parade of lighted decorated boats, Oxnard.

Mid-December. Parade of Lights, Ventura.

Other Recommended Restaurants and Lodgings

Ventura

Hungry Hunter, 2046 East Harbor Boulevard. (805) 648–5146. Choice steaks and seafood; innovative salad bar created and served at your table.

Yolanda's, 2753 Main Street. (805) 643–2700. Award-winning Mexican fare; great margaritas, salads, tacos, burritos, refried beans.

Doubletree Ventura, 2055 Harbor Boulevard. (805) 643–6000; (800) 528–0444. Offers 285 luxurious guestrooms, including 14 suites. Adjacent to San Buenaventura State Beach. Heated swimming pool, whirlpool, fully equipped health club with saunas. Restaurant and Lobby Bar. AAA rate includes full breakfast daily; special rates available

Holiday Inn Beach Resort, 450 East Harbor Boulevard. (800) 842–0800; (805) 648–7731; At the beach; 260 rooms with balconies, satellite TV; two restaurants, three cocktail lounges; heated swimming pool, exercise room. Just 1 block from the Ventura Pier. Special and seasonal rates; AAA rate includes discount.

Oxnard

Lobster Trap Restaurant, 3605 Peninsula Road, Channel Islands Harbor, Oxnard. (800) 228–6026; (805) 985–6311. In the sprawling Casa Sirena Marina Resort complex. Along with terrific panoramic views of the harbor, it's a trendy and popular spot, noted for fresh local seafood entrees, salads, crabcakes, steak, and prime ribs. Sunday buffet brunch.

Casa Sirena Marina Resort, 3605 Peninsula Road, Channel Islands Harbor, Oxnard, CA 93035. (800) 228–6026; (805) 985–6311. Premier waterside hotel, here for twenty-five years under the same management, offers 275 beautifully appointed rooms, including 30 suites, equipped with refrigerator, microwave oven, cable TV, VCR, and hair dryer, among other amenities. Besides sailboats drifting past your window, facilities feature heated swimming pool and spa, tennis, putting green, and bicycles. Dine at the popular Lobster Trap Restaurant (see listing above), enjoy live entertainment and dancing in the Guadalajara Lounge, and have a casual breakfast or lunch in the bustling La Trampita Coffee Shop. Getaway packages, meeting facilities.

Mandalay Beach Resort, 2101 Mandalay Beach Road. (800) 582–3000 (nationwide); (805) 984–2500. On the beachfront; 250 suites, each with two full bathrooms, wetbar, refrigerator, coffeemaker and coffee, microwave ovens, two TVs. Large heated pool, two spas, two lighted tennis courts. Restaurant, lounge; complimentary cooked-to-order breakfast. Special packages.

For More Information

Ventura Visitors and Convention Bureau, 89C South California Street, Ventura, CA 93001. (800) 333–2989 (in California); (805) 648–2075. Open Monday through Friday from 8:30 A.M. to 5:00 P.M. and weekends from 10:00 A.M. to 4:00 P.M.

Ventura Parks Division, City of San Buenaventura, P.O. Box 99, Ventura, CA 93002. (805) 652–4550.

Ventura Recreation Division, City of San Buenaventura, P.O. Box 99, Ventura, CA 93002. (805) 658–4726.

Greater Oxnard & Harbors Tourism Bureau, Connelly House at Heritage Square, 200 West 7th Street, Oxnard, CA 93030. (800) 269–6273 (visitor information); (805) 385–7541.

Channel Islands Visitor Center. (800) 994–4852.

Port Hueneme Chamber of Commerce, 220 North Market Street, Port Hueneme, CA 93401. (805) 488–2023.

Ojai

A putting green at Ojai Valley Inn.

Country Getaway

——————————— 2 NIGHTS ———————————

Resort • Golf • Tennis • Parks
Orange and avocado groves • Museum • Hiking and biking
Antiques • Galleries • Fishing and boating

This sleepy little country village has a special tranquillity perfect for unwinding in a three-day outing. Creative people as well as fugitives of Los Angeles's fast lanes have long been drawn to Ojai (pronounced

"O-hi") for its quiet, unhurried pace. Tucked in a deep coastal valley, extending from the 6,000-foot Topa Topa Mountains at the edge of Los Padres National Forest to the ocean, Ojai's miles of orange groves brim with golden fruit. Avocado trees drape the rolling foothills, and the hectic world seems far away. Small wonder that Ojai was the setting for the mystical, beautiful valley of **Shangri-La** in the movie *Lost Horizon,* starring Ronald Colman.

In this cozy town you can tee off at two championship golf courses, play tennis, browse and shop at fine galleries and boutiques, tour artist studios, and pedal a bike along a meandering creek down country lanes where horses graze in sunny pastures. You can visit a museum, "take it off" in style at a chic health spa resort, picnic in uncrowded parks, purchase just-picked oranges and avocados to tote home, and stay in a legendary world-class inn. Camping, fishing, and boating are available in nearby Lake Casitas, site of the 1984 Olympic rowing and canoeing events.

Day 1

Morning

Drive north on Ventura Freeway 101 to **Ojai,** 76 miles through the rural San Fernando Valley. Traveling over the Conejo Grade, you see the vast fertile plain spread out below. Both sides of the highway are checkerboarded with farms, row crops, and citrus groves.

Immediately after seeing the signs for Ventura, exit to the right on Highway 33 north to reach Ojai, 14 miles inland along a divided country road framed by voluptuous hills that turn chartreuse in spring and are sere in winter.

After Foster Park follow the one-lane rural road past Casitas Springs and small houses; you'll see bikers and horseback riders on the bike and equestrian paths that follow the road. Stop at the Big Red Barn roadside stand, at **Rancho Arnaz,** 9504 North Ventura (Highway 33) (805–649–2776), to buy fresh apple cider, fresh produce, jams, nuts, and olives. In fall this is a popular spot to pick your own apples at the adjacent orchard.

As you drive through Oak View, make note of **Oak Pit Barbeque,** on the right side of the road, to return to for sandwiches to eat there or take out on your way home (see "Other Recommended Restaurants and Lodgings").

Continue through the small village of Mira Monte, along Ojai Avenue, to the Ojai Valley Inn, on the right, and turn onto the private road to the inn.

Lunch: **Ojai Valley Inn,** Country Club Drive, Ojai. (800) 422–6524; (805) 646–5511. Dining on the broad Oak Terrace beneath a vine-covered pagoda surrounded by the lush golf course marks a carefree beginning to your holiday. Relax in the beautiful surroundings over creative sandwiches—broiled salmon on brioche or grilled Portobello mushrooms with cream cheese on flatbread, salads, soups, hot entrees; moderately priced.

Afternoon

Golfers won't waste any time teeing off on Ojai Valley Inn's renowned, challenging course. Nongolfers, with permission, enjoy tooling around this scenic, impeccably maintained course in a golf cart, rattling over rustic wooden bridges spanning picturesque creeks, and cruising fairways lined with giant sycamores and oaks. Tennis enthusiasts will soon be racing across the courts, and swimmers are equally at home in the sunny, uncrowded pools.

Others can drive, take the trolley, or borrow a bike from the inn and pedal about 1 mile into downtown Ojai. **Libbey Park,** with its splashing fountain smack in the center of town across from the Arcade, is the showcase for most local events and activities. In the charming, oak-studded small park, the secluded bowl beneath an ancient sycamore is the delightful setting for the city's prestigious annual Ojai Music Festival at the end of May, concerts, and theater. Libbey Park is also the site of the Ojai Tennis Tournament, held in April, and public courts.

Alongside, the post office, with its landmark 65-foot bell tower, was built in 1917, at the same time as the shaded, Spanish-style shopping Arcade across the street. There are no parking meters, and you'll find plenty of parking places.

The best way to see Ojai is to stroll the small downtown area. The **Arcade,** between Signal and Montgomery streets, is the city's main shopping stretch of stores, galleries, and some restaurants. You'll find more of everything on the small side streets, across from the Arcade and behind it.

Rains, 218 East Ojai Avenue (805–646–1441), Ojai's largest store and family-owned since 1917, is an attractive, well-stocked, upscale emporium featuring men's and women's apparel, giftware, kitchenware, pottery, and hardware. A few doors away, **Tottingham Court, Ltd.,** 242 East Ojai Avenue (805–646–2339), is a unique place to shop or have brunch or both. Its small tearoom offers quiche, sandwiches, salads, pastries, and true English scones with Devonshire cream from England. Among its multitude of import gift items are china, crystal, silver, babywear, and tiny collectibles.

A bit farther down, the **Ojai Indian Shop,** at 31 East Ojai Avenue (805–646–2631), has been, since 1968, a popular source for authentic Indian artifacts, baskets, masks, moccasins, turquoise jewelry, coins, and full feather headdresses for young chiefs and squaws.

Across from the Arcade, **Barbara Bowman stores,** at 139 East Ojai Avenue, make their own exclusive and handsome clothing and accessories. **Ojai Valley Museum,** 138 West Ojai Avenue (805–646–2290), has moved to new, enlarged quarters in the chapel of the Old Catholic Church. You get a glimpse of the city's past from the displays of Indian artifacts discovered in nearby excavations of the Oak Grove and Chumash tribes, who settled here thousands of years ago. View the lifelike birds and animals, together with memorabilia depicting Ojai's early pioneer life. The museum's giftshop offers T-shirts, postcards, and great children's books. (Open daily except Tuesday, from 1:00 to 4:00 P.M.) **The Ojai Chamber of Commerce** has moved and is just next door at 150 West Ojai Avenue. Here's where you can pick up maps, brochures, and other visitor information.

Next door stop by the **Massarella Pottery & Gallery,** 105 South Montgomery Street (805–646–9453), a good-looking showroom and factory displaying the owners' classic stoneware and porcelain made on the premises. If you're lucky, you can watch the potters throwing the clay and firing it. (Closed Monday.)

Dinner: **Oak Grill,** at the Ojai Valley Inn, Ojai. (800) 422–6524; or (805) 666–5511. The cozy, Spanish Mission Revival–style Oak Grill features gourmet dinners that highlight seafood stew with Pacific mussels, monkfish and cranberry beans, or braised rabbit with potato dumpling, followed by luscious desserts you've only dreamed about until now. Reservations suggested.

Lodging: Ojai Valley Inn, Country Club Drive, Ojai, CA 93023. (800) 422–6524; (805) 666–5511. Deluxe award-winning resort atop 200 rolling acres; 207 guestrooms and suites, each with private balcony or terrace overlooking the fairways; hair dryer, coffeemaker, television, minirefrigerator, turndown service. The Inn's Ranch & Stables offers guided horseback trail rides, hikes, and mountain bike rides into the national forest, and a charming children's farm. 18-hole championship golf course, driving range, putting green, golf shop; eight tennis courts (four lighted), tennis center; two heated swimming pools, whirlpool, exercise facility; two restaurants, lounge; conference center; concierge service; children's playground; complimentary bikes and Ojai trolley shuttle to town. Sunday buffet brunch. Member of Historic Hotels of America. Site of Annual Senior PGA tour event. Golf, Pamper, B&B packages available.

Day 2

Morning

Breakfast. At the inn. Generous buffet breakfast in the glass-walled Vista Dining Room overlooking the sunlit golf course and the mountains begins your day with beauty. Place your order with the obliging chef at the Omelette Bar for eggs just the way you like them, prepared with all the fixings. Then serve yourself with fresh juice, fresh fruits, quiche or crepes, eggs Benedict, waffles, French toast, ham, bacon, sausage, hash brown potatoes, hot and cold cereals, and freshly baked blueberry muffins, breads, and pastries. Hot coffee is brought to your table.

After breakfast golfers will soon be breaking par on the front nine. Or you can drive into and through the village for about another 2 miles east, to see the beautiful acres of orange groves and avocado groves, and then drive up into the foothills for spectacular vistas across the rich valley.

This most easterly end of town is where you can see the famous **Shangri-La** view as seen in the movie. At Boccali's Pizza Place, 3277 Ojai Avenue, turn right and drive partway up the hill to Dennison Grade. Stop at the stone bench on the right side of the road. The panoramic view down into the valley on a clear, bright day, as well as when the mountain ranges seem to be floating in clouds and mist, is gorgeous.

Return to Ojai Avenue and turn left to **Ventura County Soule Park,** off Highway 150 on Boardman, adjacent to Soule Golf Course (pronounced "sole").

The spacious park, edging squiggly San Antonio Creek, provides shady picnic tables, barbecue pits, a playground, tennis courts, and serene expanses of lawn and trees. Local equestrian groups hold weekend shows in Soule's horse arena, considered one of the country's finest.

Lunch: **The Ranch House,** South Lomita and Besant, P.O. Box 458, Ojai. (805) 646-2360. Follow Ojai Avenue west to the Y intersection signal. Turn right on El Roblar, turn left at Lomita, then turn left to the restaurant. This flower-filled garden restaurant is a longtime special favorite for Ojai residents and visitors. Luncheon suggestions include homemade fettucine with crab, Gorgonzola cheese, snowpeas, and mushrooms. Breads are baked daily; desserts are made in the kitchen; the wine list is notable. Garden luncheons served from May through September, Wednesday through Sunday; dinner served Wednesday through Sunday;

Sunday Champagne brunch and dinner. Closed Monday and Tuesday.

Afternoon

Driving around this rural area of Meiners Oaks, you are apt to find fresh produce for sale at private homes. Try those along La Luna, with its groves of orange trees, and those along Cuyama. Look for little stands of oranges, avocados, and berries in front or side gardens available for you to purchase on the honor system, according to directions given there.

Return to the Ojai Valley Inn for golf, tennis, or swimming and sunning. Later you might want to drive back into the village or pedal in for shopping or further sightseeing. **Bart's Books,** Matilija 302 West Street at the corner of Cañada (805–646–3755), is a collector's delight and a town pride. Go inside to browse this unusual open-air bookmart, built around a huge oak tree and offering some 100,000 new and used books, magazines, and sheet music. Shelves of bargain-priced used books line the exterior walls to accommodate after-hours book lovers, who can buy them by tossing the marked price over the wall onto the patio.

A few blocks away are the **Biblical Gardens,** on the grounds of the graceful old Presbyterian Church, 304 North Foothill Road at the corner of Aliso (805–646–1437), featuring fifty varieties of plants mentioned in the Bible; all have been authenticated, and you're in for a few surprises. Join a guided tour or pick up a map and wander about on your own. All plants are labeled, making them easy to identify.

If antiques hunting is part of your fun in visiting small villages, check out the **Antique Collection,** 236 West Ojai Avenue at Cañada (805–646–6688). A group of about twenty-five antiques dealers share a large building, with space divided into small rooms and areas. You'll find all kinds of bric-a-brac, furniture, objets d'art, books, kitchen collectibles, sterling silver items, memorabilia, and varied accessories.

Dinner: At the **Ojai Valley Inn.** The creative chef's dinner menu changes about every two weeks. Among its variety of appetizers, entrees, and desserts to choose from are tournedos of beef, rack of lamb, and fresh sea bass. Or you can happily enjoy an encore of last night's gastronomic pleasures.

Lodging: At the Ojai Valley Inn.

Day 3

Morning

Breakfast: Another splendid buffet breakfast at the inn.

Golfers will want to play another round on this well-manicured course, hit some balls on the driving range, or sharpen up their game on the putting green near the dining terrace, with Ojai's warm sun on their backs.

Afternoon

On your return to Los Angeles, try to allow time to stop at lovely **Lake Casitas.** Follow Highway 33 west to its junction with Highway 150; west from Mira Monte turn right (north) and drive about 3 miles to the park's entrance. The gleaming man-made reservoir, with 60 miles of shoreline, is surrounded by lush avocado groves.

Recreation is unlimited at Lake Casitas. Here at one of the area's largest campgrounds, visitors can rent a boat; ride a bike; fish for trout, bass, or catfish; picnic and barbecue—but no swimming. A snackbar serves breakfast and lunch. Admission (805–649–2233). After your visit to Lake Casitas, take Highway 33 back to 101 and follow it south to Los Angeles.

There's More

Golf. Soule Park Golf Course, 1033 East Ojai Avenue. (805) 646–5633. An 18-hole public course, threaded with old oaks and pine trees. Golf shop, driving range, carts; Clubhouse Restaurant; seniors' weekday rates.

Tennis. Tennis is a large part of Ojai's lifestyle. Besides courts at Libbey and Soule parks, you can play at Nordhoff High School, 0.5 mile north of the Y intersection on Highways 150 and 113, or at Matilija Junior High, just off El Paseo Road.

The Oaks at Ojai, 122 East Ojai Avenue. (805) 646–5573. Health and fitness spa resort run by noted fitness expert Sheila Cluff, who can help you take it off and stay that way. Various programs and packages.

Bike riding is one of the most pleasant ways to see the Ojai Valley, riding either through the downtown area or along the 10-foot-wide, paved bikepath separated by a fence from the road and equestrian path. A 6-mile trail begins at Fox Street and leads through scenic backroads, ending in Oak View. Pick up trail maps at the Chamber of Commerce or at rentals. Bicycles Collectibles of Ojai, 108 Cañada Street (805–646–7736), offers new mountain bikes and tandems. Get on your bike and follow the trail.

Friend's Ranch Market, 15150 Maricopa Highway. Original long-time location, 2.5 miles north of the Y intersection, is a scenic drive but may be a bit out of the way. It sells fresh orange juice, oranges, avocados, nuts, and lemons and will ship all over the United States.

Ojai's "Pink Moment." At day's end look toward the soaring Topa Topa Mountains to watch the pink-orange sunset radiate over the peaks. It bathes the sky and mountains in a luminous, blushing glow that gradually diffuses and fades. Strictly an Ojai phenomenon.

The Pottery, studio gallery of Otto Heino, 971 McAndrews Road. (805) 646–3393. This internationally acclaimed potter welcomes visitors Tuesday through Sunday. Go east on Ojai Avenue, past Soule Park; turn left on Reeves Road to McAndrew Road.

The Krotona Institute School of Theosophy, 46 Krotona Hill Highway 33 and Hermosa Road. (805) 646–2653. Courses and workshops are conducted in its serene, one-hundred-acre hilltop setting. Library houses the largest theosophical collection on the West Coast. Bookshop and library open daily from 10:00 A.M. to 4:00 P.M. and Sunday from 1:00 to 4:00 P.M. Ojai was the foundation headquarters and residence of the late philosopher Jidda Krishnamurti and was the sanctuary of author Aldous Huxley.

Krishnamurti Library, 1130 McAndrew Road. (805) 646–4948. The works have a large following, with frequent gatherings. Books and tapes for sale. Open Wednesday through Sunday 1:00 to 5:00 P.M.

Beatrice Wood Studio gallery, on Highway 150 in Upper Ojai. (805) 646–3381. It's worth a visit to see this ceramicist's work and collection of international folk art in a spectacular view setting. Look for the pink mailbox about 1 mile past the top of Dennison Grade on Ojai–Santa Paula Drive. Open by invitation only.

Gracie's Antique Mall, 238 East Ojai Avenue. (805) 646–8879. In the Ojai Arcarde, sixteen dealers show collectibles, Victoriana, and memorabilia from past generations to the 1970s, in lamps, furniture, glassware, and art.

Heart of Light, 451 East Ojai Avenue. (805) 646–3812. Ojai New Age Center and Emporium, recently expanded, houses a large selection of books, music, art, eclectic gifts. Ongoing programs and workshops feature lectures with guest speakers.

Ojai Certified Farmers Market, in the parking lot at 300 East Matilija, across from the Arcade Plaza. (805) 646–4444. Fresh vegetables and fruits, delicious breads, arts and crafts, and more. Every Sunday from 9:00 A.M. to 1:00 P.M. in summer and from 10:00 A.M. to 2:00 P.M. in winter.

Treasures of Ojai Antiques, 110 North Signal Street, at the corner of Matilija. (805) 646–2852. Here's where eighteen antiques dealers display treasures, from estate jewelry, California pottery, and home accessories to Indian rugs and art nouveau pieces.

Wheeler Hot Springs, 16825 Maricopa Highway, Ojai. (800) 994–3353; (805) 646–8131. This has been a popular retreat and health resort ever since the original lodge was built in 1891. Located six-and-a-half miles north of Ojai (just past Friend's Ranch), this secluded escape offers relaxation in private redwood tubs filled with naturally hot mineral water and select spa services, including therapeutic massage, body wraps, and facials. The restaurant features fine Modern European cuisine, and a notable wine list. Enjoy live jazz entertainment during Friday and Saturday dinner and Sunday brunch. Special packages include Hot Tub Dinner and Lunch specials for two; other specials available. No overnight accommodations; special packages are available with lodging in Ojai.

Special Events

Note: Call for admission fees.

End of February/beginning of March. Annual Senior PGA Tour Golf Event. (805) 646–5796. Senior golf superstars play the demanding course at Ojai Valley Inn.

Last weekend in April. Ojai Tennis Tournament, Libbey Park. (805) 646–2494. The oldest amateur tennis tour, since 1895.

Early May. Ojai Garden Tour of private gardens; self-guided. (805) 646–8126.

Last weekend in May. Annual Ojai Music Festival, Libbey Park. (805) 646–2094. Day and evening concerts.

Mid-June. Annual Ojai Wine Festival. Lake Casitas (800) 548–4881. Live jazz, food, art.

Late July/early August. Annual Ojai Shakespeare Festival, Libbey Park Bowl. (805) 646–WILL. Afternoon and evening performances; preshow entertainment.

Beginning of October. Annual Bowlful of Blues Festival, Libbey Park Bowl. (805) 646–7230. World's top artists.

Mid-October. Annual Ojai Studio Artists Tour. (805) 646–8126. Tours of private studios of Ojai's finest painters, sculptors, potters, printmakers. Festive reception. Admission.

Other Recommended Restaurants and Lodgings

Ojai

L'Auberge Restaurant, 314 El Paseo. (805) 646–2288. Between Cañada and Rincon; entrance on Rincon to this vintage 1910 white Ojai mansion, half-hidden by oak trees. L'Auberge enjoys an excellent reputation for noteworthy French Belgian cuisine; specialties such as New York pepper steak flambé, *poulet cordon bleu,* and desserts of raspberry ice cream dipped in chocolate. Lunch Saturday and Sunday; dinner nightly. Reservations suggested. Terrace dining offers stunning view of the rugged Topa Topa Mountains.

The Clubhouse Restaurant at Soule Park Golf Course, 1033 East Ojai Avenue. (805) 646–5685. Wrapped around a dramatic fireplace in a dining room overlooking sunny fairways. Medium-priced continental menu includes sandwiches, pasta, seafood, salads, fresh pastries. It's quite busy weekends; best to reserve. Closed Monday.

Casa Ojai Best Western, 1302 East Ojai Avenue. (800) 255–8175; (805) 646–8175. Across from Soule Park Golf Course; forty-five guestrooms, in-room coffeemakers, cable TV, nonsmoking rooms available; heated pool and spa; complimentary continental breakfast of muffins, pastry, orange juice, and coffee in lobby. Special midweek golf package.

Los Padres Inn, 1208 East Ojai Avenue. (805) 646–4365; (800) 228–3744. Thirty-one guestrooms in attractive, Spanish-style architectural and garden setting; kitchen units available. Cable TV; swimming pool and hot Jacuzzi; complimentary continental breakfast; senior citizen rates. One block from Soule Park Golf Course.

Casa De La Luna, 710 South La Luna. (805) 646–4528. B&B on the rural outskirts of town. Follow Ojai Avenue west; turn right on El Roblar to La Luna; turn left and follow the signs. A popular hideaway in the owner's former home, with seven large, well-decorated rooms and suites, each with modern private bath. On seven acres of large oaks and rambling gardens. Full breakfast cooked to order and served in large formal dining room. No pets, children, or smoking indoors.

Oak View

Avanti!, 710 Ventura Avenue. (805) 649–9001. Five minutes from Ojai. It's not much to look at from the road, but this popular, upscale, moderately priced restaurant has patrons lined up outside on Friday nights. Tasty Italian specialties range from lobster-stuffed ravioli to four-cheese pizza, with great sauces and desserts. Lunch and dinner daily. All menu items available for take-out.

The Oak Pit, 820 North Ventura Avenue, Highway 33. (805) 649–9903. This is your best pitstop on your way to or from Ojai for pork ribs and hefty hand-carved beef and ham sandwiches, barbecued beans, and chili, to eat there or take out. Help yourself to the array of fiery sauces, including "X-Rated" and "Killer." Closed Monday.

For More Information

Ojai Valley Chamber of Commerce, 150 West Ojai Avenue (in the old chapel), P.O. Box 1134, Ojai, CA 93023. (805) 646–8126. Open Monday through Saturday from 9:30 A.M. to 4:30 P.M. and Sunday from 10:00 A.M. to 4:00 P.M.

For further information about parks and camping, call the City of Ojai Recreation Department (805–646–1872) or the Ojai Ranger Station, 1190 East Ojai Avenue, Los Padres National Forest (805–646–4348).

Santa Barbara

Santa Barbara's Mission of 1786.

American Riviera

_____ 2 NIGHTS _____

Beaches • Fine dining • Mission • Wharf • Children's zoo
Botanical garden • Sailing • Biking • Whale-watching • Antiques shopping

Here's a three-day getaway to Santa Barbara, Southern California's own Riviera, a small, prosperous seaside resort community with a special panache, tucked between the Pacific Ocean and the rugged Santa Ynez Mountains. Sleek yachts dance in its snug, flag-festooned harbor, and tall, skinny palm trees frame miles of white sandy beaches dotted with picnic tables and barbecue pits.

With its festive air, profusion of flowers, slower pace, and Old World flavor, Santa Barbara is a cultural community of style, old money, and gracious living blended with the romance and tradition of its ancient Spanish heritage.

Santa Barbara's temperate weather began luring wintering Eastern socialites back in the late 1880s. Moreover, the city has always been a retreat for celebrities (Julia Child, Michael Douglas, Jonathan Winters, and Robert Mitchum, among them), who unwind in the casual lifestyle and anonymity of a small town. And when the Reagan administration's hilltop Rancho del Cielo was nicknamed the "Western White House," Santa Barbara became a world-renowned, glamorous Southern California destination.

Few cities can boast such a robust, historic past and different cultures, dating from 1782, when Spanish soldiers accompanied by Franciscan Father Junípero Serra founded Santa Barbara, establishing a military presidio and a mission. Remnants of the ancient fort still remain, and Mission Santa Barbara is the city's greatest treasure and most famous landmark.

The city was an important Spanish stronghold in the New World for forty years, until California became a Mexican territory. During the Mexican-American War, Santa Barbara became part of the United States, in 1845, and the sleepy pueblo began to stir and grow.

Day 1

Morning

Drive north from Los Angeles 90 miles to Santa Barbara on Freeway 101, also known as Ventura Freeway 101. As the road traverses the rural San Fernando Valley, through fringes of small towns like Calabasas, the low, rolling hillsides are studded with clusters of large oak trees, native to the area. Approaching Camarillo, the dramatic downswing of Conejo Grade presents a panoramic sweep of the misty green valley spread out below.

After Ventura the freeway, enlivened with a flowered divider strip of colorful oleanders, borders the glistening ocean, and there is the graceful curve of white beaches and small coves. Oil tankers far out on the horizon are camouflaged to resemble small tropical islands, even with tall palm trees waving in the distance.

The blue ocean fades in and out of sight as you note the cutoff to Lake Casitas. Passing the small town of Carpenteria, you'll see a huge Santa Claus figure looming over **Santa Claus Lane,** a year-round enclave of Christmas gift and toy stores, off Highway 101 on the ocean side. Mail posted here gets a Santa Claus postmark.

Arriving in Santa Barbara, note **Stearns Wharf,** at the foot of State Street, the town's main thoroughfare; built in 1872, it is the West Coast's oldest operating wharf, really a 3-block-long extension of State Street over the Pacific Ocean. The engaging **Dolphin Fountain** marks the beginning of State Street, as well as the entrance to the busy pier, where one can fish, shop, dine or snack, browse, and drive or stroll.

Along the pier, **Stearns Wharf Vintner's** is fun for wine tasting on its sunny terrace, and **Madame Rosinka** can read your palm with true gypsy finesse.

In the **Sea Center,** (805–963–1067), operated by the Museum of Natural History, marine life exhibits feature awesome, life-size models of whales and dolphins. (Open Sunday, Monday, Wednesday, Friday, and Saturday from 10:00 A.M. to 5:00 P.M. and Tuesday and Thursday from noon to 5:00 P.M.; admission. Public parking available on the wharf.)

From the pier the scene inland is an enchanting Dufy painting—cushy yachts preen in the sunlit harbor along the curved waterfront and the little city spreads up into the mauve foothills and the protective embrace of the mountains.

The lively area around the wharf is a fine starting point to explore Santa Barbara's charming beachfront, where cycling and jogging paths weave through **Chase Palm Park** beneath soaring palm trees. Bikes, roller skates, and **Pedalinas** (jaunty four-wheel cycles with surrey on top) are rentable across from the wharf at Beach Rentals, 8 West Cabrillo Boulevard (805–966–6733). In this same area, every Sunday from 10:00 A.M. until sunset hundreds of regional artists sell and exhibit their work in a bustling arts and crafts show held along a sunny, 1-mile oceanfront stretch.

Santa Barbara is noted for its beaches, and each has its own attractions: **East Beach** is the most popular, with bikepaths, volleyball courts, and picnic areas, plus a great cafe. **West Beach,** on the other side of the wharf, offers the best sailboarding, swimming, and sunbathing as well as beginning sailboarding lessons and rental equipment. **Leadbetter Beach,** at the breakwater with a landscaped picnic area and the Sea Cove cafe right on the sand, is well known for some of the best surfing and sailboarding.

Lunch: **East Beach Grill,** 1118 East Cabrillo Boulevard, Santa Barbara. (805) 965–8805. An upbeat spot right on the sand, with good sandwiches and grill food, where you can watch the action on the bikepaths and the ocean.

Afternoon

The **Andree Clark Bird Refuge,** at 1400 East Cabrillo Boulevard, is near the intersection of Cabrillo Boulevard and Highway 101. At this lovely lagoon and gardens adjoining the Child's Estate Zoo, you can feed and watch the many varieties of freshwater fowl. A bikeway and footpath fringe the lagoon. Park on the north side of the lagoon. (Free.)

The adjacent **Santa Barbara Zoo,** 500 Ninos Drive (805–962–6310), on a clifftop off Cabrillo Boulevard east of Milpas, was designed primarily for children in a delightful garden estate setting. The zoo features almost 500 animals, including baby elephants, big cats, giraffes, monkeys, and sea lions as well as exotic birds. A playground, snackbar, and picnic area are here too. Kids particularly love the domestic-animal petting park and the miniature train ride. (Open daily from 10:00 A.M. to 5:00 P.M. and in summer until 6:00 P.M. Admission fees, parking fee.)

Before leaving the beach area, pick up a handy destination guide at Santa Barbara Visitors Information Center, 1 Santa Barbara Street (805–965–3021), at the corner of Cabrillo Boulevard. These guides are also available at the courthouse, most restaurants, and shops.

Incidentally, from the beach at Stearns Wharf you can ride the free shuttle bus east and west on Cabrillo Boulevard to Coast Village Road and back as well as up State Street to Sola Street, just past the Museum of Art. It runs round-trip every fifteen minutes from 10:00 A.M. to 5:00 P.M. and till 8:00 P.M. on Friday and Saturday. Or you can hop on the open trolley at the wharf for a ninety-minute sightseeing tour of the city (fare). City lots in the downtown area provide free parking for the first ninety minutes.

State Street, Santa Barbara's foremost promenade, is truly one of the most attractive main streets anywhere and a favorite shopping and browsing stroll for visitors and residents alike. State begins at the ocean and leads you through the Old Town historic section and the city's important dining and shopping hub of specialty shops, galleries, and upscale department stores. You'll soon notice that traffic moves at a slower pace in sedate Santa Barbara. Along this appealing boulevard, large trees in huge planters share sidewalk space with tall eucalyptus and palm trees, decorative iron grillwork, arched passageways, and lots of flowers.

It is a planned harmony and beauty. The people of Santa Barbara are determined to preserve their city's Spanish inheritance in timeless, graceful architecture of red-tiled roofs, arched facades, benches, and courtyards. The city acquired this distinctive look following a severe earthquake in 1925 that destroyed much of the downtown section. Everything was rebuilt in a unified motif still adhered to. Even sidewalk telephone booths must conform to the red-tiled-roof theme. There is a noticeable absence of glitz. No high-rise buildings intrude into Santa Barbara's clear blue skies, and billboards have long been banned.

Along State Street you'll want to browse the charming **Paseo Nuevo,** bordered by Chapala Street, an engaging, two-level, Spanish-style mall of restaurants, fountains, courtyards, galleries, and boutiques. Farther along in the 1100 block, the 16-foot-tall sidewalk clock, with Westminster chimes, and inviting shade trees enhance the entrance to **La Arcada Court,** with its specialty shops, fountains, plants, and Acapulco Mexican Restaurant, a convenient upbeat place to snack and people-watch at the outdoor tables.

Continuing up State Street, you'll arrive at the **Santa Barbara Museum of Art,** 1130 State Street (805–963–4364), whose colorful banners welcome you to one of America's foremost small museums, boasting a prestigious permanent collection of art and ancient sculpture, plus important changing exhibitions. The Museum Bookstore is a good bet for art books and distinctive jewelry made by local artisans. Free guided tours are held Wednesday at 12:30 P.M. (Open Tuesday through Saturday, 11:00 A.M. to 5:00 P.M. Admission; free admission Thursday and the first Sunday of each month.)

Dinner: **Wine Cask,** 813 Anacapa Street, Santa Barbara. (805) 966–9463. Tucked in downtown's charming and historic El Paseo in a majestic dining room, with hand-painted beamed ceiling and baronial fireplace. Imaginative bistro-style cuisine offers delightful appetizers, such as stuffed Anaheim chiles with corn fritters. Dinner entrees highlight seared peppercorn *Ahi* tuna and ginger risotto; grilled filet mignon served with red wine sauce. Extensive wine list features selections from the restaurant's adjacent wine store.

Lodging: **Four Seasons Biltmore,** 1260 Channel Drive, Santa Barbara, CA 93108. (805) 969–2261. The city's most luxurious hotel, with 234 rooms, suites, and private cottages, on nineteen rambling garden acres. Three lighted tennis courts, two swimming pools (one beach-front), two hydrotherapy pools, private beachfront cabanas. Guestroom amenities include refrigerated minibar, clock radio, terry robes, and hair dryer. Complimentary putting green, bikes, croquet, and shuffleboard. Concierge service, four restaurants, elegant Sunday brunch. Golf arrangements with local courses.

Day 2

Morning

Breakfast: **Montecito Cafe,** 1295 Coast Village Road. (805) 969–3392. In the Montecito Inn (see "Other Recommended Restaurants and Lodgings"), the small hotel Charlie Chaplin and Fatty Arbuckle built in the 1920s and the inspiration for the song "There's a Small Hotel." This amiable cafe with laid-back service offers good, traditional breakfast fare, with southwestern and California cuisine touches, such as pancakes with caviar.

All visitors want to see the city's most famous landmark, **Mission Santa Barbara,** Laguna and Los Olivos streets (805–682–4149). Take State Street to Mission Street or to Los Olivos Street. Turn right toward the mountains and continue to the mission, situated in the scenic rural foothills overlooking the city; both streets run into it. Known as the "Queen of the Missions" for its graceful symmetry and tall twin bell towers, it is the tenth of twenty-one California missions, founded in 1786 by the Spanish Franciscan Fathers and still a Catholic parish church. The annual Italian Street Festival is held on its broad terrace. A self-guided tour encompasses the gardens, museum, courtyards, chapel, and cemetery. The small giftshop features pretty fans, books, T-shirts, souvenirs, and religious objects. (Open daily from 9:00 A.M. to 5:00 P.M. Admission; children under sixteen free.)

Since it's just 2 blocks north of the mission, you're within walking distance of the **Museum of Natural History, Planetarium, and Observatory,** 2559 Puesta del Sol Road (take Mission Canyon Road and follow the signs; 805–682–4711). The museum is housed in a rambling ranch-style building around a courtyard. The highlight is the knockout 72-foot skeleton of a giant blue whale, outside to the right of the entrance. Exhibit halls include the West's largest collection of Chumash Indian artifacts. Check out the full-scale model of a 33-foot giant squid, suspended from the ceiling in the Marine Hall. The Museum Store offers pottery, T-shirts, Indian and Southwest jewelry, and souvenir items. (Open daily from 9:00 A.M. to 5:00 P.M. and 10:00 A.M. on Sundays and holidays. Admission; free admission Wednesday and the first Sunday of each month.)

In the same quiet area, about 1.5 miles north of the mission, is the spectacular **Botanic Garden,** 1212 Mission Canyon Road (805–562–2521). Take Mission Canyon Road to Foothill Road, go right 1 block, then left on Mission Canyon Road to the garden. You'll find some sixty acres of California wildflowers and native flora, a redwood forest, and miles of nature trails. The giftshop features books, souvenirs, and native plants. Guided tours are held daily. (Open daily from 8:00 A.M. to sunset. Fee; free admission Tuesday and Wednesday.)

Drive back to the city center for lunch.

Lunch: **Chase Grill Downtown,** 1012 State Street, Santa Barbara. (805) 965–4351. Along with its checkered tablecloths and congenial atmosphere, Chase's has been voted as having the best Caesar salad for eleven years and keeps customers happy with good pasta and other Italian specialties.

Afternoon

While you're downtown, head over to another famous landmark, the **Santa Barbara County Courthouse,** in the 1100 block of Anacapa Street (805–681–4200). Considered one of the most striking public buildings in the United States, the handsome, impressive Spanish-Moorish building, completed in 1929, boasts a 70-foot clock tower and grand-scale archways and turrets, all surrounded by spacious lawns, palm trees, and lush tropical plants. The attractive interior is rich in its hand-painted ceilings, wrought-iron chandeliers, murals, and historical exhibits. From the observation deck the panoramic city view sweeps from the lavender Santa Ynez Mountains over the carpet of red-tiled roofs to the sparkling Pacific Ocean and occasionally to the Channel Islands floating in the mist 20 miles offshore. (Open Monday through Friday from 8:00 A.M. to 5:00 P.M. and weekends and holidays from 9:00 A.M. to 5:00 P.M. Free. Tour information: 805–962–6464.)

El Paseo ("The Street in Spain"), in the 800 block of State Street between State and Anacapa, remains one of the city's loveliest and oldest Spanish-style shopping and dining complexes. Built in and around the 1827 adobe home of the historic De la Guerra family, it has undergone extensive renovation and restoration and now boasts art galleries, specialty shops, sidewalk cafes, and fine restaurants.

For those hipped on history, the compact downtown area is rich in landmarks of Santa Barbara's colorful past. Among historical highlights is **El Cuartel–El Presidio de Santa Barbara** (State Historical Park), 122 East Cañon Perdido Street (805–963–3633). This is where the city began in 1782 and includes buildings that were part of the Presidio Real, the original fortress. In addition to a slide show, you'll find a scale model of the old fort and a giftshop. (Open Monday to Friday 9:00 A.M. to noon and 1:00 to 4:00 P.M. Free.)

Just south of the Presidio, the **Santa Barbara Historical Society Museum,** 136 East De La Guerra Street and East Cañon Perdido (805–966–1601), is a complex of colonial Spanish houses built in the 1800s. The museum features many exhibits, as well as memorabilia of the city's four cultural eras: Indian, Spanish, Mexican, and American. (Open Tuesday through Friday from noon to 5:00 P.M. and Saturday and Sunday from 1:00 to 5:00 P.M. Free.)

Antiques buffs will admire the string of little shops on **Brinkerhoff Avenue** at Cota, between Chapala and De La Vina. This nostalgic, charming, 1-block-long tree-shaded street, named after Santa Barbara's first physician, Samuel Brinkerhoff, is a designated Special Historic District. The original Victorian-style clapboard houses line the street in an array of bright sherbet colors, white picket fences border old-fashioned gardens. They are now antiques and specialty shops, plus some galleries, to browse for memorabilia, old treasures, and gifts. Most are open Tuesday through Sunday from 11:00 A.M. to 6:00 P.M.

Dinner: **The Palace Cafe,** 8 East Cota Street. Santa Barbara. (805) 966–3133. A longtime local favorite for hot, Louisiana-style Cajun, Creole, and Caribbean cuisine. Look for jambalaya, fresh fish, *andouille* sausage, and Key Lime Pie for dessert. Closed Monday.

Lodging: Four Seasons Biltmore.

Day 3

Morning

Breakfast: In your hotel or at **Tutti's,** 1209 Coast Village Road, Montecito. (805) 969–5809. A bright, airy local breakfast hangout, great for huge fresh muffins, pancakes, waffles, and such. Quite busy.

You're in the heart of lively **Coast Village Road,** an intimate, tree-shaded strip of posh cafes, galleries, wine shops, designer boutiques, and long-legged blonds driving gleaming Jaguars and Ferraris. After browsing the shops, take the time to drive around the residential section of affluent **Montecito,** where the wealthy people drawn to Santa Barbara during the 1890s established their luxurious estates. The millionaire migration included Rockefeller, Carnegie, Du Pont, McCormick, Cudahy, and other barons of industry, who built palatial vacation mansions in Montecito's rolling woodlands. For the scenic hillside drive, take Olive Mill Road at the end of Coast Village Road to Alameda Padre Serra. Along "APS" the famed Riviera view is a photogenic panorama over the city that reaches to the palm trees along the beachfront. Then drive back to the ocean for lunch.

Lunch: **Citronelle,** 901 Cabrillo Boulevard (in the Santa Barbara Inn), Santa Barbara. (800) 231–0431. Opened in 1991 by Michel Richard (owner-chef of Citrus, in Los Angeles), the restaurant has become a gourmet choice for signature dishes favoring scallops with sautéed Maui onions, inspired desserts, and stunning harbor views.

Afternoon

At oceanside on West Cabrillo Boulevard, the **yacht harbor and breakwater,** home to around 1,200 pleasure and working craft, grab your attention with strikingly colored flags flapping high overhead. The broad, paved walkway atop the breakwater offers a scenic 0.5-mile walking tour around the harbor, the Yacht Club, marine stores, and restaurants, along with fine views of surfers and boats. This is the departure point for shoreline tour boats and sportfishing excursions, as well as a source of boats for rent and charter.

There's More

Farmer's Market each Tuesday and Saturday is a fun place to shop. Local growers sell fruits, vegetables, nuts, eggs, flowers, and plants at reasonable prices, with puppet shows and other entertainment enlivening the scene. The Tuesday market takes place in the 500 block of State Street from 3:00 to 5:30 P.M.; the Saturday market—larger and more crowded—is held at the corner of Santa Barbara and Cota streets from 8:30 A.M. till noon. For information call (805) 963–0303.

Boating, sailing, and fishing opportunities are at the breakwater. The Sailing Center of Santa Barbara (800–350–9090) specializes in sailing classes, boat rentals, and coastal and whale-watching cruises.

Golf. You can hit the sticks at two 18-hole municipal courses open for daily play:

Santa Barbara Golf Club, Las Positas Road and McCaw Avenue. (805) 687–7087. Bordering the Earl Warren Showgrounds.

Sandpiper Golf Course, 7925 Hollister Avenue, Goleta. (805) 968–1541.

Tennis. Use permits are required, obtainable at the courts or at the Recreation Department, 820 Laguna Street (805–568–5418). Lighted courts include Las Positas Municipal Courts, 1002 Las Positas Road (six courts). Nonlighted courts include Municipal Courts, 414 Park Place (twelve courts), and Pershing Park Courts, near the intersection of Cabrillo Boulevard and Costillo Street (eight courts). All in Santa Barbara.

Hang gliding. Keep a lookout for the daring hang gliders near the bluffs at Arroyo Burro Beach. The Hang Gliders Emporium, 613 Milpas Street, Santa Barbara (805–965–3733), gives lessons.

Whale-watching. Track the big grays off the coast during their southward migration to Baja, mid-November through March, and again when they head back north, during February, March, and April. Best viewing spots are along the bluffs at Shoreline Park. Several commercial charters offer cruises, among them Sea Landing (805–963–3564). Santa Barbara.

Polo. Santa Barbara Polo and Racquet Club, 3375 Foothill Road Carpenteria. (805) 684–8667. Polo games/matches every Sunday, April through October, at 1:00 P.M.; feature match at 3:00 P.M. Admission. Phone for information and schedule.

Factory-outlet shopping. Discount shoppers should explore the stores and studios in the bargain districts of downtown State Street (600 and 1100 blocks), the industrial and light manufacturing sections around Haley and Olive streets, and lower Milpas and Salsipuedes streets.

Lotusland, 695 Ashley Road, Santa Barbara. (805) 969–9990. Tucked in the rolling hills of Montecito, the legendary thirty-seven-acre garden estate of opera singer Ganna Waleska features thirteen distinct gardens, displaying botanical environments from all parts of the world, including dramatic and exotic trees and the famed lotus-and-water-lilies pool. Two-hour docent-led tours from mid-February to mid-November are by advance reservation only. Admission.

Special Events

January 1. Hang Gliding Festival. Daring local pilots fly in precision contests and demonstrations off the ocean bluffs.

Mid-February. Compadres De Los Gatos All Breed Cat Show.

Early March. International Orchid Show, at Earl Warren Showgrounds. One of the world's most prestigious horticultural events. Santa Barbara International Film Festival. Premieres and screenings of international and U.S. films; citywide festivities.

March. During the entire month from the bluffs along Shoreline Park, you can watch the big gray whales on their northern migration.

Late April. Presidio Days. Three-day celebration of Santa Barbara's birthday and multiethnic heritage, held at the historical El Presidio.

End of May. I. Madonnari, three-day Italian street painting festival, attracts thousands of visitors and some 200 local artists, who get on their knees to create vibrant chalk paintings on the pavement of the Old Mission courtyard terrace. Enjoyable authentic Italian marketplace; Italian cuisine specialty dishes.

End of June. Santa Barbara Writer's Conference, Miramar Hotel (805–684–2250). Week-long creative writing workshop; lectures by best-selling authors. Summer Solstice Parade on State Street. A spectacular—with costumes, dancers, and music.

July 4. Independence Day Festivities. Parade, special arts and crafts show at the mission.

Late July to early August. Old Spanish Days (fiesta). Santa Barbara's biggest event, begun in 1926. A five-day festival, featuring a grand parade with gaily decorated horse-drawn carriages; Spanish marketplaces; and carnival, rodeo, and dancers.

Mid-August. Santa Barbara Museum of Natural History Wine Festival. Food and music in charming creekside setting.

Late September. Santa Barbara Concours d'Elegance. Antique and classic car show.

Early October. Santa Barbara International Jazz Festival.

Late November. Santa Barbara National Amateur Horse Show.

Early December. Christmas Parade. Costumes and floats.

Mid-December. Yuletide Boat Parade. Off Stearns Wharf.

Other Recommended Restaurants and Lodgings

Santa Barbara

Oyster's, 9 West Victoria Street. (805) 962–9888. Attractive, with open kitchen and menu posted outside to scan; specializes in oysters in many variations. Other entrees include grilled chicken and pastas. Lunch and dinner Monday through Saturday; Sunday dinner only.

Four Seasons Biltmore, 1260 Channel Drive. (805) 969–2261. A hands-down winner for consistently good food, elegantly presented. Try the ocean-view Patio terrace for lunch and buffet dinner, La Sala Lounge for high tea and the famed Biltmore Brunch, and La Marina for romantic candlelight dining. (Pricey.)

Soho, 21 Victoria Street. (805) 963–5497. A comfy yuppie hangout, with a varied California cuisine menu. Live jazz. Lunch Monday through Friday; dinner nightly. Reservations recommended.

The Harbor Restaurant, 210 Stearns Wharf. (805) 963–3311. At the end of the wharf, it's just right for grilled fish, salads, steaks, and cocktails while you enjoy some of the best views of Santa Barbara. Lunch and dinner daily; Sunday Champagne brunch.

Fess Parker's Red Lion Resort, 633 East Cabrillo Boulevard. (800) 879–2929. On the boulevard across from the beach and sprawled over twenty-four acres, each of the 360 rooms and 24 suites has a private patio and minibar. Concierge service, swimming pool, Jacuzzi, gym, sauna, three lighted tennis courts, putting green, two restaurants, and lounge.

Montecito Inn, 1295 Coast Village Road (800) 843–2017. Charming small hotel with European ambience; built by Charlie Chaplin and friends in the 1920s. Located 2 blocks from the beach; well-furnished rooms (some have refrigerator and VCR) and nice bathrooms, swimming pool, Jacuzzi, sauna, exercise room, complimentary bikes, and trolley passes. Additionally, complimentary continental breakfast is served in lobby. Good restaurant/cafe.

For More Information

Santa Barbara Conference and Visitors Bureau, 510 State Street, Santa Barbara, CA 93102. (800) 927–4688. Ask for destination guide.

Hot Spot, 36 State Street, in the Visitor Center. (800) 793–7666; (805) 564–1637. For free reservations and information about lodgings, attractions and events.

Solvang and the Santa Ynez Valley Wine Country

Solvang's windmills are delightful Old World sights.

Windmills and Wineries

1 NIGHT

Historic villages • Shopping • Mission • Lake boating and fishing • Golf
Horseback riding • Ethnic dining • Open-air theater

This two-day itinerary takes you north to "Little Denmark," where windmills spin lazily in blue skies in a fairytale village of curving streets lined with shops and cafes. You'll visit and tour wineries in acres of vineyards flourishing in rural Santa Ynez Valley, which has become one of California's richest grape-growing and winemaking regions, and you'll visit small, quiet pioneer villages that haven't quite marked the turn of the past century.

Day 1

Morning

Drive north from Los Angeles on Ventura Freeway 101 about 132 miles to Solvang, the delectable smorgasbord of Denmark tucked in the peaceful Santa Ynez Valley of rich farmlands and vineyards, located less than an hour past Santa Barbara.

Follow 101 through dramatic Gaviota Pass, with its soaring cliffs; go through the tunnel; and continue past the turnoff for splendid Nojoqui Falls Park, named for the 164-foot waterfall and including a playground and picnic area. Take the Buellton/Solvang exit, turn right onto Highway 246, and continue for about 5 miles to Solvang.

Lunch: **Greenhouse Cafe,** 457 Atterdag Road, Solvang. (805) 688–8408. In the heart of the village, with delightful garden patio. Select from the varied menu of Danish and American dishes, or savor the house specialties: *aebleskiver*—the toothsome, ball-shaped waffle—and those thin Danish pancakes. Breakfast is served all day. Open daily from 10:00 A.M. to 8:00 P.M.

Afternoon

After lunch explore Solvang's sunny streets with their brightly colored buildings and brick and cobblestone sidewalks. Danish half-timbered farm-style buildings have tall, steeply pitched roofs of simulated thatch or heavy shake shingles adorned with weather vanes, dormer windows, steeples, and hand-carved storks. Gas streetlamps glow in the evening, and buildings are outlined with tiny lights.

"The Danish Capital of America" has a storybook quality, as you stroll past fairytale murals on building facades and tall, country-style windmills that creak in the soft breezes. Some windmills house gift-shops or restaurants, and all provide ideal photo opportunities.

Solvang's inviting streets are lined with more than 200 tempting shops, whose open Dutch doors reveal arrays of fine imports, including crystal, pewter, porcelain, handcrafted candles, antiques, and clocks. You'll find dolls, trolls, leather fashions, music boxes, Old World bakeries, and famous designer names such as Royal Copenhagen, Dansk, Georg Jensen, Hummel, and Rosenthal.

Appealing restaurants and bubbling sidewalk cafes with colorful umbrellas offer great dining variety. You'll never have a better opportunity to enjoy authentic Danish specialties such as *gravlax,* smorgasbord, *frikadiller* (Danish meatballs), *bof med log* (chopped beef with onions), and don't overlook *smorrebrod,* the hefty Danish open-face sandwich that can feed a small battalion. Additionally, change-of-pace menus offer American, Italian, Mexican, continental, and even Chinese cuisine. Many Solvang restaurants close between lunch and dinner (usually 3:00 to 5:00 P.M.), European fashion; most have menus posted outside.

Solvang, meaning "Sunny Field," was founded in 1911 by a group of Midwest Danish educators who wanted to establish a Danish colony and folk school to preserve their culture and traditions in an area where settlers could farm the rich soil. Other pioneers included carpenters and workers who built the first buildings and school. The strong Danish heritage is evident in local customs and holidays. The lively Danish Days, held the third full weekend in September is when the city celebrates its Old World ties. Residents dress in Danish costume and prepare, cook, and serve traditional *aebleskiver* and sausage on the streets. There is entertainment, music, dancing, and parades.

Along Copenhagen Drive, on the corner of Alisal Road, **Rasmussen's** (1697), with wide arches and a tall roof steeple—the oldest, most complete department store in town—is known for Swedish crystal, Danish porcelain, handmade sweaters, gift items, and kitchenware. **Danish Village Gifts** (1683) features gourmet cookware and Royal Copenhagen dishes. The **Blue Windmill,** at Hamlet Square, has a fine assortment of T-shirts. You don't get to shop in a windmill every day, so explore the large one on Alisal Road; it's filled with a variety of gift items, many suspended from its tall ceiling.

On Mission Drive, the **Ugly Duckling** (1557), where music announces your entrance, is filled with gnomes, dolls, and amusing items. The **Jul Hus,** at 1580 Mission Drive, is Solvang's most unusual store, selling only Christmas merchandise year-round. This festive store where you hear Christmas music is filled with a large assortment of Christmas ornaments and decorations, toys, nutcrackers, music boxes, and the Dickens Ceramic Houses surrounding a fully trimmed Christmas tree with twinkling lights.

Stop by any of the city's six **bakeries** where they use Old Country, centuries-old recipes for favorite pastries. Don't overlook the popular, large, pretzel-shaped *Kringler,* filled with almond paste and raisins, topped with sliced almonds and drifts of sugar, and big as a suitcase. Small, friendly **Solvang Park,** at the corner of Mission Drive and First Street, is where Solvangers picnic and relax on the grass alongside the bust of Hans Christian Andersen, Denmark's prince of fairytales, in his famous top hat. You'll also find the *Little Mermaid,* a small replica of the famous bronze sculpture in Copenhagen's harbor, perched atop a rock and fountain at the corner of Mission Drive and Alisal Road.

Cross the street to visit the **Hans Christian Andersen Museum,** in the Book Loft Building, 1680 Mission Drive (805–588–2052), which honors the noted Danish fairytale writer, Denmark's favorite son and most famous figure. The small museum upstairs in the bookstore's loft is filled with copies of Andersen's beautifully illustrated books, many photos, letters, and memorabilia, including photographs of the beautiful singer Jenny Lind, the "Swedish Nightingale" with whom Andersen was said to have been hopelessly in love. This tall, stringy, long-nosed man wrote 156 fairytales and was greatly honored during his lifetime. The museum is open daily to 5:00 P.M. and is always accessible through the **Book Loft** (closed Monday). Browse the bookstore's wide selection of current, used, and collector's classics.

Drive or walk to the **Old Mission Santa Inés,** 1760 Mission Drive, established in 1804, the nineteenth of the twenty-one California missions and one of the best preserved and restored—it still celebrates daily mass. The graceful old parish church, with its beautiful gardens around a large fountain, evokes the valley's Spanish missionary beginnings. Join a guided tour or explore on your own through the Chapel of the Madonnas, which has the original worn tile floors, a 29-foot-high beamed ceiling, and hand-painted wall murals. The museum displays extensive artifacts of the Chumash Indian mission era; the giftshop shows religious artifacts and pottery. Frequently called the "Mission of the Passes," Santa Inés is the focus of many yearly events in the Santa Ynez Valley. (Open daily, 9:30 P.M. to 4:30 P.M.; admission.)

An easy, fun way to get around town is to ride the popular **Surrey Bike**—a four-wheel cycle with a red surrey on top and all passengers pedaling together like the Radio City Rockettes down the curving streets. Other offbeat sightseeing includes a twenty-minute narrated tour around town aboard Solvang's *Honen,* replica of an authentic Danish streetcar of the 1900s that is pulled by two massive, blond Belgian horses. Board at Mission and Alisal Road, daily during the summer season and weekends during the winter (fee). Romantics can see the city in an open, horse-drawn white carriage anytime from 3:00 to 5:00 P.M.; board it off Copenhagen and 1st Street.

Dinner: **Bit O' Denmark,** 473 Alisal Road, Solvang. (805) 688–5426. Start your own tradition at the oldest restaurant in town. This lovely, warm restaurant, offering fine food and service, features a gourmet Danish smorgasbord feast with an extensive variety of hot and cold delectables, plus American entrees.

Lodging: **Petersen Village Inn,** 1576 Mission Drive, Solvang, CA 93463. (800) 321–8985. AAA four-diamond rating. Discover Old World flavor in each of the forty spacious individually decorated suites, with canopied beds, antique and period furniture, TV, and turndown service. Cafe; complimentary European buffet breakfast served in dining room; wine-and-cheese hospitality in the lounge from 6:00 to 7:00 P.M.

Day 2

Morning

Breakfast: At the inn. Beautifully presented, generous complimentary buffet in the dining room includes juice, coffee, Danish pastry, rolls, ham, and cheese.

After breakfast select foods for a picnic lunch at the wineries by stopping at the **Solvang Market and Deli,** corner of 5th Street and Mission (805–688–6117). You'll find extensive deli items, buckets of chicken, and BBQ foods on weekends.

There's a mystique and romance about wine associated with the pleasurable and better things in life. The experience is enriched by driving along the peaceful backcountry roads of **Santa Ynez Valley,** with its natural beauty of pastures and orchards and acres of lush vineyards. As you visit the unpretentious wineries and unchanged, hundred-year-old villages, you are far removed from the daily bustle.

Pick up a "Santa Barbara County Wineries" map from your hotel or the Solvang Visitor Bureau (1511 Mission Drive) and follow the wine route. This one-night itinerary doesn't visit all the wineries, as you won't have sufficient time unless you plan to stay over another night, but you might mark the rest for a return visit to Solvang.

From Solvang take Highway 246 to Refugio Road; turn right and it's 1 mile to **Santa Ynez Winery,** 343 Refugio Road, Santa Ynez (805–688–8381). This family-owned winery was the first commercial vineyard planted in Santa Ynez, in 1974. With one hundred acres planted in thirteen varietals, the most popular are Chardonnay and Riesling. Tastings and self-guided tours are available from 10:00 A.M. to 5:00 P.M. daily. There are a giftshop and a picnic area.

After your wine tasting and tour, continue to the sleepy little town of **Santa Ynez,** founded in 1882. There's not much traffic in its 2-block-long business center. Drop by the **Santa Ynez Historical Museum,** on Sagunto Street and Farady (805–688–7889), where eight rooms ramble around a shady courtyard. Immerse yourself in early California history and memorabilia. The Indian Room exhibits a diorama of Chumash Indian life; the Pioneer Room displays turn-of-the-century furnishings; and the West Room shows saddles, guns, and other items. (Open Friday through Sunday, 1:00 to 4:00 P.M.)

Parks-Janeway Carriage House, part of the museum, displays about thirty-five gleaming carriages that seem right out of western movies, including the "Wells Fargo" and the "United States Mail"; silver-mounted saddles and many other items are here too, as is a gift-shop. (Open Tuesday through Thursday from 8:00 A.M. to 4:00 P.M. and Sunday from 1:00 to 4:00 P.M.)

From Santa Ynez take Edison Road north, turning left at Baseline Avenue to **Ballard,** the valley's oldest and first town, founded in 1880. Turn right on Cottonwood Street to see its landmark, two-room little red schoolhouse, set back on a broad lawn shaded by two ancient trees. The school has been in continuous use since its dedication in 1883.

From Ballard continue a few miles on 154 through a soft country-side of apple orchards, farmhouses, and ranches to **Los Olivos,** which has a flagpole in the center of the main street. Once a major Butter-field stagecoach stop, the town, with its many resident artists, has evolved into a fine-arts center for the Santa Ynez Valley. Visit historic **Mattie's Tavern** on Highway 154, built in 1896 as an overnight inn and still a warm, intimate restaurant for fine dining.

After driving around Los Olivos, go back through Ballard, turning right on Edison Road to Highway 246 to the **Gainey Vineyard,** 3950 East Highway 246 (3 miles east of Solvang), Santa Ynez (805–688–0558). This family-owned winery, begun in 1984, sits atop the family's 1,800-acre ranch. Gainey is one of the most visitor-oriented and popular facilities and features the largest tasting room in the area and good-size picnic gardens. The 12,000-square-foot winery and visitor center are surrounded by sixty-five acres of premium vari-etal grapes, producing Chardonnay, Sauvignon Blanc, Pinot Noir, Mer-lot, Johannisberg Riesling, and Cabernet Sauvignon. Daily tastings are from 10:00 A.M. to 5:00 P.M., with a $2.50 charge to taste four major va-rietals; the logo glass is your souvenir. The giftshop sells T-shirts and giftpacks.

Afternoon

Lunch: Picnic at **Gainey Vineyard.** To visit more wineries, go east on Highway 246 to 154; turn left, staying on Highway 154 to 101; then turn right on Zaca Station Road and left up the hill to **Firestone Vine-yard,** 5017 Zaca Station Road, Los Olivos (805–688–3940), the largest winery in the valley. The impressive building sits atop 260 acres of es-tate vineyards and is augmented by an attractive garden patio, a foun-tain, and picnic tables. The twenty-minute tours begin in the vineyard, go to the fermentation room, and then end in the large tasting room. Sampling is of Firestone's most popular varietals: Riesling, dry Riesling, Johannisberg Riesling, and a Merlot Rosé available only at the winery.

The giftshop features logo T-shirts, totebags, and wine accessories.

After sampling the wines, turn left on Zaca Station Road; continue on it until the name changes to Foxen Canyon, about 3 miles, to **Fess Parker Winery,** 6200 Foxen Canyon Road, Los Olivos (805–688–1545). The winery sales and tasting room opened in February 1992, though the first release was in 1989. The 714-acre ranch has 31 acres planted in Chardonnay, Johannisberg Riesling, Sirah, and Merlot. Tasting is from 10:00 A.M. to 4:00 P.M. in the barrel room, with a $2.00 fee for tasting three or four wines; you keep the logo glass. If celebrity owner Fess Parker is around, he'll autograph a bottle of wine for you.

Carey Cellars, 2.5 miles north of Highway 246, at 1711 Alamo Pintado Road, Solvang (805–688–8554), is framed by mountains and beautiful old trees and surrounded by twenty-three acres of estate vineyards. The winery was established by a family of doctors who refurbished an old dairy barn into a winery and had their first harvest in 1978. After Firestone Vineyards purchased the enterprise in 1987, the facilities were upgraded; Kate Firestone is now vintner. Carey's tasting room is in a small, rustic farmhouse with a homey front porch and a picnic area. The winery is open daily from 10:00 A.M. to 4:00 P.M. for visitors to sample its four varietals: Chardonnay, Sauvignon Blanc, Cabernet Blanc, and Cabernet Sauvignon.

To return to Los Angeles, get back on Highway 246 through Buellton/Solvang and pick up Highway 101 south.

There's More

Bethania Lutheran Church, 603 Atterdag Road, Solvang. Built in 1928, the Danish-style, rural church reflects tradition, with its replica of a fully rigged ship suspended symbolically from the ceiling. Regular Sunday worship; Danish services once a month.

Elverhoy Museum, 1624 Elverhoy Way, Solvang. (805) 686–1211. On a quiet residential street, this Danish-style farmhouse cultural museum is very browsable. Gallery and period rooms depict Solvang's pioneer past with early photos, antique furnishings, and artifacts. Open Wednesday through Sunday from 1:00 to 4:00 P.M.

Hans Christian Andersen Park, on Atterdag Road, 3 blocks north of Mission Drive, Solvang. The creekside rustic setting is relaxing for fun, picnics, and barbecues. A great place to enjoy a variety of picnic items—sandwiches, salads, and deli fare you've picked up earlier. Children's playground, and tennis courts are here too.

Festival Theatre, 2nd and Oak streets. (800) 549–7272. The Pacific Conservatory of the Performing Arts (PCPA) Theaterfest presents six plays in repertory under the stars, June through mid-October, in

Solvang's 780-seat, open-air theater-in-the-round. Inquire about hotel-theater-dinner packages.

Factory Outlets. (800) 468–4765. More than thirty factory outlets for discount shopping in fashion, home furnishings and more are located on different streets in the village. Open daily.

Solvang's Designer Outlets Center is on Alisal Road. (805) 686–9522.

Cachuma Lake and recreation area, 12 miles east of Solvang. If you're a fisherman, like to camp or go boating and hiking, and enjoy other year-round outdoor recreation, this 8-mile-long lake and environs are for you. Snackbar, general store. Admission per car. Guided "Eagle Cruises" November through February; "Wildlife Cruises" conducted year-round. Reservations: (805) 568–2640.

Golf. River Course at The Alisal, 150 Alisal Road, Solvang. (805) 688–6042. Along the Santa Ynez River; open to the public as well as guests of the Alisal Guest Ranch and Resort next door. The naturally scenic championship course features driving range, practice greens, and full-service pro shop. The River Grill Restaurant, in the rugged Clubhouse setting, with large patio overlooking the rolling greens is the perfect spot for relaxing after a round of golf or for breakfast, lunch, and dinner.

Special Events

End of February. Storytelling Festival. (805) 688–9533. International stories in a twelve-hour period, Solvang Royal Scandinavian Inn.

Early March. Solvang/Santa Maria Century Bike Ride. (310) 943–9440. One-hundred-mile bike ride.

Mid-March. Annual Taste of Solvang. Food festival weekend, live entertainment.

Mid-April. Solvang Custom Knife Show, Solvang Royal Scandinavian Inn. (805) 688–3612. Annual Easter Egg Hunt, Hans Christian Andersen Park. Easter Sunday Children's Parade.

End of April. Santa Barbara County Vintner's Festival. (805) 688–0881. Wine, food, and entertainment. Santa Ynez Valley Carriage Classic. (805) 688–4454. Exhibitors and celebrity guests.

Early May. Los Rancheros Visitadores Annual Santa Ynez Valley Trek. Riders parade through Solvang. Cinco de Mayo celebration, Mission Santa Inés. (805) 688–9533. A 10K run and day-long entertainment. Gourmet Century Bike Ride. (805) 688–6385. One hundred miles around Santa Ynez Valley.

May 18–19. Pepper Tree Art Show and Barbecue. (805) 688–6205.

Early June. Old Santa Ynez Days. (805) 688–3093. Celebrate the town's birthday in Old West style; cowboys, food, entertainment, parade.

July 4. Solvang's Fourth of July Parade.

Mid-August. Old Mission Santa Inés Fiesta. (805) 688–4815. Festive weekend of food and fun, mariachi folklorico dancing and entertainment.

Third weekend in September. Danish Days Festival. (805) 686–9380. Celebrate Solvang's Danish heritage; dancing, music, food, fun.

Mid-October. Day in the Country, Los Olivos. (805) 688–5083. Vintner's Association Wine Harvest, Rancho Sisquoc. Celebration of harvest.

Early November. Solvang Prelude. Twenty-five and 50-mile bike ride through the beautiful Santa Ynez Valley. Two-Day Pepper Tree Art Show.

Mid-November. Dixieland Jazz Festival, Solvang Royal Scandinavian Inn. Music, food, and fun.

End of November through December. Winterfest in Solvang.

Early December. Christmas Tree Lighting and Window Walk, Hometown Christmas Parade, Winterfest.

Other Recommended Restaurants and Lodgings

Solvang

Mustard Seed, 1655 Mission Drive. (805) 688–1318. Home-style American cooking, featuring sandwiches, salads, soups, and daily specials. Patio dining. Closed between lunch and dinner.

Mollekroen, 435 Alisal Road. (805) 688–4555 Across from the post office; walk upstairs to the large, sunny dining room for hearty Danish smorgasbord, including meatballs, herring, red cabbage, cold cuts, and fruit; plus American menu.

Paula's Pancake House, 1531 Mission Drive. (805) 688–2867. Popular for good food. Extensive breakfast and lunch menu features thin Danish pancakes, waffles, eggs, homemade soups, salads, and burgers. Patio dining, closed from 3:00 P.M.

Alisal Guest Ranch, 1054 Alisal Road. (805) 688–6411. Three miles down the road from city center. There's a genuine western flavor to this 10,000-acre, upscale dude ranch. Seventy-three well-furnished bungalows with studio rooms and two-bedroom suites feature wood-burning fireplace, coffeemaker, wetbar, refrigerator with icemaker. No TV, radio, or telephone mars your peaceful escape. Play golf on the

18-hole championship course, where deer watch you tee off. Heated swimming pool and spa, seven tennis courts, riding stable, private lake for fishing and boating, library, recreation/TV room, dining room, lounge with evening entertainment, conference center. Full breakfast and dinner included in two-night-minimum stay. Seasonal packages.

Danish Country Inn, 1455 Mission Drive. (800) 44–RELAX; (805) 688–2018. Warmly decorated; eighty-two minisuites with refrigerator, cable TV, video player, and hair dryer. Full complimentary farm-fresh breakfast in the attractive dining room; manager's cocktail reception.

Tivoli Inn, 1564 Copenhagen Drive. (800) 776–1484; (805) 688–0559. Look for the distinctive tall clock tower. Hospitality begins with a welcome basket of fruit and wine and continues with a complimentary continental breakfast in bed. Thirty-five well-designed suites with fireplace, TV, minibar, refrigerator; cafe and pub.

For More Information

Solvang Conference and Visitors Bureau, 1571 Mission Drive, P.O. Box 70, Solvang, CA 93464. (800) 468–6765 (in California), (805) 688–6144. Pick up a handy walking map of the village.

San Luis Obispo/San Simeon/Cambria/Morro Bay

Morro Bay's 576-foot-tall "Gibraltar of the Pacific."

Coastline and a Castle

2 NIGHTS

Mission • Wineries • Farmer's market • Artists' colony • Museum
State university • Castle/mansion • Galleries

This packed, three-day excursion takes you about 200 miles north through California's richly scenic central coast of rolling hills and pastoral land to a lovely, small college town. You'll also stop at a noted winery for a taste of its bubbly product; visit a legendary, art-filled cas-

tle; have lunch in a seaside artists' colony in the pines; and see California's "Gibraltar of the Pacific."

Note: This itinerary visits Hearst Castle in San Simeon, where reservations are required. Tours (about two hours long) are always available and can be reserved anywhere from a few hours to weeks or
months in advance. (At this writing, all tours are $14, except tour 5
evening tours, which is $25. Call (800) 444–4445.)

Day 1

Morning

Leave Los Angeles via Ventura Freeway 101 north, driving through
rural San Fernando Valley. After the turnoff for Ojai, the freeway follows the unruffled, mist-covered ocean. You're soon past Santa Barbara with no congestion, thanks to the revamped freeway, which
bypasses the city. Curving inland, you drive through dramatic Gaviota
Pass, where the road is framed with tall rugged mountains. Exit Buellton (on the outskirts of Solvang) on Avenue of the Flags, a landscaped
parkway decorated with a tall row of American flags waving in the
breeze.

Lunch: **Pea Soup Andersen's,** 376 Avenue of the Flags, Buellton.
(805) 688–5581. The original 1924 home of split pea soup. This large,
very busy restaurant includes pea soup or salad with all sandwiches
and entrees. For those in a hurry, the coffeeshop serves the same food
but has faster service than the dining room. Sunday buffet brunch is
from 11:00 A.M. to 3:00 P.M.

Afternoon

For the nearly 60 miles to San Luis Obispo, continue north on 101
in a tranquil, pastoral countryside where stately old oak trees dance
gracefully over the hillsides. Just past Nipomo and about 3 miles south
of Arroyo Grande, look for the Maison Deutz (rhymes with "Toots")
winery on the right.

The white and blue entry gates of **Maison Deutz,** at 453 Deutz
Drive in Arroyo Grande (805–481–1763), are immediately past the
large winery sign. Maison Deutz offers a range of fine sparkling wines
produced in the *methode champenoise*. Tastings of wines in a full flute
glass, accompanied by appetizers—crackers, cheeses, mustards—are
about $4.00 to $5.00 for each of three wines. Tastings are offered daily
except Tuesdays, from 11:00 A.M. to 5:00 P.M. Guided tours of the winery are by appointment only.

After your visit to the winery, return to Highway 101 north to San Luis Obispo.

Friendly and hospitable **San Luis Obispo** (say "Lewis," not "Looey") may well be one of the most likable small towns you've visited. Its rather old-fashioned, prosperous downtown area, distinguished by tree-shaded streets, offers a pleasant variety of shopping and dining, with good food served in generous amounts. Fortunately, local restaurants tend to bypass expensive nouvelle cuisine entrees of small portions and barely cooked cauliflower, favoring moderately priced, robust American-style fare instead. The city glows during its summer Mozart Festival; the weekly Farmer's Market is the hottest ticket on a Thursday night; and a rural creek meanders through the city.

Along Higuera Street, the main thoroughfare, stately, well-preserved old buildings add stability and harmony. Many buildings have been attractively recycled. The renovated Golden State Creamery, which closed in 1974, has a new life as a trendy complex for dining and shopping.

Home to California Polytechnic State University, or Cal Poly, this is a walking town. Stroll through the **Network's** skylit arcade, which has ceiling banners, bright shops, and a sandwich bar at the rear, where you tote your order out to the dining patio overlooking San Luis Obispo's picturesque creek. You'll have to go a long way to find a prettier, more natural setting.

To see where the city was founded in 1772, when Father Junípero Serra established **Mission San Luis Obispo de Tolosa,** drive around the corner or walk across the footbridge over the creek. The mission was the fifth in the chain of twenty-one California missions. In the chapel the statues and Stations of the Cross along the walls are all the originals. The first California olive trees still grow in the pleasant mission garden. (Open daily from 10:00 A.M. to 4:00 P.M. in winter and from 9:00 A.M. to 5:00 P.M. in summer, bookstore, giftshop, and museum open daily.)

Mission Plaza, the grassy landscaped area between the mission and San Luis Creek, is the focus of community events and a quiet park of benches and shade trees. Visit the adjacent Community Art Center (open Tuesday through Sunday from noon to 5:00 P.M.) and Children's Museum.

Dinner: **F. McLintocks Saloon and Dining House,** 686 Higuera Street, San Luis Obispo. (805) 541–0686. This western-style saloon, with red-and-white checked tablecloths, long bar, and moose-head decor, is where locals meet to eat and schmooze. Hearty, delicious nightly specials include beef ribs and BBQ chicken as well as hamburgers and BBQ beef sandwiches—and the chili has plenty of authority. Easy prices, large portions, excellent service.

Lodging: **La Cuesta Motor Inn,** 2074 Monterey Street, San Luis Obispo, CA 93401. (800) 543–2777 (in California); (805) 543–2777. Conveniently located, seven-year-old three-story building; seventy-two good-size rooms, bathroom with extra mirrored makeup pullman, ample storage, small balcony, clock radio, TV, dining table and chairs; heated swimming pool, Jacuzzi. Complimentary continental breakfast and afternoon tea and cookies served in the lobby. Friendly, efficient staff.

Day 2

Morning

Breakfast: At the inn. Continental breakfast served in the lobby is included in your room rate. Help yourself to orange juice, coffee, minimuffins, and sliced bagels and cream cheese. You can also tote a tray to your room.

Leave for Hearst Castle, about a 45-mile drive. Drive down Monterey Street to Santa Rosa; turn right to the freeway, taking Highway 1 to San Simeon. Alongside the rolling hills and farms in the peaceful, open country, you become aware of California's grandeur and size. You'll pass several towns to visit on your return—Morro Bay, Harmony, and Cambria, where an array of tall pine trees are raggedy green giants marching in place on the slopes. After a WELCOME TO SAN SIMEON sign where the ocean is as blue as Paul Newman's eyes, Hearst Castle is the next right.

At the visitor center board your tour bus for the fifteen-minute, 5-mile trip to the hilltop castle; the trip is accompanied by an audiotape program. (Tours begin at 8:00 A.M. and leave every ten minutes. The last tour starts at 3:00 P.M. in winter, later in summer.)

Legendary **Hearst Castle,** with its lofty twin towers atop the four-level Spanish-Moorish mansion designed by architect Julia Morgan and built by newspaper publishing tycoon William Randolph Hearst as a summer home between 1919 and 1947, resulted in this magnificent, art-filled, 165-room estate with 127 acres of gardens, pools, and terraces.

It's certainly not your everyday owner-built home, with its thirty-eight bedrooms and thirty-one baths on a quiet hilltop with an ocean view. In a forty-year spending orgy of millions of dollars and repeated forays to Europe, Hearst gathered art objects, Renaissance tapestries, paintings, silver, and ancient carved ceilings from all over.

Entire castles and monasteries were dismantled and shipped stone by stone to San Simeon.

Back in the 1930s Hollywood's star-studded guest list for lavish weekends at the castle included Clark Gable, Charlie Chaplin, John Barrymore, and Greta Garbo, plus Hearst's mistress, actress Marion Davies. There were fabulous costume balls, deluxe barbecues, picnics, and nightly banquets. Those were the golden days of Hollywood. Today's guests take guided tours for a glimpse of the lifestyle of the flamboyant millionaire who, for twenty years, lived in regal splendor atop his private mountain kingdom.

The place is so vast that there are four separate tours to see all of it. Each tour includes the two pools and takes about an hour and three-quarters. Tour 1 is suggested for first-time visitors for an overall look and includes the entire main floor of Casa Grande, a guest cottage, gardens, the outdoor Neptune Pool, the indoor Roman Pool, and the Morning Room, Billiard Room, and Theater.

On tour 1 you'll begin at the serene, 104-foot-long, exquisite marble-faced Neptune Pool filled with pure spring water. Then you'll see the eighteen-room guest cottage where Hearst lived during construction of La Casa Grande (the castle), your next stop.

The baronial, 100-by-42-foot Assembly Hall, where guests gathered for evening cocktails, is the castle's largest room, with Renaissance furnishings and ancient choir stalls. In the 67-foot-long Refectory (dining room)—whose fireplace is large enough to roast a rhinoceros—silk Sienese banners flutter from the 27-foot-high wooden ceiling imported from a sixteenth-century monastery.

The indoor Roman Pool, large enough to float the *Queen Mary,* is made of tiny blue Venetian tiles sprinkled with twenty-two-karat gold leaf. And on and on you go, viewing a mind-boggling collection of priceless art and furnishings, Egyptian pottery, mirrors, statues, and bathrooms with real gold fixtures. At the one-hundred-seat movie theater, you finally get to sit down, to watch a short movie of the good life at the castle, featuring famous stars and celebrities. All in all, it's the kind of place that makes you want to go home and burn the furniture.

Tour 2 covers Casa Grande's upper floors, including the Library, the Gothic Suite and study, the Doge's Suite, the Cloister Rooms, and the Pantry and Kitchen, where all the sumptuous meals were prepared.

Tour 3 guides visitors through the north wing of Casa Grande, three floors of guest suites with marble bathrooms and gold fixtures, and the Casa del Monte guest cottage; a short video is included.

Tour 4 (offered April through October) takes in the extensive gardens, the Wine Cellar, Casa del Mar, the largest guest cottage, and the Neptune Pool dressing rooms.

Tour 5, a two-hour evening tour offered in spring and fall, includes a living history program, with docents dressed as guests and staff; illuminated pools and gardens; and highlights of Casa Grande and Casa del Mar.

All tours except tour 5, are offered at the same fee, and all entail considerable walking and stair climbing; better wear comfortable walking shoes. The castle is open daily, except Thanksgiving, Christmas, and New Year's Day; the busiest season is late spring and summer. Hearst Castle was given to the state of California in 1958 and is a State Historical Monument. Free parking is provided. Reservations are necessary and can be charged to your credit card. Since the castle holds more treasures than King Tut's tomb, toting along a tape recorder will help you bring it all back for future reminiscing. No photo flash or tripods are permitted, however.

Leave Hearst Castle, drive across the highway, and turn right along a narrow road to **Sebastian's General Store and** small **Patio Cafe,** adjacent post office and a Union 76 gas station. Sebastian's, built in 1852, is a State Historical Landmark. In addition to stocking groceries and wines, the store has a small section filled with attractive souvenirs, toys, and postcards half the price of those in the Hearst Castle giftshop.

Return to the highway, turning right (south) on Highway 1, and continue to Cambria, 6 miles down the road. At the Burton Drive traffic signal, turn inland into this small, appealing artists' colony surrounded by pine trees.

Cambria (locals call it "Camm-bria") is frequently compared with Carmel-by-the-Sea but seems more natural, not as cutesy or as thronged with tourists. Be sure to explore both sections of Main Street—East Village, up the hill, and West Village, more in the center of town. For lunch drive up the hill on Main Street to East Village.

Lunch: **Linn's Restaurant, Bakery, & Gift Shop,** 2277 Main Street, Cambria. (805) 927–0371. A big sunny room with a gourmet giftshop and a bakery producing luscious berry pies. Linn's is noted for chicken and beef pot pie served with fruit or green salad. Other tempters include quiche, sandwiches, and Oriental chicken salad.

Afternoon

Cambria's reconverted Victorian buildings of the 1870s house one-of-a-kind shops, cafes, galleries, and lodgings. Besides Main Street, the sidestreets are worth browsing as well. On Bridge Street, **Simple Pleasures** features gifts, ornaments, and folk art for year-round holiday celebrations. **Banbury Cross,** alongside, displays old English decorative items, china, crystal, and linen.

Drive back down Main Street to Cambria's **West Village,** which resembles a faded movie set, with its small stores tucked in pretty cottages of soft colors, towers, dormer windows, and Dutch doors. In this very browsable stretch, you'll find a variety of galleries; antiques, gift, flower, and basket shops; and jeweler's and clothing stores.

The **Soldier Factory,** 789 Main Street (805–927–3804), here since 1973, makes tiny toy soldiers (54-mm size). Close to 800 different tiny military figures, painstakingly modeled and costumed represent various wars, regiments, and so on. The store is open daily from 10:00 A.M. to 5:00 P.M. You'll find the Chamber of Commerce a few doors away, should you need brochures or information.

Across the street, flanked by galleries and cafes, **Gourmet Olives, Etc.,** at 786 Main Street, features twenty varieties of California olives grown nearby and offers free olive and pickle tasting, gourmet foods, homemade chocolates, salsas, and giftpacks.

Return to Highway 1 south. In barely ten minutes turn left at the little town of **Harmony,** population eighteen. The former one-hundred-year-old dairy community is now a one-street artists' colony, with artisans working in the old warehouses. Watch glassblowers at work in Phoenix Studio Art Glass. Next door, Harmony Cellars Wine and Tasting Room, a boutique winery, features handcrafted wines made on the premises. Stop by for a taste—the $1.00 fee to taste seven wines is applied toward your purchase—browse the giftshop inside the winery. Next to the old post office, Hart & Company highlights smart hand-painted wearable art. Be sure to stroll the old brick paths around to the Pottery Works large airy showroom.

The **Old Harmony Pasta Factory** (805–927–5882), in the former creamery building, offers cozy fireplace dining of homemade pastas, chicken, scampi, pizza, wines. Dinner nightly; Sunday Champagne brunch 9:30 A.M. to 2 P.M.

Continue south to **Morro Bay,** where the enormous, 576-foot-high **Morro Rock** (the "Gibraltar of the Pacific") juts out of the water. Take the Main Street exit to the fascinating waterfront of this small fishing village and meander along the Embarcadero, with its shops, art galleries, restaurants, boat activity, and harbor cruises. Watch the players at the giant (16-foot-square) chessboard in **Centennial Park** on the Embarcadero, then take the youngsters to the **Tidelands Children's Park** to clamber on the big sculptures and the Pirate Ship, while you watch the boats in the marina. Afterward, drive back to San Luis Obispo to relax before dinner.

Dinner: **Cafe Roma,** 1819 Osos Street, San Luis Obispo. (805) 541–6800. Near the train depot Roma is consistently praised for Italian specialties and good service in its traditional candlelit dining room. Daily homemade pastas and excellent veal dishes. Lunch Tuesday through Friday; dinner Tuesday through Saturday; closed Sunday and Monday.

Lodging: La Cuesta Motor Inn.

Day 3

Morning

Breakfast: Complimentary continental breakfast served in your hotel. Or try a town favorite: **Louisa's Place,** 964 Higuera Street (805–541–0227), where everything's made from scratch. The specialties are omelets, the hotcakes are saucer-size, and the grilled ham is as tender as a new mother's smile. (Open from 6:00 A.M. to 8:00 P.M. Monday through Saturday and from 8:00 A.M. to 2:00 P.M. Sunday.)

If there's time before leaving for Los Angeles, take a walking tour or two of San Luis Obispo's **Heritage Walks,** which begin in Mission Plaza and cover many historical buildings and areas. A brochure is available from the Chamber of Commerce, 1039 Chorro Street, or inquire at your hotel.

Afternoon

En route home on Highway 1 south, stop for a look at the **Madonna Inn,** with its own freeway exit on Madonna Road. Sprawled across 2,200 acres, each of its 109 rooms is completely different, romantically awash with cupids, hearts, stained glass, and bacchanalia bathrooms. In the lobby twinkling lights cascade over a pink marble balustrade, a rose flowered carpet, and artificial plants and trees. See the powder room, of course, but the pièce de résistance is the waterfall in the men's room.

Retrace your way south to Los Angeles.

There's More

San Luis Obispo County Historical Museum, 696 Monterey Street, San Luis Obispo. (805) 543–0638. Across from the old mission; housed in the 1904 Carnegie Library Building. The museum's photos and artifacts depict the city's development from the Chumash and Salinan Indians through the mission and rancho days and the Victorian era. Open Wednesday through Sunday, 10:00 A.M. to 4:00 P.M.; closed holidays; donations welcome.

Farmer's Market, San Luis Obispo. Festive, popular open-air market is held every Thursday evening (except Thanksgiving Day or if it's raining) from 6:00 to 9:00 P.M. on Higuera Street, between Osos and Nipomo, with streets closed to traffic. Local farmers bring just-picked fruits and vegetables as well as flowers and cider. Restaurateurs barbecue chicken, ribs, and hot dogs on massive outdoor grills; food booths offer pizza, sandwiches, and desserts. There's entertainment too: jugglers, dancers, clowns, and musicians.

Farmer's Market, Veteran's Memorial Building, parking lot on West Main Street, Cambria. Held every Friday, 2:30 to 5:30 P.M., rain or shine. Fresh produce, nuts, flowers, and fun.

The San Luis Obispo Trolley offers free rides, 10:00 A.M. to 5:30 P.M. daily, as it loops through downtown from the Civic Center or Monterey Street.

Farmer's Market, Morro Bay. Every Thursday afternoon, at Young's Giant Food. 2650 North Main Street.

Morro Bay Aquarium and Marine Rehabilitation Center, 595 Embarcadero, Morro Bay. Exhibits include live marine specimens and seals. Open daily, except on Thanksgiving and Christmas. Admission. (805) 772–7647.

Morro Bay Natural History Museum, Morro Bay State Park, Morro Bay. (805) 772–2694. Realistic mammals, other animals, and fish; offers nature video, art gallery, museum store. Open daily except Thanksgiving, Christmas, and New Year's Day. Admission.

Paddlewheeler Bay Cruise, Morro Bay. (805) 772–2257. Daily cruises aboard the *Tiger's Folly;* Sunday Champagne brunch.

Special Events

January. Martin Luther King Weekend. Bird Festival, celebrating the winter bird migration to Morro Bay's Estuary. (800) 231–0592.

Late February. Mardi Gras Street Faire, Mardi Gras Jazz Festival, Pismo Beach.

Mid-April. Mission Plaza Easter Egg Hunt, San Luis Obispo. Easter Egg Hunt, Cambria. Easter Egg Hunt, Del Mar Park, Morro Bay.

Late April. Italian Street Painting Festival, San Luis Obispo.

Mid-May. Cambria Garden Tour, Antique Show, Cambria.

July 4. Fourth of July in Mission Plaza, San Luis Obispo. Picnic and fireworks display, Cambria. Fourth of July celebration, Morro Bay.

July 9–14. KCBX Central Coast Wine Classic, San Luis Obispo.

July 19. Annual Mozart Festival, San Luis Obispo.

August 4. Annual Mozart Festival, San Luis Obispo.

Early September. Central Coast Wine Festival, San Luis Obispo.

Labor Day Weekend. Pinedorado Parade and Fair, Cambria. Since 1948.

Late September. Morro Bay Triathlon. Morro Bay.

Early October. Harbor Festival, with wine and seafood. Tallship *Californian* Annual Visit, Morro Bay.

Late November. Merchants Christmas Faire, Morro Bay.

Early December. Christmas in the Plaza, San Luis Obispo. Lighted boat parade with visiting Tallships participating, Morro Bay.

December 6–24. Decemberfest, San Luis Obispo.

Other Recommended Restaurants and Lodgings

San Luis Obispo

Apple Farm Restaurant, 2015 Monterey Street. (800) 225–2040; (805) 544–6100. A breakfast winner for home-style buttermilk pancakes, Belgian waffles, fresh muffins. Lunch and dinner American-style entrees include sandwiches, chicken and dumplings, turkey, fresh seafood, salad bar. Top it all off with hot apple dumplings and fruit cobbler. Early Bird dinners from 2:00 to 5:00 P.M. daily. Best to reserve for all meals.

Linnaeas Cafe, 1110 Garden Street. (805) 541–5888. A young hangout, with garden dining, for offbeat salads, soups, and burritos. Open daily, 7:30 A.M. to midnight.

Buone Tavola, 1037 Monterey Street, San Luis Obispo. (805) 545–8000. Next to the Fremont Theater downtown. A steady winner for northern Italian cuisine, featuring all your favorite dishes.

Mango's, 1023 Chorro, San Luis Obispo. (805) 781–8306. A convenient location next to the mission; for popular Mexican specialties.

Apple Farm Inn and Trellis Court, 2015 Monterey Street. (800) 374–3705; (805) 544–2040. Victorian-style, 101-room hotel, with fireplaces and country decor. Complimentary coffee, TV, radio, terry robes, turndown service, and souvenir gift. Heated swimming pool, spa; country store, restaurant, giftshop, working Mill House. Seasonal rates.

Quality Suites, 1631 Monterey Street. (805) 541–5001. Has 138 two-room suites, each with two TVs, VCR, microwave, stereo, honor bar, refrigerator; complimentary cooked-to-order breakfast; swimming pool, spa.

Cambria

The Brambles Dinner House, 4005 Burton Drive. (805) 927–4716. West Village. The small red cottage was built in 1874 as a family residence. Everything is homemade in this multi-award-winning restaurant. Medium-priced entrees feature prime rib, grilled steaks, smoked ribs, fresh seafood, English trifle. Open Sunday through Friday from 4:00 to 9:30 P.M., and Saturday from 4:00 to 10:00 P.M.; Sunday Champagne brunch served from 9:30 A.M. to 2:00 P.M. Early Bird specials. Reservations suggested.

Cambria Pines Lodge, 2905 Burton Drive. (800) 455–6868; (805) 927–4200. Landmark lodge of 120 rooms on twenty-five hilltop acres in a rustic pine setting, with TV and coffeemakers; includes 54 fireplace suites with microwave, wetbar, refrigerator. Indoor heated swimming pool, spa, and sauna; Main Lodge building features restaurant, lounge, giftshop, and conference rooms. Seasonal rates.

For More Information

San Luis Obispo County Visitors & Conference Bureau, 1039 Chorro Street, San Luis Obispo, CA 93401. (800) 634–1414. Open 8:00 A.M. to 5:00 P.M. Free brochure.

Cambria Chamber of Commerce, 767 Main Street, Cambria, CA 93428. (805) 927–3624. Hearst Castle tickets available.

San Simeon Chamber of Commerce, P.O. Box 1, San Simeon, CA 93452. (805) 927–3500.

Morro Bay Chamber of Commerce, 895 Napa Suite #A1, Morro Bay, CA 93442. (800) 231–0592 (in California); (805) 772–4467.

Mozart Concerts, San Luis Obispo. (805) 781–3008.

Eastern Escapes

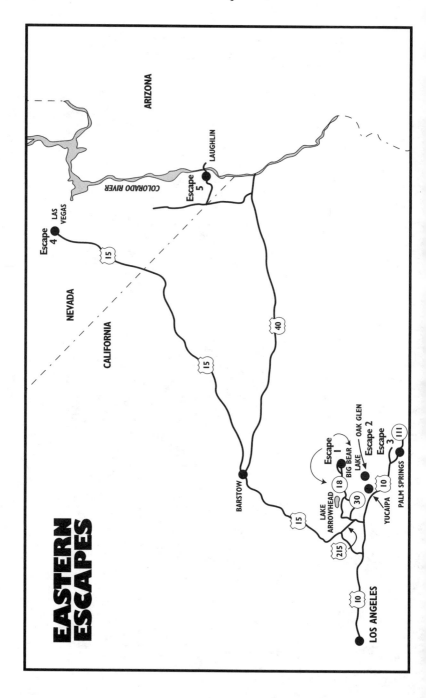

Lake Arrowhead/Big Bear Lake

The *Arrowhead Queen* paddlewheeler cruises the serene lake.

Sun and Snow at Mountain Lakes

___ 2 NIGHTS ___

Lake cruises • Zoo • Mountain biking • Alpine slide • Pine forests
Watersports • Hearty dining • Golf • Skiing and skating • Antiques

This three-day outing in the rugged and scenic San Bernardino Mountains takes you from city noise and traffic to a pair of sparkling, mile-high resort communities. Amid clear, invigorating mountain air and quiet pine forests, you'll find year-round boating, swimming, hiking, fishing, and other outdoor recreations that make these communities so stimulating to visit. The area prides itself on distinctive shopping, hearty mountain dining, and hospitality.

Lake Arrowhead, a bustling summertime getaway, becomes a serene winter wonderland with nearby skiing and snow fun. While **Big Bear Lake** is Southern California's major ski and winter sports center, it is a popular, refreshing destination in all seasons. Both rural cities are easily toured in this change-of-pace itinerary.

Day 1

Morning

For the 90-mile drive up to Lake Arrowhead, your first destination, head east from Los Angeles on I–10 toward San Bernardino, a pleasing drive through rolling countryside toward the majestic mountains. You'll probably find gasoline prices at least 15 cents per gallon higher in the mountains than in Los Angeles, so it's wise to fill your gas tank before leaving the city. Exit at California 215 Junction North/San Bernardino/Barstow. Drive through San Bernardino city and take the Highland Mountain Resorts 30 exit. Follow California 30 east to the Waterman/18 exit. Turn left on California 18 to Lake Arrowhead and ascend toward the mountains as you drive through the San Bernardino National Forest.

The marvelously scenic **Rim of the World Highway** is aptly named, as it climbs and winds around the San Bernardino Mountains up to Lake Arrowhead, at 5,200 feet. The panoramic view over the city is unparalleled as the road climbs and curves. The scenery is stark and indomitable, with tall pines covering the mountainside. Massive sand-colored boulders tower alongside the road, and the mountain air is brilliantly clear and sparkling.

After you pass the turnoffs for the familiar small hamlets of Crestline, Lake Gregory, and Twin Peaks, framed by dense forests, the road narrows and makes a few downhill squiggles. Suddenly, there's the dramatic sight of the gleaming blue Lake Arrowhead, hidden in a dense forest of sky-touching pine trees.

Continue ahead to **Lake Arrowhead Village,** an attractive, bustling, multilevel complex of some eighty shops, galleries, and restaurants sprawling around the lakeshore.

Everything in this friendly, sunny mountain town focuses on the man-made glittering blue lake. Lake Arrowhead, developed in the

1920s, became a glamorous, popular, year-round resort area for sailing and swimming in summer and for skiing in winter. The exclusive North Shore attracted wealthy vacationers and privacy-seeking celebrities. Almost everyone who was "somebody" had a second home in Arrowhead. The studios used the area for frequent movie locations and found the perfect setting for *Heidi,* starring Shirley Temple.

The privately owned, thriving village you see today is, like a Hollywood movie, a remake of the original 1923 community. The village was completely rebuilt in 1979, except for the eye-catching, red-roofed, former 1920s dance pavilion, which was restored as the Theme Building and now houses upscale boutiques.

The lower lakeshore level is the busiest, with its cluster of **shops** and restaurants that snuggle close to the water's edge. The Village Christmas Shop is filled with Christmas merchandise year-round. Just Browsing, the big main store in the village and the largest bookstore on the mountain, is ideal for gifts, mobiles, and postcards. The Village Sweet Shoppe and the Ice Cream Castle keep busy dispensing what you like best. Surrounding stores feature souvenirs, posters, clothing, T-shirts, and gifts; about a dozen factory-outlet stores highlight discounts on national chain items.

Among the Pavilion boutiques, the Leather Shop has leather gifts, wool skirts, silk blouses, and other apparel. The Harvest offers lovely country Americana furnishings of crystal, linens, and pretty afghans. Galleries, restaurants, and stores present still more variety on the traffic-free Peninsula level.

Lake Arrowhead **Children's Museum,** (28200 Highway 189; 909–336–1332), which opened in August 1991 alongside the lake, is for ages twelve and under, who'll enjoy the hands-on exhibits, various activities, and puppet theater. (Closed Monday and holidays; admission.)

Lunch: **Arriba Mexican Restaurant,** Lake Arrowhead. (909) 337–2572. In the Village here's an ever-popular lakefront favorite for hearty Mexican specialties. The lunch bunch goes for the daily chicken and fish specials in the dining room or on the sunny lakeside patio.

Afternoon

Cruising Lake Arrowhead is a memorable way to appreciate the beauty and serenity of the lake in its forest setting. During a one-hour narrated **cruise** aboard the sixty-passenger paddlewheeler *Arrowhead Queen,* your captain points out historical sites and landmarks. (No drink or food sold aboard: hourly departures from 10:00 A.M. to 6:00 P.M.; purchase tickets at Leroy's Sports Store.)

After your delightful cruise around the lake, take a short drive to **Blue Jay Village** to explore its many shops, restaurants and its ice-skating rink. Drive uphill from Lake Arrowhead Village; turn right past the Lake Arrowhead Resort on Highway 189 for about 1.5 miles, along a quiet country road where chalet-style homes are sheltered among tall trees.

In Blue Jay Village, Front Street's row of stores includes Jensen's Finest Foods gourmet supermarket, Vicki O-O's dress shop, Pat's General Store, and many other specialty shops and restaurants. Across the highway you'll find Thrifty Drug store and a strip of choice dining places.

On your return to Lake Arrowhead Village, stop at the **Ice Castle** skating rink, 27307 Highway 189 (909–337–SKATE), in Blue Jay. In this Olympic-size, covered outdoor skating center, you're apt to find a hundred or more ice skaters gliding effortlessly across the rink to lilting music. Even if you don't skate, it's fun to watch, and visitors are welcome. Many famous professional and amateur skaters practice here. (Skate rentals, snackbar, and pro shop; open year-round; admission.)

You shouldn't miss **Santa's Village** amusement park, in Skyforest (909–337–2481). It's about five minutes from the lake and appeals to the child in most of us. Head out of Lake Arrowhead Village to the Rim of the World Highway; turn left and continue east about 2 miles on Highway 18. Look for the two giant candy canes flagging the narrow highway entrance.

Santa and storybook friends welcome visitors in an enchanting outdoor forest fantasyland of little rainbow-colored picture-book houses tucked beneath tall pines. Christmas music and Disney movie songs fill the air. Besides a petting zoo, children enjoy a variety of thirteen rides, especially the giant Bumble Bee monorail that brushes lofty treetops. You'll also find toy shops, unusual Christmas ornaments, a bakery, and souvenirs. (Open daily, 10:00 A.M. to 5:00 P.M., from mid-June through mid-September and from mid-November through December; closed Christmas Day. Open weekends and holidays all other months, weather permitting. Admission includes unlimited rides.

Dinner: **The Barkley** in Lake Arrowhead Resort, 27984 Highway 189, Lake Arrowhead. (800) 800–6792; (909) 336–1511. A large, comfortable room; rich, burgundy-hued canopies over the plants match the burgundy tablecloths. Choice dinner entrees besides New York steak and prime rib include broiled half-chicken served with soup or salad, hot muffin, baked or fried potatoes; Southwestern Pasta Chicken and Rotelli is zesty with tomato, and tomatillo atop cilantro.

Lodging: **Lake Arrowhead Resort,** 27984 Highway 189, Lake Arrowhead, CA 92352. (800) 800–6792. Adjacent to the village, sprawled along the lakeshore, and featuring a private swimming beach and fishing dock, plus 261 luxurious rooms, suites, and villas, this is the largest hotel on the mountain. Heated swimming pool, health and fitness spa; two restaurants; other recreational activities. Sunday buffet brunch.

Day 2

Morning

Breakfast: At your hotel. Or opt for **Belgian Waffle Works** (909–337–5222), in the village at the edge of the lake, for delectable waffles and croissant sandwiches. Try the fruit waffle with strawberries and sliced bananas topped with whipped cream.

Leave for Big Bear Lake by driving out of Lake Arrowhead Village; turn left to Rim of the World Highway 18, and continue for about 26 miles. The road zigzags to Big Bear Lake, curving down the heroic San Bernardino Mountains; past Running Springs, which has many roadside stores; and past forests and Green Valley Lake. Massive boulders loom on both sides of the highway. The road winds and curves, the air is very clear, and the forest trees march tall on buff-colored slopes. You'll spot the sign to Big Bear Lake to the right and then glimpse the placid blue lake in its travel-brochure setting beneath tall pine trees.

Big Bear Lake is considered a premier year-round recreation area because of its variety of activities for outdoor enthusiasts of all ages—sailing, fishing, hiking, lake tours, mountain biking, watersports, snow skiing, shopping, dining, and sightseeing. From mid-November through early April, its two skiing facilities, with miles of snowy slopes, have made it a major winter sports headquarters.

Friendly and unhurried, Big Bear Lake is the ultimate escape, a world removed from crowds and freeway traffic, secure in its beautiful mountain valley on the fringe of a fairytale forest. So far the small frontier town hasn't been prettified or boutiqued. It just meanders around the glittering, 7-mile-long man-made lake, with 27 miles of undulating shoreline.

There's a satisfying feeling of open space, similar to that of small towns in Alaska, throughout this sparsely built community, sheltered as it is beneath the tall mountains that provide the long ski runs in winter. Flashes of the cobalt lake are visible through towering pines; the quiet, rural atmosphere is relaxing; the sun is richly warm, even in October; and the air is gorgeous and clear, at a nearly 7,000-foot altitude. Restaurants with sunny dining patios abound, featuring excellent food in generous portions, and there's a large choice in lodging accommodations of all types.

The focus of the city is the **Village,** a lively area along Pine Knot Avenue, which runs at right angles away from the lake toward the mountains and is the main drag, filled with shops, dining places, and people. The Village continues as Pine Knot ends up at another Big Bear Boulevard, this one having several busy blocks of more shops and restaurants. Then you're in wide-open space at the foot of the mountains and ski areas at the edge of the forest.

Lunch: **Old Country Inn Restaurant,** 41126 Big Bear Boulevard, Big Bear Lake. (909) 866–5600. Dark walnut paneling, red leather booths, a peaked ceiling, and plants provide a just-right atmosphere for large-portioned specialties, such as *Wiener schnitzel* with potato pancakes, red cabbage, and sauerkraut; also served here are Italian entrees of veal, chicken, and pasta.

Afternoon

For shopping and browsing after lunch, drive back along Big Bear Boulevard to **Pine Knot Avenue** (the Village) and turn left toward the mountains. Among the many select shops along this vibrant stretch is **Der Weihnachts Markt** (The Christmas Mart), 652–654 Pine Knot Avenue. Here for twenty years, the shop sells only imported Christmas merchandise—year-round—and there are Christmas music and a beautifully decorated Christmas tree. Big sellers are the little village houses, beer steins, and colorful, fierce-looking nutcrackers.

A few doors away, **Ice House,** at 626 Pine Knot Avenue (909–866–2464), features Mary Engelbreit gifts and interiors for the young at heart. In **Mountain Country House,** 633 Pine Knot Avenue, you'll find a large selection of country-style items, from rag dolls, stationery, teddy bears, and birdhouses to afghans, pillows, and giftware. **Teddy Bear Miniatures and Dolls,** at 583 Pine Knot Avenue, offers limited-edition dolls, such as Madame Alexander and Hildegard Guenzel, as well as other collector dolls, doll furniture, cuddly bears, and designer quilts with fine appliques.

For a relaxing respite you can tour the calm blue lake in a one-hour narrated **cruise** on the ten-passenger *Serena,* which leaves from Pine Knot Landing at the foot of the village (909–866–2628), or on the sixty-passenger *Big Bear Queen* paddlewheeler, which leaves from Big Bear Marina, Paine Road at Lakeview (909–866–3218). Both charge the same rate.

Dinner: **Big Bear Prospectors,** 40771 Lakeview Boulevard, Big Bear Lake. (909) 866–6696. Bring a hearty appetite along to this congenial local institution that offers top food and service. Despite the corny menu terms, try the excellent Whisker Licken Bear Trap Beef Ribs or other flavorful, mesquite-grilled specialties. Dinner nightly; Sunday Chuckwagon Champagne Buffet Brunch.

Lodging: **Big Bear Inn,** 42200 Moonridge Road, Big Bear Lake, CA 92315. (800) BEAR–INN; (909) 866–3471. Near the ski resorts. An upscale, small, privately owned, very European hotel, with seventy-five handsomely furnished guestrooms and three suites; Venetian chandeliers, antiques; heated swimming pool and year-round Jacuzzi; restaurant and lounge. Free shuttle to ski resorts.

Day 3

Morning

Breakfast: At the inn. Enjoy a leisurely continental breakfast of fresh fruit and assorted pastries and muffins, or sample the variety of breakfast buffet selections.

Drive up Moonridge Road to the 9-hole **Bear Mountain Golf Course** (909–585–2519) and freshen up your game. Just beyond is **Moonridge Animal Park,** a small, charming zoo in a rustic, hilly clearing at the foot of Bear Mountain Ski. Look for silvery timber wolves; bobcats; huge, black-feathered golden eagles as big as turkeys; and, of course, the big, husky black bears that gave the region its name. (Open daily, mid-May through October; admission.)

In this same area shop at the **Bear Mountain Trading Co.,** 42646 Moonridge Road, a big log cabin treasure chest filled with old-fashioned gifts, turquoise jewelry, bears of all sizes, Navajo rugs, and other temptations.

Lunch: **The Iron Squirrel,** 646 Pine Knot Avenue (in the Village). (909) 866–9121. Country French cuisine in this intimate dining room features excellent salmon and other fresh fish entrees. Another luncheon favorite is the spinach pasta with grilled Italian sausage in tomato cream sauce. For dessert the puff pastry filled with ice cream is drenched in chocolate sauce. Lunch and dinner Tuesday through Sunday.

Retrace your way back to Los Angeles. Take Highway 18 south to California 30. Go west on 30 to I–215 and then south on I–215 to I–10 west. Follow I–10 west into Los Angeles.

There's More

Antiques shopping. Lake Arrowhead and tiny neighboring hamlets are a hub of antiques stores. Among those nearby are Addie's Attic, 318 Highway 173, for home accessories and gifts; and Attic Babies. Open daily.

Way Back When Antiques, 25852 Highway 189, Agua Fria. Features heritage lace, Tiffany lamps, gourmet coffees, teas, and gifts.

Pacific House West, Highway 18 and Kuffel Canyon, Skyforest. Here's a chance to pick up beautiful estate linens, china, gifts, and Victorian silver. Open Friday and Sunday, also by appointment.

Skiing. Snow Valley Ski Resort (Lake Arrowhead), 14 miles east toward Big Bear Lake, from mid-November through March or April. Thirty-three runs, serviced by five double chairlifts, eight triples; longest run is 1.5 miles. Snowboarding with half-pipe available. Snowmaking machine capability of well over 170 acres. Full facilities include cafeteria, bar, après-ski music, rentals. General information, (909) 867–2751; recorded ski and snow report, (909) 867–5151.

Big Bear Lake's two full-service ski resorts are open throughout its long season, from mid-November through early April, whether or not there's snow. They each have high-tech snow-making systems for miles of snowy slopes:

Bear Mountain Ski Resort, P.O. Box 5812 (909) 588–2519. In the Moonridge area about 1 mile east of Snow Summit, is southern California's highest major resort, with the biggest vertical rise. At an 8,805-foot elevation, Bear Peak, the highest and most challenging, has nearly 1,700 vertical feet of continuous skiing. Eleven chairlifts include one high-speed detachable quad, one quad chair, three triples, four double chairs, and two surface Pomas. Also snowmobiling, food, instruction, rentals. Ski hotline, (310) 289–0636.

Snow Summit Ski Resort, P.O. Box 77. (909) 866–5766. One mile east of the village center; well rated by *Ski* magazine, the resort is one of the most popular. Eleven chairlifts and more than 18 miles of ski runs—the most of any Southern California ski area. Night skiing and snowboarding. Food, rentals, ski school, licensed day-care center. Ski hotline, (310) 613–0602.

Mountain biking. In Lake Arrowhead at Snow Valley, from Memorial Day through Labor Day.

In Big Bear Lake, mountain-biking terrain covers miles of forest trails and roads. During summer riders take their bikes on Snow Summit Ski Resort's Sky Chair to the mountaintop, enjoy the valley views, have lunch, and hit the riding trails. Rentals and information: Team Big Bear, in Big Bear Lake (909) 866–4565.

Boat rentals for sailing, waterskiing, fishing, and cruises. Big Bear Lake. Call Pine Knot Landing in Big Bear Lake (909) 866–2528.

The Trolley in Big Bear Lake runs through the Village with three routes. A convenient place to board is at the visitor center on Bartlett Road in the Village. Fee.

Horse-drawn carriage rides are a romantic, leisurely way to sightsee Big Bear Lake. Contact Victoria Park Carriages, Ltd., at the carriage stand location, corner of Lakeview and Bartlett.

Hiking and gold-fever trails in Big Bear Lake offer historic insight into the 1864 Gold Rush in nearby Holcomb Valley. Maps available at the Big Bear Ranger Station on the North Shore and at the Chamber of Commerce.

Alpine Slide at Magic Mountain, on Big Bear Boulevard, a half mile west of the Village in Big Bear Lake. (909) 866–4626. Hop on a scenic chairlift above the lake, then shoot down a thrilling toboggan-style slide with controlled speed. Also a water slide, miniature golf, and a snackbar. Open year-round, weather permitting.

Special Events

Mid-February. U.S. Men's Pro Ski Tour, Snow Summit Ski Resort, Big Bear Lake. Annual California Handicap Ski-a-thon, Bear Mountain Ski Resort.

Early April. Easter in the Village, Lake Arrowhead. Easter egg hunt, musical entertainment, candy.

May through October. Mountain Bike World Cup Race, Big Bear Lake. (909) 866–4565.

Mid-May. Trout Classic, Big Bear Lake. (909) 866–6260.

End of May and end of August. Big Bear Lake's Antique Car Club's Red Fed Car Show, at Redlands Fed. parking lot. (909) 505–8709. Antique cars from all over California; chili cookoffs

Early June. Fireman's Muster, Big Bear Lake. Lake Arrowhead Antique Classic Wooden Boat Show, largest in the nation. (909) 337–3715.

End of June. Rotary Art and Wine Festival, Tavern Bay, Lake Arrowhead.

July 4. Fireworks over the lake at dusk, if approved by the fire marshal, Lake Arrowhead Ice Castle Star-Spangled Ice Show, Blue Jay. Fourth of July Celebration, Rotary BBQ, and fireworks display over Big Bear Lake.

Early July. Mountain Festival Arts and Crafts Faire, Santa's Village parking lot, Skyforest.

Mid-July to early August. Old Miner's Days. Chili Cook-Off, Country Fair. (909) 866–4608.

End of August. Annual Peddler's Market antique and collectibles show, Elks Lodge, Big Bear Lake. (909) 866–9142. Annual Fall Arts & Crafts Show, Civic Center, Big Bear Lake. (909) 585–3000.

Labor Day weekend. Forty-Ninth Annual Rodeo, Big Bear Lake.

Labor Day weekend to the last weekend in October. Annual Oktoberfest, Big Bear Lake.

Early September. Rotary Art and Wine Festival, Lake Arrowhead Village.

Mid-September through October 27. Fall Fling Celebration/Oktoberfest, Lake Arrowhead.

End of November through December 29. Dickens Christmas Celebration, Lake Arrowhead.

End of November. Christmas in the Village. Christmas Tree Lighting in Big Bear City.

Mid-December. Ice Castle Annual ice show, Blue Jay.

Other Recommended
Restaurants and Lodgings

Lake Arrowhead

Woody's Boat House, lakeside (909–337–BOAT), with dining booths shaped like antique wooden boats. Offers salad bar, seafood, prime ribs, and steaks. Weekend breakfasts feature Outrageous Omelettes and Awesome French Toast.

Saddleback Inn–Arrowhead, P.O. Box 1890, 300 South State Highway 173. (800) 358–3334; (909) 336–3571. Come for B&B in this totally restored, 1917 historical landmark at the entrance to the village. Thirty-four guestrooms and cottages, with stone fireplaces, double whirlpool baths, minirefrigerator. Complimentary breakfast daily and Welcome Cocktail. Restaurant and bar. Several guestrooms are named after previous celebrity guests, including Howard Hughes and Mae West.

Romantique Lakeview Lodge, 28051 Highway 189. (800) 358–5253; (909) 337–6633. A Victorian B&B that's a nine-room hideaway offering lake views, antique furnishings, and fireplaces. Continental breakfast features huge cinnamon rolls from local bakery.

Blue Jay Village

Teacher's Restaurant, 27200 State Highway 189. (909) 336–4303. An early daytime breakfast hangout that stretches through lunch and dinner, starring home-baked ham and chili, friendly service, and home-made desserts. Seniors' discounts.

Big Bear Lake

Boo Bear's Den, 572 Pine Knot Avenue. (909) 866–2162. The inviting, parosoled patio lures lots of diners for daily seafood catches, sandwiches, ribs, steaks, and chicken.

Hansel's, 40701 Big Bear Boulevard. (909) 866–9497. Resembles a Bavarian lodge, with tall beamed ceiling and large dining patio. Continental and American dishes include chicken, goulash-stuffed potato, German sausage, and New York pepper steak.

Paoli's Italian Kitchen, 40831 Big Bear Boulevard. (909) 866–2020. Enjoy family-style pasta, veal, chicken, and seafood, served in a large, sunlit patio or indoors.

Castle Wood Cottages, P.O. Box 1746, 547 Main Street. (909) 866–2720. Each of the "theme" cottages is an adventure—for instance, the European decor of Heidi's Room, with a rock-covered Jacuzzi in front of the fireplace, a kitchen, and a wetbar. Miss Kitty's Boudoir is draped in black lace and red velvet, while Davy Crockett's Cabin has a frontier theme. Midweek rates and ski packages.

For More Information

Lake Arrowhead Communities Chamber of Commerce, P.O. Box 155, Lake Arrowhead, CA 92352. (909) 337–3715; (800) 545–5784 (lodging information). At the entrance to Lake Arrowhead Village in the Vineyard Bank Building; on weekends it's in the information booth or Thrifty Drug Store in Blue Jay Village.

Big Bear Lake Resort Association/Big Bear Lake Chamber of Commerce, 630 Bartlett Road, P.O. Box 1936, Big Bear Lake, CA 92315. (909) 866–7000.

Forest Ranger Station 76. (909) 866–3437 (for information on camping and hiking).

Oak Glen

Rural apple country provides a relaxing escape.

Apple Holiday Time

_____ 1 NIGHT _____

Apple ranches and orchards • Fresh-pressed cider • Apple pie • Museums
Animal petting farms • Giftshops

If you think Southern California doesn't have a change of seasons, you'll
discover otherwise in this one-night escape to rural Oak Glen. Located
about 120 miles from Los Angeles (on the way to Palm Springs), the se-
questered glen is tucked in the San Bernardino Mountains between Yucaipa and Beaumont, at an elevation of almost 5,000 feet.

Oak Glen is the Southland's largest mile-high apple-growing community. More than a million visitors come up year-round for its peace and beauty, to smell the lilacs and pink-and-white apple blossoms covering the slopes in springtime, to enjoy the cool summers in the mountains, to marvel at the brilliant fall foliage amid towering pines, cedars, and oaks, and to throw snowballs in winter. Above all, they come to enjoy the fall harvest of some 40 million eating apples (40,000 bushels) of more than sixty-five varieties, all sold directly to the public in one of the largest operations of its kind in the country. The apple growers also press several hundred thousand gallons of fresh cider and sell their own blends. In all the friendly apple sheds, you can taste the different apples and ciders before you buy.

In an 8-mile loop, you can visit twelve apple ranches and orchards. During apple harvest season, September to New Year's, you can buy fresh crisp apples in the apple sheds by the bag, the box, or the bushel and buy fresh-pressed cider, apple butter, apple jelly, and other apple products; browse forty specialty shops; enjoy hearty country food in five family restaurants, always highlighted by fresh baked, hot apple pie; have picnics; visit a candy factory and animal petting parks; take part in seasonal festivities; and overnight in a charming B&B. On your return home you'll visit an elegant and delightful decorative arts museum.

Day 1

Morning

Drive east from Los Angeles on I–10 and exit Yucaipa Boulevard. Follow Yucaipa Boulevard east to Oak Glen Road, turn left, and continue on up to **Oak Glen.** The quiet rural road is nearly deserted during the week as it meanders past horses and cows grazing in sun-dappled fields and continues up the valley to an altitude of 5,000 feet to Oak Glen, then loops down the other side of the glen to Cherry Valley and Beaumont.

Oak Glen families have been growing apples up in this beautiful sheltered canyon for more than a hundred years, on 450 rolling and fertile acres. Generations of persevering mountain pioneers and their families still run many of the original orchards and ranches in traditional, unsophisticated mom-and-pop operations that preserve the glen's authentic and unpretentious rustic character. They are reminders of the time when horse-drawn wagons filled with apples plodded down dusty dirt roads; and a handful of homesteaders held out against fierce weather, Indian warfare, and marketing setbacks. Remnants of Oak Glen's spirited pioneer days linger everywhere.

Though the area is delightful to visit in any season for an old-fashioned holiday in the country, from September to October is when roadside sheds and ranchers' apple barns are crammed with fresh, just-picked apples (not waxed), plus tangy, fresh-pressed cider to tote home. This is delicious raw cider, not pasteurized or sweetened and not at all like that sold in your local supermarket. And everywhere there's the tantalizing, fruity aroma of apples and freshly baked apple pie. The glen's apple orchards are open daily during apple harvest season. Varieties of apples include MacIntosh, Jonathon, Gravenstein, Rome Beauties, Red and Gold Delicious, Fuji, Gala, Granny Smith, and other familiar names, as well as some new ones. Additionally, several ranches invite the public to join in the fun of seasonal U-pick crops on weekends for raspberries, pears, apples, and pumpkins.

Note: Days and hours are subject to change.

One of the first ranches you come to is **Parrish Pioneer Ranch,** 38561 Oak Glen Road (909–797–1753), where in fall a tumble of fat golden and orange pumpkins brighten the entrance to the vintage red barn and salesroom of the oldest apple ranch in the canyon. It was founded in 1866 by Enoch Parrish, who traded his four-mule team and wagon for a homestead site of 160 acres, built a three-room log cabin, and planted the first apple trees in Oak Glen in the late 1860s. He later bought additional land and built a large house for his family of nine children; it is the oldest all-wood house in San Bernardino County.

Parrish is open daily year-round from 9:00 A.M. to 6:00 P.M.; seventeen varieties of apples are on sale from late autumn into the new year. The apple barn is stocked with apple cider, apple butter and nutmeats, dried fruits, jams and jellies, and Granlund's hand-dipped chocolates. There are a good restaurant and bakery, snackbar, duck pond, and country animals to pet.

The 1876 Parrish House, now an antiques shop, displays American furniture, kitchen decor, glassware, old trunks, and collectibles from the Victorian era to the present.

Farther along, **Law's Restaurant, Cider Mill, and Ranch,** 39392 Oak Glen Road (909–797–1642), is where the Law family opened Oak Glen's first apple shed, in 1938, and is still growing many varieties of apples. The small restaurant began in the apple packing shed when Teresa Law started baking apple pies to sell with coffee to customers in the early 1950s. The pies proved so popular that the family soon built a coffeeshop above the shed and added other buildings.

Lunch: **Law's Oak Glen Restaurant.** (909) 797–1642. The chalet-style building's dining room offers views over the valley. Lunch favorites are homemade split pea soup and meatloaf sandwiches. The menu also offers hamburgers, a variety of sandwiches, good chili, and chicken salad. Save room for Law's famous apple pie; they bake about 200 on weekends during harvest season. Before leaving the restaurant, take a peek at the fascinating apple-peeling-and-coring machinery in a small room adjacent to the kitchen, where apples are prepared for the pies. Open January through September, Wednesday through Sunday from 8:00 A.M. to 7:00 P.M. After September, open Tuesday through Sunday from 8:00 A.M. to 7:00 P.M., Monday 8:00 A.M. to 3:00 P.M.

Outdoors the cider mill and apple shed are filled with bags and boxes of apples, gallons of apple cider, apple butter and preserves, gourds, Indian corn, and pumpkins. After September, open daily from 9:00 A.M. to 5:30 P.M.; closed most weekdays after December 1st. The Apple Tree country gift shop, run by Teresa Law, features Beatrix Potter books and figurines, baskets, and pretty kitchen items.

Just up the road, **Oak Tree Village,** 38480 Oak Glen Road (909–797–2745), began in 1961 when a young couple were successful selling apples and apple pies from a shed on their orchard and built a small restaurant. They later added a delightful animal park—where children can still feed deer, sheep, goats, and pigs—then added Mountaintown, where lifelike wolves, Kodiak and polar bears, and rare birds are in a simulated natural habitat. The yellow clapboard complex features a sweet-scented Candy Kitchen where you can watch candymakers hand-dipping chocolates and making caramel apples and fudge, while you inhale the delectable scent of chocolates and other sweets simmering in the big copper kettles. Browse the twenty-three specialty shops, two restaurants, and snackbars. During apple season live country music is presented weekends at the Peacock Pavilion. (Open daily year-round, 10:00 A.M. to 7:00 P.M.; during apple season, to 5:00 P.M.)

Afternoon

Around the curve of the road, **Snowline Ranch,** 39400 Oak Glen Road (909–797–3415), here since 1898, features thirty varieties of apples, chestnuts, and U-pick raspberries. Look for honey, apple butter, syrups, and decorator baskets. (Open daily after September 1, from 9:00 A.M. to 5:00 P.M.; weekend barbecues.)

At the crest of the hill, an ancient wagon overflowing with big golden pumpkins highlights **Los Rios Rancho,** 39160 Oak Glen Road (909–797–1995), the largest apple ranch in Southern California and a family-operated spread since 1906, when Howard Rivers bought his 350-acre ranch. They offer twenty-six varieties of apples in the packing shed salesroom, a cider press, and fresh cider. Gourmet giftshop features apple blossom honey, apple butter, jams, even apple noodles; exotic baskets; gourds, squash, and minipumpkins. The bakery is popular for fresh hot apple pie, applesauce cake, lunch sandwiches, and country barbecues on weekends. Pony rides are available weekends from Labor Day through October; there are farm animals, and picnic areas, additionally are U-pick raspberries every weekend into mid-September and U-pick apples on weekends mid-September through October. (Open daily beginning September 1, from 9:00 A.M. to 5:30 P.M.; Christmas through August, open Wednesday through Sunday from 10:00 A.M. to 5:00 P.M.)

As you continue down the loop past Oak Glen Inn, your overnight lodging, you're soon at Oak Glen's greatest historical treasure, the old one-room, two-story **Oak Glen School House,** built of stone in 1928. Photos of Presidents Calvin Coolidge and Herbert Hoover hang on the walls above the still-in-use wood-burning stove. The schoolhouse has been restored as a museum and offers insight into the area's past. Weekend tours during apple season (909–797–1691).

Below the crest of the hill, **Wilshire's Apple Shed,** 11925 Oak Glen Road (909–797–8731), has been growing apples since Joseph Wilshire bought his land in 1876 from an Indian for $50; the grant deed to his acreage was signed by President McKinley. The apple shed has been open since the early 1950s and is run by the fifth generation of the Wilshire family. Apples are still sold in pretty paper bags with handles. Additionally, you'll find gourmet food, coffee, gift items, antique apple labels, and dried cranberries. (Open daily, 9:00 A.M. to 5:00 P.M., through December.)

The Enchanted Loft (909–790–1171), perched high atop the apple barn, is a fantasy world of Wee Forest Folk and tiny mice people, Raikes Bears, Brambley Hedge, and other well-known lines for special gifts. (Open April through August from Friday through Sunday, 10:00 A.M. to 5:00 P.M.; closed January through March.)

Another downward curve in the road leads to **Riley's Farm & Orchard,** 12253 South Oak Glen Road (909–790–2364). Here's where thousands of people show up yearly during different seasons to pick their own apples, pears, and raspberries. Grab a U-pick bag at the store, hop into the wagon (or walk out to the orchard), and pick yourself some really fresh fruit right from the tree or the raspberry patch. You can press your own cider, pet the country animals, and browse the General Mercantile store. (Open weekends April to August 6 from 10:00 A.M. to 5:00 P.M. and Saturday and Sunday from noon to 5:00 P.M.; closed Easter Sunday. Open daily August 7 through September 20 from 10:00 A.M. to 5:00 P.M. and by appointment.)

Dinner: **Oak Glen Inn.** Light dinner is included in your accommodation at the inn as many restaurants in the area close early. Hearty, heavy minestrone soup is served with homemade focaccia, followed by luscious homemade desserts of either chocolate cappuccino cake or cranberry cake with cheesecake filling and orange sauce. In summer it's lighter fare of pasta, various breads, and desserts. Dinner is served from 5:00 to 7:00 P.M.

Lodging: Oak Glen Inn Bed & Breakfast, 39796 Pine Bench Road, Oak Glen, CA 92399 (909) 797–7920. The owners (your hosts) built this attractive, three-story gray-and-white clapboard country inn in 1991, on more than two acres of land that include a small orchard of various fruit trees. A fantastic variety of seventy-five different herbs edges a lovely, flower-filled garden; there's lots of open space where dogs, cats, and ducks casually roam. Five romantic, air-conditioned guestrooms with private bath and balcony are each named for a different variety of apple—Granny Smith, Rome Beauty, and so forth. Furnished in appealing country decor of antique rocking chairs, ruffles, and Victorian lace. No room phones, and the TV is up on the third floor in "Granny's Attic" game room. Upscale clientele. Accommodations include light breakfast and light dinner, afternoon snacks and beverages. No smoking, children, or pets. Reservations required.

Day 2

Morning

Breakfast: **Oak Glen Inn.** Serve yourself from two nicely set tables in the sunny dining room. Fruit juice, fresh Danish or muffins, and coffee.

Later, go off to the village to browse the stores and visit other ranches and orchards. Be on the lookout for old farm implements, wagons, and numerous historic relics of the early days of apple farming. Then treat yourself to a hearty country-style brunch.

Brunch: **Apple Dumplin's Restaurant & Bakery,** located in the old converted equipment barn built in 1867, at Parrish Pioneer Ranch. (909) 797–0037. Stained-glass apples gleam in the windows, and the original ceiling beams are visible. All-you-can-eat country-style buffet brunch is served on Saturdays, Sundays, and holiday Mondays, year-round. Help yourself at the long buffet table to apple crisp, apple muffins, fresh melons, strawberries in season, pancakes, French toast, hot and spiced apple slices and cherries, scrambled eggs with cheese, seasoned potatoes, sausage, bacon, country gravy, biscuits . . . and more. The prized apple dumplings, served daily, are cored and peeled apples stuffed with sugar and spices, baked in a pie crust, and served hot in a bowl; cider and cinnamon sauce is poured over it, and the dumpling is topped with ice cream. From 8:00 A.M. to noon. Seniors' 10 percent discount.

Regular daily breakfast menu offers omelets, pancakes, waffles, ham or bacon and eggs, served with potatoes, fruit garnish. Daily 8:00 A.M. to noon. Dinner, served till 6:00 P.M., includes fried chicken with biscuits and honey.

Afternoon

Departing Oak Glen to visit the **Edward-Dean Museum of Decorative Arts** 9401 Oak Glen Road, Cherry Valley (909–845–2626) en route home, continue down Oak Glen Road toward Beaumont. Driving through the piney San Bernardino National Forest, you'll find that the air is crisp and cold, the sycamore trees are a hundred shades of gold in the pale winter light, and the panoramas of the tall mountain ranges in the near distance constantly changing.

As you drive down the rural valley following a woodsy stream, the museum is on the right, set well back from the road in the midst of sixteen beautifully landscaped acres. In the modern eight-room museum, the stunning antique collection consists primarily of European decorative arts—furniture, paintings, tapestries, porcelains, important Oriental pieces, and sculpture dating from the third century B.C. to the present.

The best part, however, is that you feel you've somehow stumbled into an eighteenth-century home and are a guest, not a museum visitor, where the charm of the period is evoked by the arrangement of furnishings and art objects. The museum was built in 1957 by Edward Eberle and Dean Stout, an interior decorating team, to showcase their growing personal collection of antiques. When the partners retired, they gave the museum in its entirety to Riverside County, in 1964, for an art and cultural center.

Each room is named for a distinctive feature. In the spacious Pine Room, with its splendid seventeenth-century carved pine paneling, in addition to an impressive eighteenth-century Waterford crystal chandelier are cabinets displaying Chinese and Tibetan bronzes, Wedgwood, Meissen, and Spode porcelains. A rare 1804 pianoforte and an unusual paperweight collection are highlights in the Blue Room. The North Gallery's changing art exhibits combine works of current artists with those of artists of the past. (Open Tuesday through Friday from 1:00 to 4:30 P.M. and Saturday and Sunday from 10:00 A.M. to 4:30 P.M.; closed Easter Sunday and legal holidays.) Donations welcomed.

From here follow Beaumont Avenue down to join I–10 west to Los Angeles.

There's More

Orchards in Oak Glen High Country Orchards, 38695 Oak Glen Road. (909) 797–4249. Apples, cider, jams, jellies, antique gift items, collectibles. Open daily, 9:00 A.M. to 5:00 P.M., after September 2.

Wood Acres, 38003 Potato Canyon Road. (909) 797–8500. A unique small family orchard specializing in gourmet dessert and antique apples. Open daily after September 15 through apple season.

Jo's Raspberry Patch, 38309 Oak Glen Road. (909) 797–1212. U-pick raspberries. Open from the end of July through September.

Yucaipa Regional Park, 339 Oak Glen Road, Yucaipa. (909) 790–3127. At the gateway to Oak Glen, this lovely park offers a variety of recreational activities. In a scenic setting surrounded by the nearby San Bernardino and San Gorgonio mountain ranges, the park features a unique one-acre swim lagoon with two 350-foot water slides, white sandy beaches, two lakes stocked seasonally for year-round fishing, shady picnic grounds, snackbars, pedalboat rental, overnight campgrounds, equestrian trails, and summer concerts under the stars. Admission.

Mousley Museum of Natural History, 35308 Panorama Drive (corner of Bryant Street), Yucaipa. (909) 790–3163. Louis B. Mousley began collecting quartz crystals and seashells as a child, encouraged by his great-grandfather, a sea captain who brought him shells from exotic world ports. Mr. and Mrs. Mousley built a museum for their large collection and presented it to the county of San Bernardino, which dedicated it as a branch of the San Bernardino County Museum in September 1970. The world-class collection of 65,000 seashells is the largest such display in the country. Also here are major mineral and rock specimens, fossils, artifacts, and ceremonial objects. Open Thursday through Sunday from 1:00 to 5:00 P.M.; tours by appointment; Donations welcome.

Special Events

Note: Call for admission fees and specific dates.

January. Winter Wonderland in the Glen.

February. Valentine gifts and goodies.

Early March. Easter Egg Hunt, Easter activities.

Mid-April. Annual Oak Glen Apple Blossom Festival. Festival activities Saturday and Sunday at Law's Restaurant, Cider Mill, and Ranch. Apple Blossom Festival arts and crafts, Saturday and Sunday at Los Rios Rancho. Annual Apple Pancake Breakfast, crowning of Apple

Blossom Queen at Oak Tree Village. Cherry Festival Queen Pageant in Beaumont (909–845–9641).

End of May. Memorial Day weekend Frontier Rendezvous, Living History in Oak Knoll Park. U-pick daffodils and other spring flowers, Los Rios Rancho. Memorial Day Arts & Crafts Fairs.

Memorial Day to end of June. Cherry picking and buying. For information and orchard locations, call Cherry Grower's Association, (909) 845–3628.

Early June. Annual Gem and Mineral Show, Yucaipa Community Center, First Street and Avenue B. Two days.

Mid-June. Annual Corn Feed, Saturday and Sunday at Parrish Pioneer Ranch. Annual Cherry Festival, since 1978, to celebrate cherry harvest: carnival rides, live music, parade, food and game booths. Admission. Call Beaumont Chamber of Commerce (909–845–0541) or Cherry Valley Chamber of Commerce (909–845–8466), or write to Beaumont–Cherry Valley Cherry Festival Association, P.O. Box 126, Beaumont, CA 92223.

July. Christmas in July Sales, Oak Glen.

Early August through September. Oak Glen Raspberry Festival. (909) 797–2745. Raspberry U-Pick begins at four ranches.

Mid-August. Oak Glen Western Days. Country music, stunt shows, western-style BBQ at Apple Dumplin's Restaurant, Parrish Pioneer Ranch. (909) 797–0037.

September. Annual Oak Glen Fall Harvest Festival begins. (909) 797–6833.

Beginning of September. Hog Heaven Hoedown, Riley's Farm & Orchard.

Labor Day weekend. Arts & Crafts Show, Westernaires Old West Gun Show, Los Rios Rancho. Annual Arts & Crafts Fair—pony rides, live entertainment, clowns, at Oak Tree Village.

End of September. Art in the Glen, Yucaipa Art Association, at Oak Tree Village.

Early October. Mountain Music Festival, Saturday and Sunday. Folk singers, children's concerts at Peacock Pavilion, Oak Tree Village. (909) 797–4020. Gala Halloween Festivals.

Early November. Yucaipa Art Association Show, Oak Tree Village.

Mid-November. Blue-Gray Ball, Riley's Farm & Orchard. Antebellum attire; reservations required.

End of November. Annual Lighting of the Glen Thanksgiving Weekend, Parrish Pioneer Ranch. Carolers sing, Santa Claus visits; complimentary hot spicy cider.

Early December. Breakfast with Santa, Puppet Show, Parrish Pioneer Ranch. Two days, by reservation only. Dicken's Christmas in the Village. Special Dickens Faire, three weekends. (909) 797–4020.

Mid-December. Old St. Nick Christmas caroling, Riley's Farm & Orchard. Winterfest—Cherry Valley/Beaumont. (909) 855–9555.

Other Recommended Restaurants and Lodgings

Apple Annie's Restaurant, in Oak Tree Village. (909) 797–7371. The pine-paneled restaurant is a nice snug spot, or you can eat in the indoor garden patio with the waterfall and pretty plants. Hands-down favorite is the honey-stung chicken—fried chicken with a honey batter. Next is the seaside platter, which combines deep-fried cod, scallops, and shrimp. For dessert French crumb apple pie topped with brown sugar and cinnamon, or opt for regular good old-fashioned apple pie. The very popular Pig Out Pie is layers of apples and pecans topped with crunchy crust. Open daily, year-round, from 9:00 A.M. to 5:00 P.M. After lunch or dinner it's fun to stroll the wide veranda and browse the shops.

Casa Trejo Too, across the road from Oak Tree Village. (909) 790–9534. Good homemade Mexican food for lunch and dinner. Days and hours vary; call ahead.

Creekside Kitchen. (909) 797–9394. Good soups, pretty sandwiches, and first-rate baked goods. Breakfast and lunch. Hours and days vary; call ahead.

Oak Glen Resort, 38955 Oak Glen Road. (909) 790–3463. Membership campground and RV park; all recreational vehicles, including tents. Small convenience store. Oak Tree Tavern/Restaurant (closed Wednesday and Thursday) serves breakfast, lunch, and dinner; open to nonovernight guests.

Best Western El Rancho Motel, 555 Beaumont Avenue, Beaumont. (909) 845–2176. AAA; fifty-five units, with four two-bedroom units, shower or combination baths; air-conditioned; heated swimming pool, indoor whirlpool; cable TV; restaurant; no pets.

Golden West Motel, 625 East 5th Street, Beaumont. (909) 845–2185. Member, Budget Host Inns. twenty-four guestrooms, two two-bedroom units; air-conditioned; cable TV, movies, radios, shower-baths. Small pool, whirlpool, pets. Seniors' discounts.

For More Information

Oak Glen Information. (909) 797–6833. Year-round events.
Oak Glen Apple Growers Association. (909) 797–1005.

Yucaipa Valley Chamber of Commerce, 33733 Yucaipa Boulevard, P.O. Box 45, Yucaipa, CA 92399. (909) 790–1841.

Beaumont Chamber of Commerce, 450 East 4th Street, Beaumont, CA 92223. (909) 845–0541.

Cherry Valley Chamber of Commerce. (909) 845–8466.

Cherry Growers Association, 10700 Jonathan Avenue, Cherry Valley, CA 92223 (909) 845–3628.

Palm Springs/Coachella Valley

Ancient palm trees frame rocky gorge in Palm Canyon.

Desert Retreat

2 NIGHTS

Swimming and sunbathing • World-class resorts • Fine dining • Shopping
Botanical garden • Desert wildlife center • Indian canyons • Aerial tramway
Water park • Horseback riding • Golf and tennis tournaments

The dry desert climate and radiant sunshine have lured sun-worshipers since the 1930s, when Palm Springs was a small-town winter haven for movie stars. Its natural splendor, glamour, deluxe resorts, and lush golf courses enhance its reputation as a posh playground and home for presidents and celebrities, who frequent local shops and restaurants and have city streets named for them.

The desert area is one of Southern California's most popular weekend getaways, boasting winters of more sunny days and less rainfall than other regions. Summer temperatures soar to one hundred degrees or higher, but the drastically reduced hotel rates are irresistible and the season is getting longer. Evenings are always cool; dress is casual. But you don't have to be Elizabeth Taylor or a VIP to enjoy the seductive sunshine in this cactus paradise. There are accommodations and restaurants for all budgets.

The Palm Springs season begins October 1 and runs through the end of May. The busy "high season" is from mid-January through mid-April.

Favorite good-life pursuits are swimming and lounging around the pool in the lazy sun, as well as swinging a golf club or tennis racquet. You'll also visit Indian canyons, tour wildlife and garden centers, bike along sun-washed streets, shop in indoor air-conditioned malls, and enjoy people-watching in sidewalk cafes.

This three-day desert jaunt explores the mystique and romance of Palm Springs and the neighboring desert communities of the widespread Coachella Valley, where snowcapped lavender mountains frame groves of towering date palms and emerald golf fairways.

Day 1

Morning

For the one-and-a-half-hour, 110-mile trip to the desert, head east from Los Angeles on San Bernardino Freeway I–10.

The tall, majestic gray mountains are topped with snow. After Beaumont, roadside billboards advertise **Desert Hills Factory Stores,** 48–850 Seminole Road (909–849–6641), in Cabazon. If you're a dedicated discount shopper, go ahead and take the Cabazon Main Street exit, turning left past Hadley Fruit Orchards. The sprawling outlet center showcases one hundred leading names in fashion and home furnishings, with prices reputed to be 30 to 60 percent below retail. The stores are open daily from 9:00 A.M. to 8:00 P.M.; Sundays are quite crowded. (Make a note to return to Hadley Fruit Orchards en route back to Los Angeles, to check out its large variety of dried fruits, nuts, and other edibles.)

Return to I–10 heading toward Palm Springs by turning left at the small road sign and left again on I–10 east. You soon feel close enough to the tall mountain ranges to almost touch them. The windy

San Gorgonio Pass at the junction of Highway 111 and I–10 is the site of one of California's three large **wind farms,** where 4,500 wind turbines resembling silvery windmills spinning in the sun generate enough electricity for some 93,000 homes.

At the junction follow 111 into **Palm Springs,** curving around the tall mountain. Just past the city limits, **Palm Springs Aerial Tramway**'s cable cars whisk you up 8,516 feet to the cool wilderness of Mount San Jacinto State Park in a fifteen-minute ride. In the brisk mountain air, you'll have breathtaking views and opportunities for hiking, cross-country skiing, and a picnic; a restaurant and giftshop are here too. The cars run year-round every fifteen minutes. (Fare.)

At **Palm Springs Visitors Information Center,** 2781 North Palm Canyon Drive (800–347–7746), you can pick up maps and brochures, make hotel reservations in the city of Palm Springs, and purchase souvenirs. On North Palm Canyon Drive, lined with palm trees, **Loehmann's Plaza** houses the discount clothing store and other specialty discount stores.

Lunch: **Billy Reed's,** 1800 North Palm Canyon Drive, Palm Springs. (760) 325–1946 is a convenient dining stop at the northern entrance to the city. You'll like the looks—and the food—of this large, rambling popular restaurant with Victorian furnishings. The moderately priced menu features French dip and other sandwiches, salads, chicken, a kids' menu, fast service, and a full bar.

Afternoon

Palm Canyon Drive is inviting to stroll, with its many shops, cafes, and galleries. There's ample parking space, and you won't find parking meters. The city still retains its village atmosphere, even though it is quite busy Saturday nights and usually crowded with college students during the Easter spring break, when adjacent desert cities are quiet. Palm trees are illuminated at night, and midweek canyon strolls are highlighted by festive street fairs and sidewalk parties. **Villagefest,** held every Thursday evening along Palm Canyon Drive, with streets closed to traffic, is a lively combination of old-fashioned street fair and block party. It features music, a farmer's market, sidewalk vendors, and fun.

For quick insights into the city's history, stop at the **Village Green Center,** 219–223 South Palm Canyon Drive (760–323–8297), where several small museums share a garden setting and fountain. Miss Cornelia White's House, built in 1894 and made entirely of railroad ties, displays paintings, bibles, photos of memorabilia, and the town's first telephone, complete with hand crank.

The McCallum Adobe, the town's oldest building (1885) and the family home of Judge John McCallum, the city's founder, contains photographs and the collections of the Palm Springs Historical Society. Both historical sites are open Wednesday and Sunday from noon to 3:00 P.M. and Thursday, Friday, and Saturday from 10:00 A.M. to 4:00 P.M. (Nominal admission.) Ruddy's General Store Museum, a re-creation of an old-fashioned general store of the 1930s and 1940s, displays hundreds of authentic items of that bygone era. Open Thursday through Sunday, 10:00 A.M. to 4:00 P.M., weekends only from July through September. (Nominal admission.)

Next door, the Agua Caliente Cultural Museum Information Center displays historical artifacts and photos of Cahuilla Indians, the city's first settlers. Open Wednesday through Saturday from 10:00 A.M. to 4:00 P.M., Thursday 6:00 to 9:00 P.M., and Sunday noon to 3:00 P.M. Closed June to October. (Free.)

Up the street you'll find **Desert Fashion Plaza,** an elegant indoor shopping mall of more than one hundred shops. With its striking marble floor and a huge fountain, the mall is anchored by Saks Fifth Avenue. Around the corner and just behind the mall, the stunning **Palm Springs Desert Museum,** 101 Museum Drive (760–325–0187), with its sunken sculpture garden and Annenberg Theater, presents changing exhibitions, along with its permanent collection of Western and contemporary California art. (Open year-round; closed Monday and major holidays. Admission.)

To visit **Moorten Botanical Garden,** 1701 South Palm Canyon Drive (760–327–6555), follow South Palm Canyon Drive about 2½ blocks past Lyon's Restaurant; it's on the right-hand side of the road. Wander through more than two private acres of 3,000 varieties of desert plants, including giant cacti, and birds. All plants are labeled; the dirt paths are cool and shady under the tall plants. Pick up a map showing different trails and plant locations. The old red-roofed adobe house with the sunny green lawn is the owner's residence. (Admission.)

Afterward check in at your hotel (see "Lodging" below). Since this is Palm Springs, you'll probably want to enjoy some swimming and sunbathing before going on to dinner.

Dinner: **Rock Garden Cafe,** 777 South Palm Canyon Drive, Palm Springs. (760) 327–8840. Dine inside or on the surrounding flower-filled patios under colorful umbrellas. You'll find good menu variety and good service for steak or prime rib sandwiches, hamburgers, and other entrees and a delightful salad bar with dinner.

Lodging: **L'Horizon,** 1050 East Palm Canyon Drive, Palm Springs, CA 92264. (760) 323–1858. Quiet luxury in a handsomely decorated hotel. Twenty-two rooms/suites (some with kitchens), with minirefrigerator, TV, and other amenities, situated around a large swimming pool on two beautifully landscaped, grassy acres of orange trees and flowers, all framed by Mount San Jacinto. You can't beat the location or the warm hospitality, which includes complimentary continental breakfast, plus daily *Los Angeles Times* and complimentary use of bicycles, library, horseshoes, and croquet.

Day 2

Morning

Breakfast: At L'Horizon. Relax over a beautifully served continental breakfast (included in your room rate) of fresh fruit juice, a thermos of coffee, tea, or hot chocolate plus fresh pastry, brought to your lovely room or the private poolside patio in the desert's bright morning sun.

To see the unusual **Oasis Waterpark,** 1500 Gene Autry Trail (760–325–7873), drive east on East Palm Canyon Drive to Gene Autry Trail, then turn left for about 1 mile, till you see the tall slide. The twenty-one-acre family water playground features water slides, innertube rides, food, private cabanas, and a health club. (Open daily mid-March to Labor Day; weekends only September 25 to October 27. Admission.)

Follow South Palm Canyon Drive to its end for a visit to the magnificent **Indian Canyons,** settled centuries ago by ancestors of the native Agua Caliente Indians, the city's largest landowners. Palm Canyon, the most accessible, is remarkably beautiful, with its thousands of native *Washingtonia filifera* fan palm trees. A fifteen-minute scenic drive through the quiet foothills leads you up to a small Trading Post, crowded on Sundays; it sells jewelry, T-shirts, artifacts, and Indian souvenirs. Follow the pathway down to the canyon floor and a dramatic, 15-mile-long rocky gorge of waterfalls and mountain streams alongside a towering grove of palm trees said to be more than 1,500 years old. (Open daily September to June and weekends in summer; admission.)

Lunch: **Cedar Creek Inn,** 1555 South Palm Canyon Drive, Palm Springs. (760) 325–7300. Lots of greenery and airy French country decor. It's noted for innovative specialities of seafood, pasta, a large salad bar, and handsome sandwiches. Bread made on the premises, and desserts are dazzling.

After lunch why not return to your hotel for a refreshing, leisurely swim and a bit of relaxation in the warm sunshine?

Afternoon

Neighboring desert resort communities cut a distinctive swath east and south across the Coachella Valley. To get to the **Living Desert Reserve,** 47900 Portola Avenue, Palm Desert (760) 346–5694), drive east on Highway 111 through Rancho Mirage, where Eisenhower played golf, Gerald Ford tees off, and you can stand on the corner of Bob Hope Drive and Frank Sinatra Drive.

Turn right from Highway 111 at Portola Avenue and continue for about 1.5 miles to the 1,200-acre wildlife center and botanical park. Maps guide you to the exotic horned Arabian oryx, slender gazelles, bighorn sheep clambering the hillsides, and other animals as well as to the aviary, picnic areas, and hiking trails. If you're lucky, you'll meet docents displaying live animals and birds. The Tortoise Shelf bookstore/giftshop additionally sells cool, refreshing ice cream. (Open daily September through July. Hours vary. Admission.)

Take Portola Avenue back to Highway 111 to explore **Palm Desert,** another celebrity haunt of designer golf courses, deluxe resorts, and El Paseo Drive, a fashionable stretch of carriage trade shops, galleries, and cafes with inviting patio dining.

The Coachella Valley's palm groves have flourished since the 1800s. Considered the "Date Capital of the World," the area produces about 99 percent of America's dates, harvested from 250,000 date-producing palms that thrive in the brilliant desert sun, intense heat, and natural underground water supply.

Continue easterly where, at Indian Wells city limits, a dramatic grove of tall date palms looms on the right side of the highway beneath the massive mountain range. Another grove is farther along. At harvesttime you can watch the agile date pickers high up in the trees. Across the highway the deluxe high-rise Hyatt Grand Champions Hotel and Renaissance Esmeralda Resort share two well-manicured golf courses.

Among the many date ranches open to the public, **Shield's Date Gardens** roadside store, at 80–255 Highway 111, Indio (760–347–0996), has been growing, packing, shipping, and selling many varieties of dates since 1924. Here you can also purchase local grapefruit and oranges; enjoy the house drink specialty, a refreshing date milk shake; and watch a movie, *The Romance and Sex Life of the Date.* Shield's is open daily, except on Christmas.

To get to the **Fantasy Springs Casino,** 84–245 Indio Springs Drive (760–342–5000), on Indian reservation land (about 30 miles southeast of Palm Springs), continue toward Indio on Highway 111 to Auto Center Drive; turn left, drive over the bridge to I–10, and then turn right at the sign for the casino. The vast, twenty-four-hour casino, which opened in January 1992 and expanded in early 1995, is crowded with casually dressed patrons and features off-track satellite wagering, bingo, poker, blackjack, etc., pan card casino, a restaurant, and a bar. To return to Palm Springs, go back to the first stop sign and turn left onto I–10; go past another stop sign, then turn right at the first traffic signal on Highway 111 Palm Springs. You're soon back at your hotel in time for some exhilarating swimming and relaxing before going out to dinner.

Dinner: **Le Vallauris,** 385 West Tahquitz Canyon Way, Palm Springs. (760) 325–5059. Better wear your Guccis to this fine French restaurant, with its romantic courtyard and flower-filled dining room. Besides pasta, fish, lamb, and seafood, menu specialties include lobster ravioli with truffle sauce and grilled breast of duck with potato pancake. (It's also a great place to see celebrities.)

Lodging: L'Horizon.

Day 3

Morning

Breakfast. At your hotel. After breakfast there's time for more swimming and sunning on your last morning in the desert.

Lunch: **Las Caseula Terrazza,** 222 South Palm Canyon Drive, Palm Springs. (760) 325–2794. Have your last lunch in Palm Springs at everybody's favorite spot for tasty Mexican cuisine and people-watching.

Afternoon

Try not to leave town too late in the day, particularly on Sunday, when traffic heading out of the city gets very heavy.

To return to Los Angeles, drive north on Indian Canyon Drive, following it around to North Palm Canyon Drive and the wind turbines as it becomes divided Highway 111, then I–10 west. On the way home you can stop and shop at **Hadley Fruit Orchards** (909–849–5255), about 20 miles from Palm Springs in Cabazon. Take the Apache Trail exit and park in front. Besides a wine-tasting salesroom, Hadley offers a wide selection of California dates, dried fruits, nuts and bakery items, plus a small snack area; it's open daily from 7:00 A.M. to 9:00 P.M. To get back on I–10 west to Los Angeles, drive down the frontage road past the discount factory stores, turn left at the second stop sign, and turn right on I–10 west. Stay on it all the way to Los Angeles.

There's More

Golf is the leading desert sport, with more than eighty courses to play. Deluxe resorts feature their own; other hotels can generally provide tee time for their guests at nearby private links. These golf courses are open to the public:

Palm Springs Golf Course, 1885 Golf Club Drive. (760) 328–1005. Eighteen holes.

Canyon South Golf Course, 1097 Murray Canyon Drive. (760) 327–2019. Eighteen holes.

Mesquite Golf and Country Club, 2700 East Mesquite Avenue. (760) 323–1502. Eighteen holes.

Tommy Jacobs' Bel Air Greens, 1001 South El Cielo Road. (760) 322–6062. Nine-hole executive course, night driving range; bar and restaurant.

Tahquitz Creek Palm Springs Golf Resort, 1885 Golf Club Drive. (760) 328–1005. Two 18-hole championship golf courses, open to the public, with great views of Mount San Jacinto.

Tennis enthusiasts can try 600 courts. Besides hotel facilities, you'll find free court time at the following:

Demuth Park, 4375 Mesquite Avenue. Four courts.

Palm Springs High School, 2248 East Ramon Road. Six courts; free weekends, holidays, and summer.

Ruth Hardy Park, Tamarisk and Caballeros. Eight courts.

Bicycling was part of the Palm Springs lifestyle long before it became a national sport. Miles of bike trails are well marked. Maps are available in the Leisure Center, 401 South Pavilion Way, and at rental shops. Some hotels offer complimentary bike use to guests.

Horseback riding. Smoke Tree Stables, 2500 Toledo Avenue. (760) 327–1372. Daily rides following desert trails in mountains and Indian Canyons.

Tours. Desert Adventures Jeep Tours (760–864–6530) takes you for guided, narrated tours of the Coachella Valley, including Indian Canyons.

Celebrity Tours (760–770–2700) offers guided one- and two-hour sightseeing tours to movie stars' homes, country clubs, and other attractions.

Gray Line Tours, 455 East Tahquitz Way (800–638–1839; 760–329–9609), has daily celebrity tours.

Covered Wagon Tours, P.O. Box 1106, La Quinta (760–347–2161), requires reservations for its two-hour narrated tour through the Coachella Valley Preserve aboard authentic, mule-drawn covered wagons. Tour only or with chuck-wagon–style dinner and singalong dinner. Fee.

The Ice Chalet, 72–840 Highway 111, inside the Palm Desert Town Center mall. (760) 340–4412. Large ice rink is a neat way to cool your heels; boutique and rental skates here too.

Offbeat shopping. In Cathedral City try Trader's Discount Place, 62–555 East Palm Canyon Drive (760–328–4425). For one-stop bargain shoppers, this indoor swap meet has thirty-five specialty stores featuring jewelry, shoes, gift items, golf clubs, and other merchandise at reportedly good prices and values. Open Wednesday through Saturday from 10:00 A.M. to 6:00 P.M. and till 5:00 P.M. on Sunday.

In Palm Springs, North Palm Canyon Drive has become home to almost a dozen antiques and art boutiques, vintage clothing shops, and furniture stores. Among them are Patsy's Clothes Closet (4121 East Palm Canyon Drive; (760–324–3825), featuring a good collection of Chanel and other designer suits, barely worn clothes from Escada and Donna Karen, and celebrities discards, and the Village Attic (849 North Palm Canyon Drive; 760–320–6165), where you can browse through 1950s furniture, lamps, tuxedo chairs, and other items.

Hot air ballooning. Soar high above the desert on a warm, clear breeze:

Balloon Charters. (760) 327–8544.

Sunrise Balloons. (800) 548–9912.

Produce shopping in Indio. Sun and Citrus Packing Co./Ranch Market, 81–150 Highway 111, (760) 347–2442. Visitors are welcome to watch luscious grapefruit from nearby ranches being sorted and packed for market; on sale at adjacent Ranch Store. Closes at 4:30 P.M.

Jensen's Dates & Citrus Gardens, 80–65 Highway 111. (760) 347–3897. Stroll the garden shaded by citrus and tall date palms, then browse the country store for dates and a variety of fresh fruits and gift-packs.

Indio Orchards, 80–521 Highway 11. (760) 347–7536. Attractive garden and flowers surround this Spanish-style house whose nice, cool country store is stocked with seasonal fruits—huge strawberries, oranges, dates, and more.

Special Events

Early January. California Gold Cup, Eldorado Polo Club, 50–950 Madison Street, Indio.

Don Drysdale's Hall of Fame Annual Golf Classic.

The Nortel Palm Springs International Film Festival. Sixteen days.

Call Visitor Center or box office (760) 778–8979 for dates and other information.

Mid-January. Annual National Collegiate Tennis Classic.

Annual Bob Hope Chrysler Golf Classic with celebrity pro-am stars.

Mid-February. Annual Date Festival. Indio. Ten days. Agricultural exhibits, and Riverside County Fair, junior fair, nightly Arabian Nights Pageant, carnival rides, exhibits.

Palm Springs Annual Invitational Senior Olympics. For all sports.

Annual Palm Springs Mounted Police Rodeo. Parade, cowboy dance.

Annual Frank Sinatra Celebrity Invitational Golf Tournament, Palm Desert. Fashion show and luncheon as well.

Early March. *Newsweek* Champions Cup Tennis Tournament, at Hyatt Grand Champions Tennis Stadium, Indian Wells.

End of March. La Quinta Annual Art Festival. Juried show features fine art of 200 artists.

Annual Nabisco Dinah Shore LPGA Major Tournament, Mission Hills, Country Club, Rancho Mirage.

Mid-April to August. Palm Springs Angels baseball season. Home games at Angels Stadium, Sunrise Way and Baristo Road.

Early July. Independence Day fireworks displays throughout the desert resorts.

Mid-November. Chrysler Grand Prix of Palm Springs. Two-mile road race.

End of November. Annual Christmas Tree Lighting Ceremony, Desert Fashion Plaza.

Early December. Annual Christmas Tree Lighting Ceremony, at the top of the Palm Springs Aerial Tramway. Celebrity guest and entertainment, 6:00 P.M. Palm Desert Annual Golf Cart Parade along El Paseo. For more information call (800) 417–3529.

Other Recommended Restaurants and Lodgings

Palm Springs

Eveleen's, 664 North Palm Canyon Drive. (760) 325–4766. A dressy, romantic place for intimate dinners of excellent traditional French cuisine and service. Specialties include roast duck with Grand Marnier plum sauce and steak Eveleen.

Blue Coyote Grill, 445 North Palm Canyon Drive, Palm Springs.

(760) 327–1196. A congenial, upscale downtown spot for good south-western and gourmet Mexican cuisines, with sizzling *fajitas* and mariachi Mexican entertainment.

Elmer's Pancake & Steak House, 1260 South Palm Canyon Drive. (760) 327–8419. Friendly place, with prompt service, for pancakes, sandwiches, steaks, salads, and burgers. Crowded Sunday morning.

Hyatt Regency Suites Palm Springs, 285 North Palm Canyon Drive. (800) 233–1234; (760) 322–9000. Luxury hotel in the heart of downtown, with 192 one- and two-bedroom suites; swimming pool, whirlpool; two restaurants, lounge; golf and tennis arranged at country club.

Riviera Resort & Racquet Club, 1600 North Indian Avenue. (800) 444–8311; (760) 327–8311. Expensively refurbished, with 462 rooms and 36 suites on seventeen acres. Large swimming pool; 18-hole putting green, nine tennis courts, basketball, volleyball, and bocce courts.

Palm Desert

Doug Arango's Fine Foods, 73695 Highway 111. (760) 341–4120. Diners enjoy the imaginative California cuisine and home-baked breads, Matzobrie and eggs, pasta, and specialty chicken.

Marriott's Desert Springs Resort & Spa, 74855 Country Club Drive. (760) 341–2211. The area's largest resort, with 884 deluxe rooms on 400 acres of lush grounds and lakes. Spectacular lobby waterfall; lagoon with gondolas. Two 18-hole golf courses, 18-hole putting course, twenty tennis courts, five swimming pools, health spa; ten restaurants.

Rancho Mirage

Westin Mission Hills Resort, Dinah Shore and Bob Hope drives. (760) 328–5955. Has 512 deluxe rooms amid 360 acres; two 18-hole golf courses, seven lighted tennis courts, three swimming pools, whirlpools, fitness center, two restaurants, lounge, pool bar.

Bangkok Five/Cuisine of Thailand, 69–930 Highway 111. (760) 770–9508. Along the city's noted Restaurant Row in the Atrium Design Center. Smart-looking, chic lunch and dinner favorite for delectable Thai dishes such as *Tom Kha Kai* (spicy chicken coconut soup with lemongrass), *Thai Satai* (tender chicken, beef, or pork on skewers with curry peanut sauce), and other flavorful specialties.

The Ritz Carlton, 68–900 Frank Sinatra Drive. (760) 321–8282. High above the city, tucked in twenty-four quiet acres. Mobil four-star-,

AAA-diamond-rated elegant resort features 240 guestrooms and suites, plus Club Floor. Guestroom amenities include honor bar, minirefrigerator, TV, clock radio, marble bathroom, hair dryer, small private balcony, daily newspaper. Concierge service; three restaurants, lobby lounge and bar; huge swimming pool and whirlpool, fitness center, ten lighted tennis courts; access to nearby golf courses. Seasonal rates. Overnight valet parking fee or free self-parking.

Indian Wells

Hyatt Grand Champions Resort, 44–600 Indian Wells Lane. (760) 341–1000. AAA four-diamond, Mobil four-star award winner, featuring 336 deluxe guestrooms and suites on thirty-four acres; two championship 18-hole golf courses, twelve tennis courts and stadium, four swimming pools, two spas, health/fitness center; three restaurants.

La Quinta

La Quinta Resort and Club, 49–499 Eisenhower Drive. (760) 564–4111. The Coachella Valley's oldest hotel has been a favorite retreat for celebrities and stars since it opened in 1926. Its 640 guestrooms and suites are situated in Spanish-style casitas rambling along forty-five acres of flowers and towering palm trees. Accommodations include private patio, minirefrigerator and/or icemaker, large bathroom, TV, and other amenities. The resort has five restaurants, two lounges, twenty-five swimming pools, thirty-eight spas, five championship golf courses, thirty tennis courts, pro shop, fitness center, meeting facilities, pleasant shopping arcade. Sunday Champagne brunch. Seasonal rates; golf and tennis packages.

For More Information

Palm Springs Visitor Information Center, 2781 North Palm Canyon Drive, Palm Springs, CA 92262. (800) 347–7746. Provides maps, brochures, hotel reservations. Open daily.

Palm Springs Desert Resorts Convention & Visitors Bureau, 69–930 Highway 111, Suite 201, Rancho Mirage, CA 92270. (800) 417–3529.

Las Vegas

Las Vegas's famed neon-lit hotel casino strip.

Gambling and Glitter

3 NIGHTS

Gambling casinos • Shopping • Golf and tennis • Antique car collection
Factory-outlet stores • Museums • Resort hotels • Musical shows

This jaunt takes you 300 miles northeast of Los Angeles to the internationally famous "Gambling Capital of the World," the "City That Never Sleeps." This twenty-four-hour party town is neon-lighted glitzy, crowded, and noisy, with fast-paced casinos offering plenty of action, mega-resorts vying for fantasy themes, showgirls in lavish musical productions, inexpensive food buffets, gourmet restaurants, trendy cafes, and magicians who make little white birds appear from red silk scarves. Bugsy Siegel, the playboy mobster who built the Flamingo Hotel in 1946 as a 105-room "carpet joint" where all employees wore tuxedos, said, "Come as you are—enjoy yourself!"

Day 1

Morning

From Los Angeles take San Bernardino Freeway 10 east past Ontario/Upland to I–15 north to Las Vegas via Barstow. Look for I–15 about a half-hour from downtown Los Angeles; at the I–15 TWO MILES sign, stay to the right for Barstow–Las Vegas/215 north, follow the curve, and you're on I–15 north toward the smoky lavender mountain range. The freeway curves to the left for Barstow and climbs as you enter San Bernardino National Forest. The road travels through curving, barren landscape and lots of boulders, and it climbs again as you reach Cajon Summit, an elevation of 4,900 feet.

Just south of Barstow, the midway point between Los Angeles and Las Vegas, take the Lenwood exit for lunch; gas, if you need it; and **discount shopping.** Factory Merchants Outlet Plaza (2837 Lenwood Road, Barstow; (619) 253–7342), in a large cluster of white buildings, houses fifty manufacturer-owned outlet stores that claim savings from 20 to 70 percent off retail prices and include such well-known names as Bugle Boy, Evan Picone/Gant, Toys Unlimited, Bass Shoes, Johnston & Murphy, Levi's, Lenox, and Adolfo II. Turn left on Mercantile Avenue into the parking lot. Stores are set among grassy courtyards, red-brick paths with planters, and covered walkways in an attractive complex. (Open daily from 9:00 A.M. to 8:00 P.M.) Closed Thanksgiving and Christmas.

Lunch: **In-N-Out Burger,** 1561 Lenwood Road, Barstow. (800) 786–1000. Large, busy fast-food eatery with long lines that move quickly for hamburgers, fries, coffee, or soft drinks. With many pleasant young people in the kitchen and behind the counter, service is pretty fast.

Afternoon

Many drivers prefer to fill their gas tank here at the halfway point, even though gas is more expensive than in Los Angeles or Las Vegas,

as 150 miles of long, deserted road lie ahead. After lunch return to
I–15 north; it curves left for Las Vegas, and you drive through magnificent scenery, enjoying the grandeur and peace of the desert, which is
ringed with mauve mountains and filled with perky Joshua trees amid
the scrub. You climb to 4,000 feet again at Halloran Summit Road for
quite a distance. When you cross the Nevada state line, where gambling is legal, the first thing you see is Whiskey Pete's Casino, along
with other gambling halls.

The Las Vegas city high-rise skyline is visible beyond the mountains
as you arrive, after a five-hour drive. Take exit 34 to the Las Vegas
Strip, beneath low-flying planes from nearby Las Vegas McCarran International Airport. Drive down Las Vegas Boulevard, also known as
the Strip, past many hotels with familiar names: Excalibur Hotel, a
white castle with moat and drawbridge, 4,000 rooms, different colored
towers, and a medieval Disneyland look; the Tropicana Resort, with
lush landscaping, waterfalls, and massive Easter Island–type sculptures; and the Alladin Hotel, Bally's, and majestic Caesars Palace.

Las Vegas hotels are different from others because you enter
through areas of labyrinthine, bustling casinos filled with people playing slot machines, blackjack, roulette, craps, poker, keno, bingo, pan,
and sports book wagering. You may find it difficult to have a drink at
the bars, since those counters too are covered with video poker machines whereby players feed the machines and have a drink. Bars are
open twenty-four hours. Though hotels have their special features and
glamorous window dressing, the casinos are the focal point. Better
bring a sweater along, as many of the casinos have their air-
conditioning set to nearly freezing.

The tables at different casinos have different betting minimums.
Slots are from 5 cents to $5.00 to a special $100 and $500 slot ma-
chine. All over the casinos you hear the steady sounds of slots
whirring and beeping and the winning clatter of coins dropping, mur-
murs of dealers, conversation, people walking, talking, cocktail wait-
resses offering drinks to players—there's constant movement, noise,
color, and people. Day and night run together. It's a great place for in-
somniacs; there are no clocks in the casinos and hardly any water
fountains.

Dinner: **Crown Room,** Flamingo Hilton, Las Vegas. 3555 Las Vegas
Boulevard, (702) 733–3111. Las Vegas hotels are noted for lavish buffet dining at inexpensive prices. You pay as you enter, before dining,
but be sure to retain your receipt, as the hostess asks for it. The
Crown Room has two large, separate restaurants, with two different
extensive buffets, one American and the other following an international ethnic menu that is changed monthly. The American buffet includes salad bar, cold cuts, fried chicken, hand-carved roast beef, beef

bourguignon, mashed potatoes, vegetables, and many other items.
The second buffet offers similar foods but adds tasty ethnic specialties.
For dessert you can make your own sundae with ice cream, chocolate
syrup, whipped cream, pineapple, and nut bits, plus elaborate pastries

Lodging: **Flamingo Hilton,** 3555 Las Vegas Boulevard South, Las
Vegas, NV. (800) 732–2111; (702) 733–3111. Centrally located on the
Las Vegas Strip, this is the second largest resort in the world, with
3,642 luxe rooms and suites, eight restaurants, two heated swimming
pools, Jacuzzi, health spa, four lighted tennis courts, game arcade,
conference facilities, and tour lobby for group travel. Aside from slot
machines and video poker, offers fast-paced casino games of
chance, including craps, blackjack, Pai Gow Poker, Sic Bo, Big Six
Wheel, keno, and mini-Baccarat; free lessons in all its table games.
Bugsy Siegel's suite in the original Garden Building, with its escape
routes and tunnels, has been razed to add a rambling swimming
pool. A plaque marks the original site and tells the story of the
hotel's beginnings and how Bugsy was gunned down in 1947 in Los
Angeles.

Day 2

Morning

Breakfast: **Food Fantasy,** Flamingo Hilton. (702) 733–3333. A
pretty room with cafeteria-style service, where short-order cooks will
prepare your eggs and bacon, waffles, and other specialties while you
wait. Coffee is served at your table.

Since most visitors come to Las Vegas to try their luck, they soon
join the throngs in the lively casinos. Others may prefer to relax in and
around the large swimming pools. Still others like to see more of the
town and drive along the Strip, to visit the different shops and hotels.
Hotels are widely spaced, with many entrances through acres of
convention-hall-size casino rooms—you'll find yourself doing as much
walking as driving. **Caesars Palace,** across from the Flamingo Hilton,
is acknowledged as one of the city's finest and, with its fountains and
sidewalk people-movers, most flamboyant hotels. Self-park in the covered structure and take the people-mover into the casinos, or park in
the lot near valet parking. Valet parking is free at most hotels, and you
usually tip $1.00 when the attendant delivers your car. But chances are
good that there'll be a considerable wait, so you're better off parking
your car yourself. At some hotels you may try to park in the fifteen-

minute Registration Zone, if there's a space, for just a quick look-around.

The **Forum Shops** in Caesars Palace attract many visitors with an hourly spectacle. About seventy upscale specialty shops and restaurants, including Gucci and Louis Vuitton, encircle an elaborate fantasy rotunda of an ancient Roman piazza with tall marble columns and marble floors. In the center of an ornate, massive fountain reminiscent of the Trevi fountain in Rome, realistic, robotic, animated figures of Bacchus (god of merriment), Apollo, and Venus perform on the hour in an entertaining ten-minute show.

Alongside Caesars Palace, the **Mirage Resort** is another showpiece offering many diversions, including its magnificent 100-foot waterfalls cascading into rocky lagoons; its lobby atrium filled with tall, exotic trees reaching to a glass dome ceiling; and its tropical fish aquarium behind the front desk. Additionally, in a special pool you can watch five bottlenose dolphins dive and play, but there's an admission. The Tiger Habitat is home to five beautiful royal white tigers featured in the nightly shows of magicians Siegfried and Roy and is on view twenty-four hours. The Three-Minute Volcano, at the Mirage's front entrance 100 feet above the rocky lagoon, erupts on the hour from dusk to 1:00 A.M.—the earth rumbles, there's thunder, eerie red coals glow, and the water roils in the lagoon.

Hotels in Las Vegas are lit up with electric and neon lights that move, go on and off, up and down, and sideways in different, gaudy colors and shapes, and you see kitsch you never thought possible on such a large scale.

Driving toward downtown, you pass many wedding chapels in little white cottages of fanciful design and whimsy. Las Vegas is considered the "Marriage Capital of America," with no red tape or blood test or waiting period required. More than thirty-five wedding chapels perform quickie marriages twenty-four hours a day.

Continue to Fremont Street, known as Glitter Gulch, where every inch of every building is ablaze with lights and you can take a snapshot without using a flash—at midnight! Glitter Gulch became even more spectacular when the Fremont Experience, a $70-million project, opened in December 1995 and transformed it into a 5-block pedestrian mall lined by hotels and casinos. Arching overhead, a 90-foot-high electric signboard canopy of two million lights features a dynamic, computer-generated light and sound show. The lowest-price gas station in town is just below Fremont Street, on the corner of Ogden and Las Vegas Boulevard—cheaper than Los Angeles and far less than Barstow. Many fine lower-priced restaurants are also in this vital area.

Lunch: **The Flamingo Room,** Flamingo Hilton. (702) 733–3333. Pretty, airy room in pink and blue decor, popular for its attractive seafood salad bar with many choice dishes and for its views of the gardens and swimming pool.

Afternoon

Las Vegas was discovered in 1829 by a party of traders who found abundant waters in its artesian springs. Later, in 1844, John C. Fremont led his first overland expedition west and stopped here. His visit is commemorated with his name on many hotels and businesses. In 1855 Mormon settlers arrived and built a fort, now preserved as a historic site. Las Vegas (Spanish for "The Meadows") became a city in 1905, when the railroad made it a definite stop on its route east from California.

Gambling was forbidden by law in Nevada until it was legalized in 1931, during the Great Depression. The first hotel built on the Las Vegas Strip was the El Rancho Vegas, in 1940. Several others followed, and the Las Vegas Strip was on its way.

After World War II, resort building in Las Vegas began to flourish. The Desert Inn opened in 1950; the Sahara and the Sands, in 1952. The nine-story Riviera, built in 1954, was the first high-rise. The Dunes, Hacienda, Tropicana, and Stardust were built between 1955 and 1957. In 1989 the 3,034-room Mirage mega-resort opened; the 4,000-room Excalibur opened in 1990. And three new major mega-resort hotel/casinos opened in late 1993: the colossal, pyramid-shaped Luxor Hotel, featuring a full-scale reproduction of King Tut's tomb; Treasure Island Adventure Resort, themed around a small Caribbean village, with hourly cannon battles between two pirate ships; and the 5,005-room MGM Grand Hotel, Casino, and Theme Park, claiming to be the world's largest hotel.

Las Vegas also calls itself the "Entertainment Capital of the World," with such regular heaadline entertainers as Liza Minelli, Englebert Humperdink, Diana Ross, and Johnny Mathis. Many hotels have their own musical production shows in which lissome, long-legged singing and dancing Las Vegas showgirls are lavishly costumed or half-costumed. Some visitors see two musical shows in different hotels each night and additionally watch the lounge entertainment.

If you're an antique car buff, the **Imperial Palace Hotel & Casino,** 3535 Las Vegas Boulevard South (800–634–4441), has more than 200 antique classic automobiles on display. It's worth the long hike through two casinos, then up the elevator to the fifth floor. The stunning collection of splendid, gleaming cars includes a 1922 Renault, a 1931 burgundy Pierce Arrow, a 1920 Minerva, a 1929 Cord with front-wheel drive, a separate room of Model J Deusenbergs, and a 1932 Stutz Rollsten convertible. Also here, among the many gorgeous gleaming cars, are Adolf Hitler's bulletproof armored Mercedes-Benz, and Benito Mussolini's 1939 Alfa Romeo. (Open daily, 9:30 A.M. to 11:00 P.M.; pick up a free admission ticket as you enter the hotel.)

Across from the Desert Inn, the **Fashion Show Mall** encompasses Neiman Marcus, Saks Fifth Avenue, Dillards, Robinson-May's, Macy's and more than 140 boutiques and an international food court. Additionally, most hotels have their own giftshop and exclusive boutiques. In another area about 1 mile east, the **Boulevard Mall,** 3538 Maryland Parkway at Desert Inn Road (702) 732–8949 is a major shopping hub, and the largest shopping center in Nevada, with Sears, Marshall's, J.C. Penney, and other department stores; more than 140 specialty shops and restaurants; a food court and fast-food eateries; and lower prices than the Strip.

Dinner: **Alta Villa,** Flamingo Hilton. (702) 733–3333. It's much easier to dine in your hotel than to drive elsewhere, especially since hotels have many dining choices. This small, intimate room, tucked in a corner on the lower level, features Italian cuisine, including stuffed scampi, pizza, and pasta specialties served with soup or salad, in a quiet, relaxed atmosphere. Reservations required.

Lodging: Flamingo Hilton.

Day 3

Morning

Breakfast: **Bally's Big Kitchen** buffet, Ballys Casino Resort, 3645 Las Vegas Boulevard South, Las Vegas. (800) 534–3434; (702) 739–4111. You need to thread your way through one of the largest and busiest casinos in Las Vegas, then take the mirrored escalator up to the second floor to a pleasant, cheery dining room with windows offering views of the Strip. Pay as you enter and save your receipt. The Big Kitchen buffet, set in a smallish, rather plain, cafeterialike kitchen, offers scrambled eggs, bacon, ham, pancakes, and French toast. There are also hand-carved roast beef and ham, and you serve yourself bagels, croissants, muffins, and pastries.

See more of Las Vegas or spend time in your favorite fashion before you leave for the five-hour trip back to Los Angeles.

There's More

Grand Slam Canyon, adjacent to Circus Circus Hotel Casino. (704) 794–3939. A five-acre, nongaming indoor amusement park, features roller coasters, tunnels, caves, and a water flume ride down a mountainside, as well as other rides and games.

Debbie Reynolds Movie Museum, 305 Convention Center Drive. (702) 734–0711. Located in the Debbie Reynolds Hotel, the museum houses Debbie's collection of movie memorabilia, set pieces, props, costumes, and posters from the 1930s to the 1960s. Besides a movie/video presentation, you'll see costumes and sets from *Cleopatra* and *Ben Hur* and Judy Garland's ruby slippers from *The Wizard of Oz.* Admission.

Factory-outlet shopping. Balz Factory Outlet World, 7400 Las Vegas Boulevard South (corner Warm Springs Road). (702) 896–5599. In this thirty-six-acre, enclosed, climate-controlled mall you'll find savings up to 75 percent on famous-name manufacturers' items in seventy different outlets and shops. Open Monday through Saturday from 10:00 A.M. to 9:00 P.M. and Sunday to 6:00 P.M.

Las Vegas Factory Outlet Stores of America, 9155 Las Vegas Boulevard South. (702) 892–9090. Open-air, Spanish-style mall of more than fifty stores, selling famous-name manufacturers' bargains; plus a sports/casino-style bar. Open Monday through Saturday from 10:00 A.M. to 8:00 P.M., Sunday to 6:00 P.M.

Circus Circus, 2880 Las Vegas Boulevard South. (800) 634–3450; (702) 734–0410. Walk up the ramp to the arcade/midway to see the high-wire and trapeze artists, unicyclists, and other circus acts and to play carnival games.

Ethel M. Chocolates Factory & Cactus Garden, 1 Sunset Way, Henderson. (702) 458–8864. Free self-tour in which you watch them make caramels, nut clusters, and liqueur-filled chocolates and receive a free sample. Afterward visit the large cacti garden. Open daily, 9:00 A.M. to 7:00 P.M.

Guinness World of Records Museum, 2780 Las Vegas Boulevard. (702) 792–3766. This new museum houses photographs, plaster creations, and records of the world's fastest-talking, tallest, and fattest man; bizarre figures; and some musical records of Michael Jackson. Open daily, 9:00 A.M. to midnight. Admission.

Hoover Dam and Lake Mead are 30 miles from the Strip; bus tours leave daily. Dedicated in 1935, Hoover Dam is one of the world's great engineering marvels. Guided thirty-five-minute tours take visitors deep within the awesome, 726-foot (seventy-story-high) dam to the banks of generators and provide information on the history and inner workings of the dam. Be prepared for long lines, though the tours leave every few minutes. A new, three level, 110-foot-diameter circular visitors center opened June 21, 1995, with 400-car parking garage, rooftop overlook, rotating theater, exhibit gallery, and two high-speed elevators to transport guests, and trim the long lines. Lake Mead, one of the largest man-made lakes in the United States, offers 550 miles of recreation, with boating, fishing, waterskiing, and camping. Admission.

Liberace Museum, 1775 East Tropicana Avenue (corner of Spencer). (702) 798–5595. Take Las Vegas Boulevard to Tropicana Avenue; turn left (east) for about 2.5 miles. The popular small museum exhibits personal items of the flamboyant entertainment personality who wore elaborate sequinned jackets and fur-trimmed capes and made the candelabra famous. Features include fifteen pianos, one covered completely with rhinestones. In the Car Gallery, ornate, customized cars are covered with gold glitz and rhinestones, and a Rolls-Royce Phantom V is covered with thousands of mirror tiles. The Costume Gallery displays jewelry and furs. Open Monday through Saturday from 10:00 A.M. to 5:00 P.M. and Sunday from 1:00 P.M. Admission.

Wet 'n Wild Water Park, 2601 Las Vegas Boulevard. (702) 737–8819. Water-oriented family recreation in flumes, wave pool, slides, water roller coaster, fountain, and lagoons. Open daily May through October, 10:00 A.M. to 8:00 P.M. Admission.

Golf. Las Vegas boasts many fine golf courses, and, with a lot of sunny days, it's best to reserve a tee time.

Desert Inn Country Club, 3145 Las Vegas Boulevard South. (702) 733–4444. Directly behind the hotel and casino; 18 holes. Open only to Desert Hotel Inn guests and their guests. Green fee includes cart.

Desert Rose Golf Course, 5483 Club House Drive. (702) 431–4653. Eighteen-hole championship course.

Las Vegas Municipal Golf Course, 4349 Vegas Drive. (702) 646–3003. Eighteen holes, with night driving range, pro shop, lounge, and coffeeshop.

Hilton Country Club, 1911 East Desert Inn Road. (702) 796–0016. Eighteen-hole championship course, driving range, pro shop, snackbar, lounge.

Tennis. Most large hotels feature courts for guest use.

Special Events

Late January. Triple Mini Slot Tournament, Riviera Hotel.

February 6–27. Las Vegas International Marathon, Vacation Village Hotel.

February 28–March 2. $200,000.00 Slot Tournament, Imperial Palace Hotel.

Late March. Annual Angel Planes Airfest, Boulder City Airport. Great American Train Show, Cashman Center.

Mid-April. Clark County Fair, Logandale. Henderson Industrial Days, Henderson.

April 20–May 13. World Poker Championship Series, Binion's Horseshoe Hotel.

End of April to May 2. Spring Jamboree & Crafts Show, Boulder City.

Mid-June. $100,000.00 Slot Tournament, Imperial Palace Hotel.

End of October. Henderson Expo, Henderson Convention Center.

December 3–11. National Finals Rodeo Cowboy Christmas Gift Show, Cashman Field Center.

December 3–12. World Championship National Finals Rodeo, Thomas and Mac Center.

Other Recommended Restaurants and Lodgings

Las Vegas

Dining is inexpensive in Las Vegas, and the operative word is *buffet,* featured throughout the day at most hotels. The largest buffet is at Circus Circus; the longest line is the one you're standing in. Prices vary, as do the specialties offered. Brunches are also appealing, especially Sunday Champagne brunch, with all the bubbly you can drink. Because of price and enjoyability, you'll usually find long buffet lines. At most buffets you pay before you enter the dining room. One way to avoid standing in line is to prepay your meal. Walk around the line to the cashier and tell him or her that you want to return in a half-hour or an hour (whatever time you desire) and that you'd like to prepay your meal to avoid waiting. Get a receipt. Play the slots, watch TV, and return later—present your receipt to the cashier and you'll be seated immediately, without standing in line. Worth a try.

If you don't enjoy standing in buffet lines, try the coffeeshops. The wait for your order may be interminable, but you'll be sitting down. Other alternatives for breakfast include McDonald's, in the basement of the Barbary Coast Hotel, across from Caesars Palace. Pancakes, scrambled eggs, biscuits, bacon, and sausage are reasonably priced and served hot, which is more than you can say for many breakfast buffets. Plus no line, no wait.

Celebrity Deli, 4055 South Maryland Parkway at Flamingo Road, in the Boulevard Mall. (702) 733–7827. Deli lovers rate it tops for corned beef and pastrami sandwiches and for its friendly atmosphere.

Circus Circus Steak House, 2880 Las Vegas Boulevard South. (800) 643–3450. Residents favor this handsome, walnut-paneled room for great steaks grilled in an open hearth.

Gold Coast Hotel & Casino, 4000 West Flamingo Road. (702) 367–7111. Across I–15; the Monterey Room is noted for excellent Chinese specialties at lunch.

Hugo's Cellar, Four Queens Hotel, 202 East Fremont Street. (702) 385–4011. Look for the large yellow neon sign. In this upscale spot for gourmet dinners, Caesar salad is prepared tableside, specialties include tender rack of lamb, and women guests receive a rose.

Palace Station Hotel & Casino, 2411 West Sahara Avenue. (702) 367–2411. Where the Amtrak station is right in the hotel. Frequent visitors recommend the Feast as one of the best buffets in town.

Union Plaza Hotel, 1 Main Street. (702) 386–2110. Second-story Centerstage Restaurant, with glass-domed ceiling, offers first-rate steaks and chicken, plus a great view of Glitter Gulch.

Caesars Palace, 3570 Las Vegas Boulevard South. (800) 634–6661. Ranked number one in town, with 1,500 elaborately appointed rooms and suites, cable TV, two heated swimming pools, spa, four tennis courts, Omnimax theater, three casinos, six gourmet dining rooms, deli, buffet restaurant, lounges, and food court. Forum Shops, conference facilities, Roman gardens, $100 slot machines.

Sahara Las Vegas Hotel & Casino, 2535 Las Vegas Boulevard South. (800) 634–6666; (702) 737–2111. Has 2,100 guestrooms with garden or Strip views, two heated swimming pools, health club, large casino and Pan game room, five restaurants, lounges, convention center, special rates.

Hard Rock Hotel & Casino, 4475 Paradise Road (adjacent to the Hard Rock Cafe). (800) 427–3762, (702) 693–5000. The world's first rock-and-roll hotel, where 340 rooms and suites offer views over the city, is decorated with rare memorabilia from rock music legends. A 90-foot Fender Stratocaster guitar sits atop the hotel porte cochere, and a chandelier of thirty-two saxophones hangs in the resort's entry.

Note: Experienced visitors recommend joining the free Slots Clubs in the casinos; get your name on the hotel mailing list of members eligible for discounts on rooms and food, special rates, and other perks not available to nonmembers. Sign up at the Slot Club booths in your hotel's casino. Additionally, check out your hotel *Fun Books*—they contain coupons for free cocktails, discounts, and other goodies.

For More Information

Las Vegas Visitors Center at the Convention Center, Las Vegas, NV 89109–9095. (702) 892–0711.

Las Vegas Chamber of Commerce, 711 East Desert Inn Road, Las Vegas, NV 89109. (702) 735–1616.

Laughlin

Laughlin's hotel-casinos are on the Colorado River.

Gambling on the Riverfront

_____ 2 NIGHTS _____

Gambling casinos • Resort hotels • Davis Dam • Factory outlet stores
Museum • Entertainment • River Walk • Swimming • Ghost town

This three-day excursion is to a small, friendly riverside gaming resort city tucked in a hot, dry desert area in the southwest corner of Nevada at the edge of Arizona. Scenically located on the sunny banks of the Colorado River, Laughlin offers casinos and high-rise resort hotels that are geared to those who like to gamble on a less expensive scale than is found in Las Vegas and who prefer a slower-paced, more relaxed, and uncrowded small-town atmosphere.

There are ferryboat cruises, strolls along the River Walk, a small historic museum to visit, and the clear, dry desert air.

Don Laughlin, who founded the burgeoning town and owns the Riverside Resort Hotel & Casino, wants everybody to feel welcome and "have a good time."

Day 1

Morning

Leave Los Angeles via San Bernardino Freeway 10 to **Laughlin, Nevada**, about 286 miles, via Barstow. (The route to Barstow is the same as to Las Vegas.) Past the ONTARIO/UPLAND signs, look for I–15 north, about a half-hour from downtown Los Angeles; I–15 goes past Rancho Cucamonga and curves left as you enter the San Bernardino National Forest toward Barstow. In the barren desertscape of sand and scrub, armies of skinny Joshua trees march in the sun.

You pass the cutoff to Arrowhead as I–15 curves to the left for Barstow, and the road goes up and down as you travel through lonely miles of boulders and sand, climbing steadily and easily to Cajon Summit, at 4,900 feet.

Just before reaching Barstow, which is about midway between Los Angeles and Laughlin, exit at Lenwood to have lunch (there are many fast-food places), fill the gas tank, and browse the discount outlet stores. Fast-food places include Arby's, Del Taco, Carl's, Jr., Quigley's Restaurant, KFC, In-N-Out Burger, and Denny's. The food seems to be interchangeable. What you want is fast service and to get back on the road.

Lunch: **Denny's,** 1201 E. Main Street at I–15, (619) 256–0022. This pleasant and busy coffee shop is convenient for a quick, refreshing stop for hamburgers and other sandwiches, fries, soups, salads, coffee, and soft drinks; plus daily specials.

Afternoon

After lunch explore the **Factory Merchants Outlet Plaza** (2837 Lenwood Road, Barstow (619–253–7342), where fifty manufacturer-owned outlet stores offer reported savings of 20 to 70 percent off retail prices. You'll find such familiar names as Corning/Revere, Black &

Decker, Reebok, Anne Klein, Toys Unlimited, and Levi's. The stores, grouped attractively along covered walkways and grassy courtyards, are open daily from 9:00 A.M. to 8:00 P.M.

Lenwood also provides an opportunity to tank up for the nearly 150-mile drive in to Laughlin, even though gas is higher-priced here than in Los Angeles.

Before you continue to Laughlin, you can take in an adventure from the rousing Old West at nearby **Calico Ghost Town,** a restored 1800s mining town and registered California Historic Monument. P.O. Box 638, Yermo, 92398; (800) 862–2542, (714) 254–2122; a San Bernardino County Regional Park. Go north of Barstow on I–15 for about 8 miles, exit on Ghost Town Road and follow the signs.

Tucked in a quiet canyon surrounded by multi-colored mountains that give the town its name, Calico was a booming silver mining town between 1881 and 1896. In its heyday the city bustled with twenty-three businesses, a general store, a school, twenty-two saloons, a Chinatown, redlight district, and a population of more than 1,200.

When silver was discovered in the Calico Mountains on March 28, 1881, hundreds of eager prospectors rushed to the booming scene. In 1883, borax was found in Mule Canyon, 3 miles east. Between 1881 and 1907 some 500 mines in the rich Calico Mining District produced more than $86 million in silver and $45 million in borax products.

By the mid-1890s, when silver prices dropped drastically, the silver mines closed. By 1907 borax mining had also stopped. The miners left for greener fields and, like many other cities, Calico became a ghost town. It dozed in the desert sun until Walter Knott, founder of Knott's Berry Farm, bought the town in 1951 and began restoration of the buildings from old photographs. After restoring part of the town, Knott donated Calico to San Bernardino County in 1966.

Join Calico's half-million yearly visitors who drop by to re-live the bygone period of the colorful 1880s with reminders of the rough'n-ready old American west. It's fun to stroll the wooden sidewalks of the hilly old camptown with its faded pioneer storefronts and picturesque old and weathered wooden buildings. Watch the daily gunfight stunts on Main Street, pan for gold, browse the stores and shops, try the shooting gallery, or follow the honky tonk piano music to Lil's Saloon for food and drink.

Other Ghost Town attractions include riding the narrow gauge railcar, touring the Maggie Mine, and visiting the Mystery Shack and the melodrama Playhouse. Admission includes a ride on a mining tram from the canyon floor parking lot to Calico's lively main street, plus a forty-five-minute guided, narrated history-walking tour of the town. Camping sites in canyons below town offer full hookups, cabins, and a bunkhouse. Rates include admission to the town site. To reserve, call (714) 254–2122. Additionally, Calico celebrates its spirited past with popular year-round festivals. Open daily year-round except Christmas. Townsite hours are from 7:00 A.M. to dusk; shops are open from 9:00 A.M. to 5:00 P.M. Admission and parking fee, attraction fees.

Return to Barstow via I–15 south to 40 east to get to Laughlin.

From Barstow follow I–40 east past Daggett, Newberry Springs, and Ludlow, through barren hilly desert to the Needles/Park Avenue exit (about 144 miles and two and a quarter hours). Take the Park Avenue exit, turn left, and follow Park Avenue to River Road, about 0.5 mile. Turn left on River Road to Laughlin (about 20 miles). You come into Laughlin from the south past the new high-rise developments and little Laughlin City, snuggled in the desert hills, and curve down Casino Drive past Harrah's to the strip of neon-lighted hotels.

All of the city's brightly lighted casino hotels are located on aptly named Casino Drive, and most of them back up to the Colorado River, with scenic views and promenades along the water. **Laughlin** is likened to an Old West boomtown and claims to be the fastest-growing gaming resort destination in the country, visited by more than five million visitors annually.

The city has grown rapidly from the small, river-town fishing village where in 1966 enterprising Don Laughlin bought a bankrupt eight-room motel on six acres of the Colorado River. He used four rooms for the family and rented out the other four, charged 98 cents for all-you-can-eat chicken dinners, and added twelve slot machines and two gaming tables. The residents named the town after him, and other casino hotels are still coming in.

Laughlin is now a flourishing city of about 8,500, with nine hotel-casinos, one casino, and two motels, and is rapidly becoming a popular destination for those who like fast-action gambling but at low-minimum tables as well as less expensive dining and accommodations and plenty of slots. It's less crowded than Las Vegas, has less glitz, and offers the romance of the mighty Colorado River.

The slots are the most popular **gambling** attraction, as they accommodate all budgets and are convenient to play at any hour. All the casinos also offer video poker, keno, 21 machines, blackjack, poker, bingo, roulette, and sportsbetting.

The large casinos are bright and airy. Picture windows frame the sunlit river and the Arizona mountains just across the water—in contrast to Las Vegas, where casino windows are definite no-nos. Some casinos permit guests to take photographs. All the hotels feature top-name entertainment or production shows.

As in Las Vegas, inexpensive buffet dining on a grand scale is a big attraction for economy-minded visitors. Nearly every Laughlin resort offers all-you-can-eat buffets, and many hotels regularly feature specialty buffets or Champagne buffets Saturday and Sunday.

Dinner: **Bountiful Buffet,** Edgewater Hotel & Casino, 2020 South Casino Drive, Laughlin. (800) 67–RIVER. Walk through the casino to the windows along the river side; then take the escalator or elevator downstairs to the large buffet and dining room, where you pay as you enter. This is a well-priced, well-run buffet, where the food is good and the hot entrees are kept hot, as they should be. The appealing variety includes tasty fried chicken (fried in pure canola oil), mashed potatoes, fresh vegetables, a meatless entree, stewed fruits, cole slaw, beef stew, hand-carved ham and roast beef, and rolls and muffins. Make your own sundae for dessert, adding to your ice cream toppings of pineapple, chocolate syrup, nuts, and whipped cream, and snaffle some luscious pastries as you pass them. Like Las Vegas, Laughlin is a cash-and-carry town: No credit cards are used in restaurants or casinos, nothing is charged to your room, everything is cash. Well, perhaps if you're a big shot or high roller or VIP . . .

Lodging: **Edgewater Hotel & Casino,** 202 South Casino Drive, Laughlin, NV 89028. (800) 67–RIVER; (702) 298–2453. At twenty-six floors high, this is the tallest hotel in town; 1,470 fair-size guestrooms and large bathrooms, including nonsmoking rooms on request, all with color TV (no remote). Many rooms overlook the scenic Colorado River, tucked below the mountain ranges. Heated swimming pool; free gaming lessons offered daily in the twenty-four-hour casino; the largest buffet in Laughlin, plus three other eateries. Seniors' discounts.

Day 2

Morning

Breakfast: Bountiful Buffet, Edgewater Hotel & Casino. Extensive array of breakfast foods includes scrambled eggs, French toast, bacon, potatoes, sausage, corned beef hash, ham, oatmeal, and other power foods, such as fresh fruits. But like searching for the Holy Grail, you just can't find hot scrambled eggs in breakfast steamers. Unless you get lucky.

After breakfast take a pleasurable walk along the narrow ribbon of the Colorado on the **River Walk,** a promenade that follows the water and connects the hotels. You can watch the pretty paddlewheeler ferries going past and jet-skiers racing by. Across the river in Arizona, the jagged edges of the charcoal mountains glint in the morning sun. The river is clean and clear, with many large fish visible swimming close to the shoreline, and offers numerous recreational activities, including fishing and waterskiing, scenic tours, and dinner cruises.

Take a **cruise on the river** aboard the 120-passenger USS *Riverside,* which leaves from Don Laughlin's Riverside Resort Hotel & Casino dock, for a ninety-minute narrated cruise in a 65-by-18-foot luxury cruiser specially designed to sail under the Laughlin Bridge to the Davis Dam and back.

The observation deck offers more sun and better viewing on this smooth, pleasant ride. The Laughlin Bridge, which opened to traffic in 1987, cost Don Laughlin $3.5 million to build. "It took four years and thirty-eight different city, state, county, and national agencies to get the bridge approved," says Laughlin. "And it took less than three months to build it!"

The cruise narrator advises that the mighty, 1,400-mile-long Colorado River runs from the Rockies through the Mohave Valley and almost to the Sea of Cortez in Mexico, providing hydroelectric power, public water, and irrigation to parts of California, Nevada, and Arizona. The 200-foot-high **Davis Dam** was completed in 1953 to control flash flooding of the area and to generate hydroelectric power; free self-guided tours are available weekdays from 9:00 A.M. to 4:00 P.M. The boat sails close to the dam and turns about, continuing past the hotels as you learn a bit about each one—the Flamingo Hilton, the Edgewater, the Colorado Belle, and Harrah's, with its private beach. As the boat turns about again, your attention is directed to the opposite riverbank and **Bullhead County Park,** where many trees mark the old Bullhead City boundary line.

Lunch: **Colorado Cafe,** Harrah's Laughlin, 2900 South Casino Drive, Laughlin. (800) 447–8700; (702) 298–4600. Enjoy sit-down lunch in the pretty cafe with patio umbrellas and a make-believe grape arbor. In the airy and bright room, you feel far away from the noise and bustle of the casinos. The lunch menu offers cocktails, sandwiches, and salads; hamburgers with fries are a good choice.

Afternoon

Most visitors prefer to return to the casinos for their favorite game. Others can drive along Casino Drive to see the different hotels. You might want to drive across the Laughlin Bridge to the Arizona side to visit the **Colorado River Museum,** on Highway 95 (702–754-3399). Drive across the bridge and turn left at the first signal (Locust Avenue) for the museum, 0.5 mile north of the bridge at Davis Camp. The small museum, which opened in February 1992, exhibits a model display of the 1871 Fort Mohave, early trapper equipment, a square Steinway grand piano shipped around the Horn to San Francisco and then to Colorado before the turn of the century, and other historical artifacts and memorabilia of Laughlin, Bullhead City, and the surrounding area. (Open Wednesday through Sunday, 10:00 A.M. to 3:00 P.M.)

Dinner: Bountiful Buffet, Edgewater Hotel-Casino. (As in Las Vegas, guests tend to dine in their hotels for convenience.) This extensive, hearty, inexpensive buffet features the same basic nightly foods, with a few changes. Help yourself to fruits, salad, good fried chicken, vegetarian entrees, fish, hand-carved baked ham, roast beef, and chicken-fried steak. You get to splurge on desserts—ice cream sundaes with lots of toppings and fancy pastries and cakes.

Lodging: Edgewater Hotel Casino

Day 3

Morning

Breakfast: **The Garden Room,** Edgewater Hotel-Casino. (800) 677–4837. If you tire of breakfast buffets, the coffeeshop is a good alternative, particularly for waffles and pancakes. This is a pleasant room, though service is rather slow.

After breakfast enjoy a last look at the Colorado River as you walk along the sunny River Walk and watch the boats go back and forth. Or play the casino games till it's time to leave for Los Angeles. Check-out time is an early 11:00 A.M., but you can turn in your room key and linger a bit.

Afternoon

Retrace your way back to Los Angeles heading south on Casino Drive to Needles Highway; turn left, continue until Park Road, and turn right to I–40 into Barstow.

There's More

Horizon Outlet Center at Casino and Edison drives. The new enclosed 250,000 square-foot, two-story mall with art deco motif features some fifty upscale designer and brand-name factory stores and shops (including Reebok, Guess?, Levi's, and Leathermade), offering prices of 20 to 70 percent off retail.

Katherine Landing, 9 miles north of Laughlin at Lake Mohave. Resort marina on the Arizona side. The former mine district is an RV recreation facility with full hookups, boat rentals, marina, launch ramp, fishing, swimming, and sandy beaches with barbecue and picnic areas, plus restaurant and lounge. Motel accommodations.

Laughlin River Tours, Inc. (800) 228–9825; (702) 298–1047. *Little Belle* river cruises. Authentic-looking, nostalgic, 150-passenger double-decker sidewheeler riverboat offers one-and-a-quarter-hour narrated cruise daily; leaves from the Edgewater Hotel Casino dock. Enclosed lower deck features a full-service bar; upper deck is canopy-covered. Cruise goes back and forth to the casinos, from Riverside Resort to Harrah's, and includes narration about the area, the river, and the casinos. Fare; purchase tickets at *Little Belle* ticket booth at the Edgewater Hotel & Casino dock.

Special Events

Calico Ghost Town. Call to verify prices and times of events (800) 862–2542. May 10, 11, 12. (Mother's Day Weekend) **Annual Calico Spring Festival** with old time Bluegrass hootenany, two-day fiddle, banjo, guitar, and band contest and more. Admission.

October 11, 12, 13. (Columbus Day Weekend) Calico Days celebrates the town's glory days with wild west parade, national gunfight stunt championship, various 1880s games and contests. Admission.

First weekend in November. (Calico Fine Arts Festival/Western Art Fest) Sixty foremost western artists display work, American Indian dances, gunfights and bluegrass music. Admission.

December. Christmas in Calico. Tree lighting and Christmas carols. Admission.

January. Annual Laughlin Rodeo Days.

Mid-April. Harley-Davidson annual River Run motorcycle rally.

End of April. Laughlin–Bullhead City Chili Cook-Off.

End of June. Laughlin River Days.

End of October. Riverflight balloon rally.

Mid-December. Annual Parade of Lights, Lake Mohave Resort.

Other Recommended Restaurants and Lodgings

Laughlin

Colorado Belle Hotel/Casino, 2100 South Casino Drive. (800) 458–9500; (702) 298–4000. On the banks of the Colorado River; 1,238 rooms and suites, some with scenic river views, on this 608-foot-long authentic replica of a three-deck Mississippi paddlewheeler with an adjacent six-story hotel. Very attractive facade, with red and white trim; it looks as though it's floating on the water. Enclosed courtyards, two heated swimming pools and spa, casino, five restaurants, lounge entertainment, giftshops, video arcade. Free ferryboat rides across the Colorado River.

Harrah's Laughlin, 2900 South Casino Drive. (800) 447–8700; (702) 298–4600. In a widespread, rambling, Spanish-style complex; 1,658 rooms and suites, with two heated swimming pools, secluded riverfront beach, five restaurants, lounge, nonsmoking casino area, children's arcade, health club, RV area, and shuttle to casino.

Note: Experienced visitors join the free Slot Clubs in the casino to get on any of the hotel's mailing lists for special rates, room and food discounts, and other perks unavailable to nonmembers. Sign up at the Slot Club booths in your hotel's casino. Additionally, scan your hotel's *Fun Books* for coupons for free cocktails and other goodies.

For More Information

Laughlin Visitor Bureau, 155 South Casino Drive, P.O. Box 502 Laughlin, NV 89029. (800) 452–8445, (702) 298–3321.

Index

About the Author

Eleanor Harris, a knowledgeable traveler and photojournalist, is an expert on Southern California and has written about its vacation attractions for such publications as *Los Angeles* magazine, *Travel & Leisure, National Motorist, Cruise Travel,* and *Westways.* She is a self-syndicated columnist and former dining editor, as well as a painter, expert cook, architectural consultant, and sometime golfer. She lives with her husband, Ben, in Beverly Hills, where they raised two daughters.